CONQUEST AND COALESCENCE

The Shaping of the State in
Early Modern Europe

Edited by
MARK GREENGRASS

Edward Arnold
A division of Hodder & Stoughton
LONDON NEW YORK MELBOURNE AUCKLAND

© 1991 Edward Arnold

except for chapter nine by Peter Baumgart © 1984 Böhlau Verlag

First published in Great Britain 1991

Distributed in the USA by Routledge, Chapman and Hall, Inc.
29 West 35th Street, New York, NY10001

British Library Cataloguing in Publication Data

Greengrass, Mark
   Conquest and coalescence : the shaping of the state in
   early modern Europe.
   1. Europe, early modern
   I. Title
   940.1

   ISBN 0-7131-6563-4

Typeset in Linotron Ehrhardt by
Rowland Phototypesetting Limited
Bury St Edmunds, Suffolk
Printed and bound in Great Britain for
Edward Arnold, a division of Hodder and Stoughton Limited,
Mill Road, Dunton Green, Sevenoaks, Kent TN13 2YA by
St Edmundsbury Press Limited, Bury St Edmunds, Suffolk

Contents

Maps and Figures

Contributors

Mark Greengrass is Senior Lecturer in Modern History at the University of Sheffield. He is a specialist in the history of sixteenth- and seventeenth-century France and has published *France in the Age of Henri IV: the struggle for stability* (London, 1984) and *The French Reformation* (Oxford, 1987).

Peter Partner taught at Winchester College from 1955 to 1986 and is an associate Fellow of the Deputazione di Atoria Patria per l'Umbria. He has written extensively on the history of Renaissance Rome as well as the contemporary history of the Near East. His publications include *The Lands of St Peter; the papal state in the Middle Ages and the early Renaissance* (London, 1972) and *Renaissance Rome* (London, 1976). His latest study, *The Pope's Men: the Papal Civil Service in the Renaissance* will appear shortly with Oxford University Press.

John Elliott was Professor of History at the Institute for Advanced Study at Princeton from 1973 until 1990 when he took up his post as Regius Professor of Modern History in the University of Oxford and Fellow of Oriel College. He is a Fellow of the American Academy of Arts and Sciences, a Member of the American Philosophical Society, and his writings on Spanish history in the early modern period are well-known and widely acclaimed. His recent publications include *The Count-Duke Olivares* (New Haven and London, 1986) which won the Wolfson Literary Prize for History and *Spain and its World, 1500–1700* (1989).

Christian Desplat is Professor of Modern History at the Université de Pau et des pays de l'Adour. His doctoral thesis on 'Pau et le Béarn au XVIIIe siècle. Groupes sociaux, attitudes mentales et comportements' was completed in 1978. He has published extensively on the history of Béarn, including the magnificent provincial history (with P. Tucoo-Chala), *La Principauté de Béarn* (Pau, 1982).

Alain Lottin is President of the Université de Lille III. The personal diary of an inhabitant of Lille in the second half of the seventeenth century inspired the study of his *Vie et mentalité d'un Lillois sous Louis XIV* (1968). He subsequently produced the remarkable study of the city in the seventeenth century, entitled *Lille, citadelle de la contre-réforme?* (1984). He also directed a pioneering research project on the history of the family, whose results were published in *La désunion du couple sous l'Ancien régime* (1975).

Ciaran Brady is a Fellow of Trinity College, Dublin. His doctoral thesis on *The*

Government of Ireland, c.1540–1583 was completed in 1980 and he has published a number of important articles on sixteenth-century Irish history. He has also co-edited *Natives and Newcomers: the Making of Irish Colonial Society, 1534–1642* (1986) and *Ulster: an Illustrated History* (1988).

Daniel Szechi is Professor of History at Auburn University, Alabama. His book on *Jacobitism and Tory Politics (1710–14)* (1984) is an important revaluation of the importance of Jacobitism and its role in English politics, sustained in a series of more recent important articles.

Robert Evans is Senior Research Fellow at Brasenose College, Oxford and University Reader. His recent books include *Rudolf II and his World: A Study in Intellectual History (1576–1612)* (Oxford, 1973) and *The Making of the Habsburg Monarchy (1550–1700)* (Oxford, 1979).

Peter Baumgart is Professor of Modern History at the University of Würzburg. He is a distinguished historian of the Prussian state and has directed numerous volumes devoted to its spectacular consolidation, including *Bildungspolitik in Preußen zur Zeit des Kaiserreichs* (1980), *Ständetum und Staatsbildung in Brandenburg-Preußen* (1983), *Expansion und Integration* (Cologne, 1984) and, most recently, *Kontinuität und Wandel, Schlesien zwischen Österreich und Preußen* (Sigmaringen, 1990). He has also collaborated in the historiographical volume devoted to the great German historian Otto Hintze, *Otto Hintze und die moderne Geschichtswissenschaft* (1980).

Zenon Kohut is Senior Research Specialist in the Library of Congress, Washington, USA. He is a specialist in the history of Ukraine, his most recent publication being the major study *Russian Centralism and Ukrainian Autonomy: Imperial Absorption of the Hetmanate 1760s–1830s* (Cambridge, Mass., 1988).

Preface

Every day of late, or so it seems, Europe has seen more flags being put out. The star-spangled banner of the European Community is amongst a small minority of newly-invented ones, a symbol, as some would see it, of Europe's coming political integration within a super-state. But for the rest, they are old flags, hidden flags, but now brought out from behind the bookcases of the past. They are symbols of *l'Europe des régions*, waved in the past year (1989) by Slovenes demanding the right of secession, by Ukrainians asking for their Uniate church to be legal once more, by Lithuanians declaring their independence, by Montenegrins bringing home the bones of their last king, by the Scots demanding their 'independence within Europe'. Meanwhile, the Basques and the IRA have gone on bombing. Old flags sometimes shroud the darker chapters of Europe's past.

This is a vivid contemporary reminder that, although we choose to imagine Europe's political structure in the form of a small number of unitary and integrated nation states, it has been so only in the relatively recent past. In the foothills of modernity, Europe's political structure was, in fact, very different. It was dominated by a multiplicity of regional political entities. Although for the most part smaller than nation states, these were, as recent events remind us, remarkably durable and robust, only gradually surrendering their independence, or slowly accepting a destiny of coalescence within a larger entity.

The active shadow of the past upon the present is one stimulus to the preparation of this volume. Another is the shadow of the present upon the past, the kind known to English historians as 'Whiggish'. An older generation of historians tended to reduce the political history of Europe to the creation of nation states (with Germany and Italy as cases of arrested development which proved the rule). In this they were doubly mistaken. For one thing, they supposed that national identity and historical destiny were the peculiar rationale of this process and of these particular developments. And, for another, they tended to assume that the larger nation states were those which were best suited, even predestined, to dominate the European map. Historical enquiry was thus weighted towards the 'successful' few. Who could say as they look at the questions on European history examination papers today that the tendency does not still, to a degree, exist?

The case-studies in this present volume set out with a different agenda. Instead of studying Louis XIV from Versailles, or Philip IV from the Buen Retiro palace, or Frederick the Great from Potsdam, the perspective they offer is from the periphery – from Flanders, Portugal and Bohemia. Aspects of the complexity of Europe's political development emerge from each case-study. There were rarely, it seems, easy ways forward for those with decisions to make in the smaller regional entities in early modern Europe when confronted with the prospect of coalescence, sometimes under the threat of armed force, within a larger political framework. At the same time, in place of the facile assumptions about the state-building ambitions of Europe's rulers, each case-study presents a more complex and variegated reality. Both ruler and ruled thus contribute to the shaping of Europe's political framework.

Why case-studies? They cannot, of course, present the whole picture but they are often a solution to a difficult research problem where the patterns are not obvious to the naked eye, a welcome resource. Even though, predictably, they do not succeed in solving the problem, they do at least offer the prospect of viewing it at closer quarters. In any case, this volume is concerned not with 'the European state' (as though it were a consistent and homogeneous entity, which is a political–scientific abstraction, rather than a historical reality) but with the European states. There is a sense, too, in which this volume is premature. A major collaborative research project, funded by the European Science Foundation and involving historians from across Europe and beyond, is currently devoted to 'The Origins of the Modern State in Europe, 13th–18th Centuries'. Seven working groups are tackling some important themes.[1] With a slight sense of casting the long shadow of the past over the present, they are due to report and publish their findings in 1992, the year of Europe's closer integration. Yet this volume, by addressing itself to Europe's peripheries rather than its centres, by focusing not just on those states which succeeded in imposing their identity upon others, those which 'made it', but also on those which were, in these over-simplistic terms, 'unsuccessful', complements the grand agenda of the European Science Foundation project. It attempts to explain how the absorption of such territories into these larger entities had embedded within it much of the turbulence of more modern and contemporary European political experience.

All save one of the chapters to this volume were specially commissioned from the contributors. They were mostly completed by early 1989 and their authors have borne with patience the delays which sometimes attend collaborative volumes of this kind. The editor owes them all a considerable debt of gratitude. In addition, the volume has benefitted from the knowledge of Linda Kirk, the editorial assistance of Jennifer Hunter and Peter Derlien as well as the gentle persistence of my publishers.

M. Greengrass
Sheffield
May 1990

1. These are: 'War and competition between state systems'; 'Economic systems and state finance'; 'The legal instruments of power'; 'Ruling classes and agents of the state'; 'Representation, resistance and sense of comunity'; 'The individual in political theory and practice'; 'Iconography, propaganda and legitimation'.

1

Introduction: Conquest and Coalescence

MARK GREENGRASS

As you cross from France into Spain through the Eastern Pyrenees, you pass successively through two villages, Palau and Aja.[1] Each is visible to the other and no more than a quarter of a mile lies between them. Both once belonged to the old county of Cerdanya; both once had a shared political identity, a common Catalan culture and economic destiny. Yet for over three centuries they have been on opposite sides of an invisible boundary dividing France from Spain. The division was created when France annexed the northern Catalan county of Roussillon and 33 villages of the adjoining county of Cerdanya in the Treaty of the Pyrenees and its accompanying protocols in 1659–60. Although the frontier's exact territorial locations were unclear until the second half of the nineteenth century, both communities had already, before that time, become assimilated into two broader but separate identities, their common inheritance surviving but being overlaid as they became integrated into the political and cultural lives of France and Spain.[2] The experience of these two villages is echoed across Europe – in the communities and regions of the Savoyard piedmont of northern Italy, in Flanders and Hainault, the provinces of Vauban's 'iron frontier', among the villages and small towns in Overijssel and Gelderland when the Dutch Republic constructed its 'great wall' in 1605 to defend the line of the Ijssel and Waal rivers and doubtless in many parts of Europe elsewhere.

The peculiar feature (though it may not be unique in world history) of Europe's political past is the unusual perception that states should be viewed as primarily territorial, rather than legal, religious, cultural or dynastic entities.[3] The fact that Europe had a system of multiple territorial polities rather than an enduring imperial tradition was established at an early date. Its stronger states were already well in place around its core economic regions (the Ile de France, the Thames basin, Rhenish Flanders, the Po valley and the other fertile river plains) by the central Middle Ages (c.900–1200).[4] What is striking in the course of the later Middle Ages and early modern periods is the way in which the number of states declined as their power grew. It has been claimed that there were something like a thousand independent polities in Europe in the fourteenth century. At the beginning of the sixteenth century, this had decreased to just below 500. By 1789, it had again fallen to under 350. The changes of the Revolutionary and

Napoleonic periods were considerable, particularly in Germany where the 294 or so territories with pretensions to being regarded as states shrank to 39 by 1820. In 1900, there were just 25 nation states. Some of these were ancient and well integrated, especially the states whose political geography and institutions had most been shaped by the existence of an integral core economic region from the central Middle Ages onwards.[5] Others were new identities forged in the crucible of nation-state politics in the nineteenth century. For all, 'swallowing' and 'being swallowed up' were fundamental features of Europe's political past.

These estimates are no more than indicative of a long, irregular and uneven process. It is extremely difficult to determine the independent political entities in fourteenth-century Europe. The political map was dominated by a skein of feudal dependencies. The relationships between élites were determined by patterns of law which governed regalian rights. Charters of privilege, exemption and immunity in the hands of individual bishoprics, independent cities, corporations, or regional estates provided the basis for rights to rule. Whilst 'territoriality' had clearly existed in the ancient world (in, for example, its peace treaties), it was often overlaid in medieval Europe by the more prevalent notions of feudal jurisdiction and dependency. Frontiers became zones of overlapping jurisdictions rather than precisely demarcated and delimited boundary lines. Similarly, whilst it is possible to find the notion of *potestas absoluta* (absolute authority) in the *Digest* and *Institutes* of Justinian, the jurists of the Middle Ages sought, in their glosses upon Roman Law texts, to attenuate the absolutist conclusions which they found there.[6]

By the sixteenth century, the estimate of the number of political entities in Europe is more reliable but there are still uncertainties. Many arise from the statelets of the German Empire. 'No one ever succeeded in compiling a rational list of the sovereign units in Germany' observes the historian Gerald Strauss.[7] Seventeenth-century jurists debated the degree to which territorial princes in the Empire had rights to conclude treaties with other powers and resist the will of the Emperor.[8] In 1667 Pufendorf described the Holy Roman Empire as a political irregularity and a monster. Leibniz tackled the question by excluding the smallest Imperial counties on the grounds that these units could not realistically defend their sovereign existence.[9] A century later, however, Jean-Jacques Rousseau defended the existence of these small states as the equivalent of the tiny weights which one might use to keep a pair of scales in balance, the means by which the European state system kept in overall equilibrium.[10]

A further dilemma concerns the frequent dynastic unions of states in the early modern period. Should dynastic conglomerates, often fragile and ephemeral conjunctures, count as having integrated one territory to another? If so, the constituent elements which together made up the vast inheritance of the Habsburgs – the '18 crowns' of Emperor Charles V – should be regarded as one integrated unit. How, too, should one acknowledge the nominal condominium between the Scandinavian kingdoms, agreed at the Union of Kolmar in 1397, but in practice barely followed, or that arrived at between Poland and Lithuania, or the confederation of the 11 cantons of Switzerland? Another problem concerns the difference between legal status and reality. The principality of Moldavia was nominally independent but, in practice, it was subjected by turns to Turkish, Hungarian and Polish overlordship. Finally, there were a number of political organisms whose overlords were in no real position to exercise control over them. This was the case with the Hanseatic towns of the Baltic such as Lübeck, as well as the area to the south of the Gulf of Finland controlled by the Teutonic Order of Knights, both subject theoretically to the Holy Roman Emperor but in practice almost entirely independent of Imperial jurisdiction. Large old-established states, new principalities, dynastic empires, city states, confederations, a continuing widespread acceptance of the ideal of universal world monarchy in the Holy Roman Empire and the spiritual and temporal jurisdiction of the Papacy – Europe's basic political fabric contained a rich variety of traditions. Homogeneity should neither be expected of it or imposed upon it by reading history backwards.[11]

Laying out Europe in the block colours of a modern map was not the way in which contemporaries would have represented this variety. International treaties and aristocratic declarations of loyalty to a sovereign lord continued to contain expressions of political relationships in terms of personal oaths of allegiance.[12] French kings tried to avoid territorial boundaries being specified in treaties for they were as difficult to define as they were hard to enforce.[13] In this, they received the willing collusion of localities in frontier zones who saw ample scope for exploiting jurisdictional conflicts. French monarchs of the early modern period preferred the infinite possibilities of juridical extension permitted by feudal institutions. Throughout the sixteenth and seventeenth centuries, sovereignty was still the exercise of authority within different domains (seigneurial, ecclesiastical, juridical, etc.). These domains were often not delineated territorially with great precision and, if they were, their limits often did not coincide with one another. Sovereignty was still alienated to princes in the form of specific grants of a feudal nature, such as an appanage to a prince. Enclaves (or exclaves, depending on one's perspective) such as those in the Rhône valley at Orange (a principality of the house of Orange-Nassau until it was occupied by Louis XIV in 1680) and the nearby papal state of Avignon (which Louis XIV failed to retain but which was finally integrated into France in 1791) were not anomalies. Older perceptions and patterns of lordship died hard.

By the end of the eighteenth century, an estimate of the number of European states in existence becomes a little easier. 'Territoriality' was more in evidence. International treaties tended to start with the assumption that peace was best established on the basis of mutually recognized independent sovereignties. Rulers were much more exercised by the territorial integrity of their states. Louis XV declined, for example, to annex the Austrian Netherlands which the *maréchal* de Saxe had conquered for him in the course of the War of Austrian Succession. As the marquis d'Argenson stated later in his memoirs: 'This is no longer a time for conquests. France must be satisfied with its greatness and extension. It is time to start governing, after spending so much time acquiring what to govern'.[14] The Emperor Joseph II offered the same Austrian Netherlands to Louis XVI in 1778 in return for more than a third of Bavaria, a partition treaty which would have realized the ideal, long cherished in Vienna, of acquiring a compact block of Habsburg territories centred on the Danube.[15] Although the major eighteenth-century wars often appear to be dynastic disputes, that component often did not run deep. Frederick II cited his claims to inherit Silesia in public as his motive for invading that province but scoffed at them in private.[16] Eighteenth-century conflicts, so often wars of *succession* by name were, in reality, more often wars of territorial *partition* along rational lines, with the prey being the smaller, or the weaker, states such as Poland, Silesia, the Spanish Netherlands or Tuscany. At the same time, rulers placed a greater reliance upon geographers to provide a more accurate representation of state frontiers and employed commissions of lawyers and surveyors to settle the precise configuration of frontiers on the ground where this had been historically a sensitive issue. When the commissioners for the border in the Pyrenees set to work in 1780, they were shocked at the way in which local 'thoroughfare' treaties (*lies et passeries*) cut across borders leaving communities 'mixed up, confused and intertwined'.[17] In 1771, the two French surveyors, Chauchard and Jolly, who were detailed to map out the frontier from Dunkirk to Landau in northern Alsace, found they had to work over a strip of territory three or four leagues (*c.*10 miles) wide in order to undertake their task.[18]

In this slow transformation, it is possible to imagine a kind of political Darwinism at work, with the politically fit surviving at the expense of the weak. It was always the prerogative of smaller states to feel threatened by larger neighbouring states and to seek protection, often by diplomatic alliances. Yet it is a plausible hypothesis that the optimum dimensions of the political entity changed over the period from 1500 to 1800. Europe's smaller states had retained much of their viability in comparison with the 'Leviathans' through the sixteenth century.[19] A small principality such as Béarn, for example, constructed a new fortification at Navarrenx on the latest Italian lines, could raise a citizen army, and maintained a fiscal and judicial bureaucracy which would have compared favourably with the absolute French monarchy's government across the border in Gascony.[20] Other recent studies of the statelets of Germany in the sixteenth century have emphasized their vigour and ability to adapt to changing circumstances, especially in the context of the Reformation.[21] By the end of the seventeenth century things had begun to change. It was not Frederick the Great's sense of aggression which made him regard the acquisition of Silesia as fundamental to securing Prussia's place among Europe's 'Great Powers'.[22] His perceptions of the increasing disadvantages of being small were shared amongst other German statelets in the eighteenth century.[23] Europe's major states had grown dramatically more powerful to the disadvantage of their smaller neighbours.

Yet how can historians measure the power of a state? They often resort to a small number of measurable (or potentially measurable) variables; the territory it controls, its population density, its fiscal potential, the number of its officials and the strength of its armed forces. In practice, most of these elements are difficult to assess, let alone to compare from one political entity to another over several generations. Even the most basic measure in terms of the growth in the size of the armed forces of major states is open to all kinds of objections.[24] Yet, in the very crudest terms, the increases in armed forces (*see Table 1.1*) reflect the significance of what has been termed the 'military revolution' of the early modern period.[25] Its effect upon the political fabric of Europe's states was profound.[26] But it has not been generally noted how much it worked in favour of the larger political units. It was partly as a consequence of military change that the institutional framework of the larger European states in turn grew more elaborate. The numbers of state

Table 1.1 Europe's armies, 1500–1800

Spain	Spanish empire	Netherlands	France	England	Venice	Prussia	Russia	Austria	Date
28 000			28 000	20 000	30 000 (1509)				1520s
45 000	150 000		50 000	30 000					1550s
86 000	200 000	20 000	80 000						1590s
85 000	300 000	50 000	150 000						1630s
	100 000	110 000	100 000	70 000	26 000				1650s
	70 000	100 000	120 000	63 000					1670s
50 000		39 000	(<)350 000	87 000		39 000	90 000	100 000	1700s
			330 000	91 000		143 000	330 000	200 000	1750s
				100 000		160 000		200 000	1770s
50 000			156 000	100 000			500 000		1789

officials as a percentage of the overall population probably expanded more substantially in Europe's leading states than in their smaller counterparts.[27] There were political 'economies of scale' to be realized which worked against smaller states and to progressively greater effect. The small principality of Hesse-Cassel, for example, paid off and reduced its military forces at the end of the Thirty Years War, leaving just 600 infantry and 40 landsknechts. Then Landgraves Wilhelm III and Charles found the necessity of a standing army inescapable and, by 1688, this military force had risen to over 10 000. An alliance with the United Provinces and England provided a subsidy which helped with its maintenance until the third decade of the eighteenth century, by which time the expenditure on its army was *higher* than the *total* revenues of its taxation. In 1727, George II of England and Hanover took over the entire army of 12 000 soldiers as a mercenary force which was maintained from English revenues, eventually employing it in the War of American Independence.[28] Senses of national identity were also more readily summoned to the aid of Europe's Leviathans and at the expense of its pygmies.

If we concentrate on these elements of state power alone, its officialdom, its fiscal base and its military power, then state-building is inevitably seen as a process which begins from the centre. From this perspective, peripheral regions, independent or autonomous territories must be militarily 'conquered', juridically rendered subservient, institutionally 'integrated' or culturally 'assimilated'. The efforts of Europe's great 'state-makers' become interpreted in terms of the cohesion and vigour of their actions, and the visionary foresight they displayed, towards this goal.

This volume provides a series of case-studies with which to view Europe's state-making from the other end of the telescope. The small-scale territorial aggrandizements, the partial integrations of independent provinces, the piecemeal reshapings of the political jigsaw of Europe from *c.*1500 to *c.*1800, allow the historian to investigate the early modern state in action, to survey its aspirations and its limitations. From this perspective we may assess how effectively these states wanted, and were able, to change traditional allegiances and reshape new loyalties. We may evaluate what stood in the way of a greater degree of integration. By looking at case-studies from a cross-section of the major states of Europe over a period of three centuries from the perspective of the relatively neglected smaller-scale political units which were in the process of being absorbed, we shall understand more about the strengths and weaknesses of the early modern state.[29]

As one reads these case-studies, an interesting alternative hypothesis about European state-building also begins to appear. We realize how cautious and prudent Europe's state-makers often were, how dominated by the historical logic of the state tradition of the past in their own regions, even when faced with fortuitous and manifestly opportune circumstances in which to increase their authority and impose their will. We discern how aware rulers were of the importance of sustaining local identities and accepting regional differences. We note how they ignored at their peril the will and determination of the local élites in the process of forging new loyalties. We see how the sense of wider national belonging did not simply, or quickly, supplant local identities, but co-existed alongside them. So an important additional perspective is added with the hypothesis that local society could be a motive force in the formation and consolidation of the European state, that local notables were capable of both opposing and exploiting the state for their own ends, and that successful integration was not just the conquest and absorption of the small by the large but also the coalescence and continuity of local and wider interests within a larger politial framework.

Conquest

In a complex civilization with a long tradition of political thought, power is inevitably viewed, and exercised, in an ambiguous way. Conquest was a dramatic exercise of power and it is not therefore surprising that it evoked contradictory responses. On the one hand, the rulers of early modern Europe often seemed in no doubt about the virtues of heroic conquest. Classical antiquity had provided them with models for martial conquerors such as Alexander and Julius Caesar and they readily identified with them at convenient moments. The 'warrior popes', Alexander VI and Julius II, exploited the Roman imperial traditions at the beginning of the sixteenth century, despite the apparent incongruity. In the course of the summer of 1506, Pope Julius II personally commanded the armies of the Papal State against Giampaolo Baglioni, the ruler of Perugia, and then marched on Bologna. In a single campaigning season, he extended the authority of the Papal State to Umbria and Emilia-Romagna. Round the streets of Bologna he was carried in imperial fashion through 13 hastily constructed triumphal arches to the cathedral and, when he returned to Rome, his arrival was timed deliberately to coincide with Palm Sunday (28 March) 1507. His route followed the Via del Corso where the ancient Arch of Domitian was embellished with paintings and statues so that, as one observer remarked, it was as if the emperor himself had returned to celebrate another triumph. Near Ponte Sant'Angelo, there was a triumphal *carro*, drawn by four white horses in accordance with the practice of Roman triumphs. On the car was a globe (the symbol of universal dominion) from which grew an oak tree with golden acorns (the emblem of the pope's family, the Della Rovere). From this ceremonial vehicle, 10 youths waved palm branches. Finally, facing the Vatican stood a replica of the Arch of Constantine, decorated with a pictorial account of the history of Julius' military campaign. To mark his triumph, Julius issued a commemorative medal with an inscription which explicitly linked his triumphs with his imperial namesake: *IVLIVS CAESAR PONT[IFEX] II.*[30] Conquest was thus glorified and sanctified, for Julius II had entered Rome as a second Julius Caesar, heir to the majesty of Rome, and in the likeness of Christ, whose Vicar he was.

Machiavelli was amongst the many contemporaries to have been impressed by this event. He subsequently devoted a good deal of attention in *The Prince* to the lessons of antiquity for princes such as Julius II and Cesare Borgia who annexed new territories. He told them how best to incorporate their gains into a state – a Machiavellian combination of fear and favour which was prudent and unrealistic in almost equal measure.[31] In the sixteenth century, Machiavelli's remarks, reflecting his acknowledgement of power as a force potentially unlinked to law or moral virtue, often appear to have been either ignored or vehemently rejected and criticized. But, reinterpreted in the works of the political philosophers of the seventeenth century, they formed the basis for renewed speculation about conquest and its legitimacy.

Meanwhile, outside the Italian principalities, imperial conquest was also picked up in France. It glorified, to a degree legitimized, the French Italian expeditions. Francis I was pictured in commemorative medals as a Roman emperor and, following the battle of Marignan (1515), the city of Rouen erected an equestrian statue to the conqueror to mark the occasion of his *joyeuse entrée* to the city – just as the city of Florence, newly restored to Medici hands, had done two years earlier for the Medici pope, Leo X. Perhaps the most remarkable presentation of the conquest theme in Renaissance France comes in the form of the illuminated manuscript of the *Commentaries of the Gallic War*. Completed around 1520 for the French king by his tutor, the text consists of Caesar's *Gallic Wars* reworked in the form of dialogue between Caesar and Francis I. The illustrations depict the French king chatting to Julius Caesar in the forest at Fontainebleau and the park in the château at Cognac, two conquerors swapping notes.[32]

The glorification of conquest is not difficult to discover elsewhere in early modern Europe. Yet it also produced hostile responses. Erasmus and Thomas More translated Lucian's *Dialogues* from Greek into Latin, with their satirical references to conquerors and every aspect of the quest for martial glory. Erasmus was still at work on it in Rome when Julius made his triumphal entry. He had witnessed the ceremonial procession of the pope at Bologna and it was evoked in a satirical vein which drew upon Lucian when he came to write *In Praise of Folly* and, later on, the anonymous *Julius exclusus*.[33] The German humanist, Ulrich von Hutten had been in Rome and witnessed Julius' ceremonial entry and wrote scathingly about the quasi-imperial tyranny which it implied.[34] Thomas More's reactions were similarly critical towards the imperial aspirations of contemporary princes: 'Most kings are . . . more anxious, by hook or by crook, to acquire new kingdoms than to govern their existing ones properly'.[35] The Spanish humanist and Latin secretary to Charles V, Alfonso de Valdés wrote a tract in the wake of the Sack of Rome which sharply criticized conquering aspirations and, in another treatise in 1528–9, presented the conquering ruler suddenly being converted to virtuous rule and abandoning his expansionist aims, ruling henceforth only for the good of his people.[36] Conquerors, by implication, were bad rulers, careless of the well-being of their subjects.

In Spain there was a more complex debate about the moral justifications for conquest. It reflected the continuing importance to contemporaries of ideas of the 'just war' and the 'law of nations'. The debate was stimulated, at least in the first instance, by the complex question of the legitimacy of the dominion exercised by Spain and Portugal in the New World. The questions for which resolution was sought included: whether the Indians enjoyed lawful title to their lands, whether the Emperor or the Pope could seize their lands, whether 'discovery' gave any right of lawful possession, whether the fact that they had not received the Christian faith provided adequate reason to subjugate them, and whether, in the event of their having customs which involved 'sins against the law of nature' (such as cannibalism), that provided just cause for subjection. The arguments were based upon expositions of scholastic notions of the natural law which governed human society and of the law of nations which governed its political society. Notions of what constituted tyranny and what was involved in a just war were not far away.[37]

Political thinking about conquest in early modern Europe drew upon and reflected these ambiguities. When François Hotman wrote his *Francogallia*, he began it with a description of Gaul 'before the Romans reduced it to a province'.[38] The Roman conquest had removed the ancient freedoms of the Gauls. Yet it was another conquest, this time of the liberating Franks, which partially resurrected the liberties which had been lost by the Gauls.[39] Theodore Beza, in the *Right of Magistrates*, published in 1574, argued the case for the duties of magistrates to oppose a usurping or invading ruler. Yet he accepted that, although the act of invasion might itself be the act of a tyrant, it could nevertheless be a prelude to a legitimate government, providing that it secured the voluntary and lawful consent of the governed.[40] In the seventeenth century, Hobbes argued that conquest was as legitimate as dynastic succession.[41] His critics seized on the fact that 'Master Hobbes saith . . . "a sure and irresistible power confers the right of dominion and ruling over those who cannot resist"', that he had asserted 'by the law of war, whatsoever the victor obtaineth is his right: *ius est in armis*'.[42] His critics followed Beza and others who argued that conquest was not legitimate until it had received some specific consent from the conquered.[43] Mankind's state of nature was not a perpetual struggle for hegemony and natural law was reinforced by human prudence to limit conquest to the rights of self-defence.[44] There was a debate over whether the Norman invasion had been a conquest and the extent to which the Normans had absorbed the customs and institutions of the Anglo-Saxons.[45]

Such ambiguities scarcely influenced royal image-mongering in the seventeenth century, which continued to draw on well-established conquering themes. When the walls of Louis XIV's Paris were taken down, some of the old city gates were replaced with *arcs de triomphe* such as that at the *porte* St Denis, constructed in 1672, or those at the *portes* St Martin and Ste Antoine in 1674, to celebrate his conquests in the first phases of the Dutch War. So overburdened with pyramids and geometric shapes were they that one contemporary English observer likened them to the contents of a cheesemonger's shop in London.[46] Conquest became the central feature of the internal decorations at Versailles in the period at the height of Louis XIV's expansionism at the end of the Dutch war in 1678. The programme for the Le Brun ceiling in the famous *Gallerie des glaces* centred on the conquests of the recent war, with scenes portraying the order to attack three places in Holland at the same time, the crossing of the Rhine, the capture of Maastricht and the taking of the city and citadel of Ghent.[47]

Yet bare-faced conquest won few friends and the pillars on which diplomatic theory and practice rested throughout early modern Europe remained those of legal title and dynastic right. When the Papal State undertook its expansion in the sixteenth century into Bologna and Romagna, it was on the basis of legal claims to suzerainty over those regions. Even its faltering footsteps towards the river Po in the middle of the seventeenth century, the last moment when the Papal State seems to have taken its territorial potential in Italy seriously, were justified in terms of papal suzerainty over the duchy of Parma and its right to distrain the duke for unpaid debts owed to papal bankers.[48] Despite Philip II's show of military force in the annexation of Portugal, he prudently laid great stress on his dynastic rights to the throne. Conquest was what happened to non-Christian infidels.[49] The French crown's strategies of exploiting a combination of dynastic claim and legal title to adjacent territories had been fundamental to the expansion of the French state.[50] Louis XIV's justification for his acquisition of Flanders on the basis of the terms of the Treaty of the Pyrenees, which included the details of his marriage to Marie-Thérèse, was entirely within the long-established traditions of French dynasticism. Dynastic high politics was fundamental to the state-building perceptions of early modern Europe.

It should not be forgotten, however, that there were circumstances in which dynasticism reinforced the existence of small, independent territories in Europe. In Germany, partible inheritance survived as the basis of dynastic succession until the early eighteenth century.[51] This was in marked contrast to the much more restrictive primogeniture, a feature of all European dynastic monarchies (with the additional restriction of the succession to the eldest males alone in those monarchies where Salic law prevailed). There were doubtless good reasons for this Germanic survival but it certainly ensured that its political fragmentation continued until the Napoleonic Wars.

Integration

'Integration', as we know from recent experience in debates within the European Community, invites a discussion of meaning and objectives. Much recent commentary on the origins of the modern state in Europe has taken the definition to be the integrated nation-state structure which finally matured in Europe in the nineteenth century. Historians have then tried to explain by what internal processes and mechanisms this degree of integration was arrived at. The problems may be investigated in every locality of Europe's states but they are posed in a particularly acute form in those regions which were newly acquired. What conclusions emerge from the inevitably partial and selective case-studies investigated in this volume?

The absolutism of the Papal State is one of the more remarkable and paradoxical political developments of the sixteenth century. From an undistinguished political and financial basis in a state which straddled the Apennines towards the close of the Middle Ages, Rome pieced together a sizeable portion of central Italy which, within a couple of generations, became the most respected force in the peninsula.[52] Even a century later, its efforts to expand towards the river Po were taken seriously by other Italian powers as a bid for hegemony. Superficially, such developments may be accounted for by institutional changes. These were certainly significant. The Apostolic Chamber became a training-ground for the principal state officials. These officials were subsequently employed as governors, treasurers and commissioners in the different regions of the Papal State. The revenues from the Papal State were handled by the Chamber too and, by the middle of the sixteenth century, the Papal State had a uniform direct tax in the form of the 'Triennial Subsidy'. By 1600, the Papal State provided three times the revenues it had contributed a century previously and nearly 80 per cent of all papal income. The Papal State's bankers had an enviable reputation throughout Europe. Partly on the basis of their loans, its military fortifications were impressive too. The fortress (*rocca*) at Ostia, constructed by

Julius II's uncle, Cardinal Giuliano della Rovere, was the most advanced fortress anywhere in Italy around 1500 and the reconstruction by Paul III of the perimeter wall around Rome itself after the Sack of Rome in 1527, although unfinished, was a tribute to Renaissance military architecture at its most elaborate.

Yet, as Peter Partner emphasizes, the Papal State should not be interpreted in too modern a light. The rectors, treasurers and commissioners of the Papal State had extensive powers but their authority was, in practice, limited by the autonomy of urban and regional privileges which the Papal State was not prepared to challenge systematically. At the same time as papal administrators were centralizing the Papal State, popes were creating new quasi-independent fiefs for their political clients and allies such as the Farnese, the Rovere and the Varano families. Even the existence of a common legal framework for the Papal States is doubtful and, whilst the right to appeal a legal case to Rome was one means of centralizing the state, the papacy also created apostolic vicariates where there were no direct rights of appeal from the apostolic vicar to the state's tribunals. The larger towns of the Papal States such as Bologna and Orvieto retained their autonomies which extended over the surrounding countryside. Sometimes these privileges were challenged by the Papal State, particularly after open revolt. But such privileges were also regularly confirmed or won back after a while. There was no observable coherent strategy of administrative integration. The higher clergy, who, if nowhere else in Europe, might at first sight have been expected to be the compliant agents of the Roman curia, turn out to have been recruited from leading local families whose interests they were often more engaged in advancing than those of the state or of the Catholic Church. There was a striking contrast between the slow implementation of the Counter-Reformation in the bishoprics of the Papal State and its success in some of the dioceses in northern Italy. Venality of office was widespread in the Apostolic Chamber and nepotism and patrimonial influences continued unchecked within state administration. Papal bankers used their credit to advance the interests of their families both within the church hierarchy and within the Papal State administration. In short, Peter Partner's study of the Papal State is an object lesson which demonstrates that there were practical limits to political integration through administrative means in the sixteenth century. Although a sophisticated sixteenth-century political entity, the Papal State did not become the basis for an integrated territorial state as perceived in the nineteenth century.

Spain's monarchy was a union of the crowns of Castile, León, Navarre and Aragon and, with them, the territories of Catalonia and Valencia. The 'Reconquest' of southern Spain had both helped to cement the 'union' of the crowns and also to preserve the independence of its separate components. The regalia of the crowns and their regalian rights were each kept distinct. The separate identity of each kingdom was retained along with its privileges and customs. Each was administered separately by a particular council of state. Territorial integration did not progress much further than dynastic union.[53] Although the Emperor Charles V's minister, Mercurio Gattinara, dreamt of a closer integration of the various component parts of the Spanish empire, including Castile and Aragon, by means of a common council, currency, legal framework and administrative organization, he convinced few, least of all in the Spanish peninsula, and his ideas remained unrealized.[54]

The union of the crown of Portugal with the others in the Spanish monarchy was yet another dynastic conjuncture, but it was one of immense political importance. The Portuguese monarchy was a considerable power in the sixteenth century, endowed with an overseas empire. It had a sizeable merchant fleet which would prove invaluable to Philip II in the elaboration of the Armada. It had a close working relationship with its leading merchant entrepreneurs and other foreign merchant bankers at Lisbon. The ground floor of the royal palace in Lisbon was given over to the *Casa da India* and the *Casa da Mina*, the offices which controlled the royal monopoly over foreign commerce and through which the monarchy maintained close links with both native and foreign merchants. The royal domain was alienable, but such alienations were always revocable. The monarchy had an established sense of its primacy within the Portuguese polity which was not questioned. Its powers over the church were considerable, especially its rights to a tithe (*dízimos*) on all Brazilian sugar production and its rights to nominate to all ecclesiastical benefices in the colonial empire (*padroado*).[55]

The terms of accession agreed by Philip II before the Portuguese Cortes guaranteed a remarkable degree of continuity to Portuguese institutions and culture once the dynastic claim to the Portuguese throne had been recognized. His minister, Cardinal Granvelle, following in Gattinara's footsteps, would have preferred to see a closer degree of integration and a reshaping of its government. But this turned out to be beyond the scope and outside the fundamental traditions of the Spanish monarchy. Personal monarchies like the Spanish Habsburgs of the sixteenth century regarded the loyalty of their subjects as of greater importance than the integration of their various dominions. The problem of consolidating the governance of a new territory like Portugal was perceived largely in the sense of providing access to the sources of patronage and favour. This could be addressed by deciding how long the monarch should spend in Portugal, what sort of viceroy or viceregal council should be instituted during his absence, and how to prevent the Portuguese from feeling that they were being excluded from favour and patronage. Institutional change and administrative reforms created resentments and, whilst a measure of corruption in local institutions might be eliminated, it was more important to maintain the monarchy's extensive regalian rights rather than attempt any measure of fundamental reform which might damage those rights. In any event, the problems in northern Europe were of more pressing and lasting concern. Whilst the loyalty of the Portuguese was not in doubt, why should the Spanish monarchy hazard that loyalty in the uncertain process of change?

John Elliott shows how, when integration was finally contemplated in relation to Portugal, it was not the culmination of a long strategic process but an abrupt change of direction by a monarchy which was faced with almost insuperable problems of resources. Count Dube Olivares, Philip IV's remarkable minister, saw closer integration of the various dominions of the Spanish monarchy, with a greater uniformity of laws and institutions, a closer knitting together of its various military and economic spheres and the expansion of its financial basis, as the only way to ensure its overall survival. The change in direction occurred quickly and, whilst not without support in Portugal itself, it alienated important parts of the country's élite. Even if Olivares was fully aware of these resentments, he was in no position to accommodate them, given Spain's overwhelming commitments during the Thirty Years War. The successful Portuguese revolt of 1640 was interpreted by Spanish contemporaries as a savage sign of internal decline; its loss, along with that of Catalonia, was interpreted in the light of Spanish decline, and has been ever since. There were successive invasions during the years 1657–9 to try to recover the territory. In 1663, and again in 1665, there were attempted invasions leading to the terrible defeats at Ameixiala and Villaviciosa. The latter is reckoned to have hastened the old Spanish king Philip IV to his grave. It is one of the paradoxes of the revolt in Portugal that its restored monarchy exploited the risks of invasion to begin to set in place a Portuguese-style absolutist monarchy and undertake some of the reforms which had eluded the Spanish. Whilst the success and permanency of the revolt rested on French and English assistance, the revolt is a good example of the underlying weakness of purely dynastic unions of a kind common in early modern Europe. At the same time, it is indicative of how the state-making imperatives of warfare and the integrative aspirations of statesmen, when faced with an administrative structure which apparently perpetuated separatism, could produce such fatal results.

All the case-studies for this volume could have been chosen from the experience of the French monarchy alone. Its dominance within the European polity was overwhelming and its progressive territorial expansion was extraordinary, as is demonstrated by crude estimates of its surface area as given in Table 1.2.[56]

The feudal monarchy of Louis IX was already very powerful and highly integrated. With a territorial integrity matched only by that of England, it had a taxable capacity which was already impressive. Its revenues were at least comparable with those which it raised in the sixteenth century and which were by then the envy of Europe.[57] The French monarchy, in contrast with that of Spain, had a tradition of piecemeal annexation and integration. It had incorporated feudal principalities which had never formed part of its domain. First Toulouse and Champagne, then Brittany, Gascogny, Burgundy and Flanders were united and absorbed into the French kingdom not as separate entities but as integral parts of it, ruled by a monarch whose jurists were the first in Europe to articulate the concept of sovereignty. This would have been an impressive achievement even had these regions been similar to the French domain to which they were conjoined. But they were fundamentally different in linguistic background, legal tradition, customs and history. In addition, they were mainly less developed economically than the Ile de France, less densely populated and less open to the outside world. The French monarchy therefore faced enormous problems of incorporating its new acquisitions which were still being felt at the end of the sixteenth century.

The costs were very high. There was an ineluctable diplomatic consequence in terms of the fears aroused amongst its neighbours at this 'monster', a continent in

Table 1.2

*c.*1200	150 000 kms²	1678	528 000 kms²
1453	350 000	1684	550 000
1598	464 000	1789	528 000
1659	495 000	1919	550 000

itself, a super-state. These fears were symbolized for most of the early modern period by the conflict between the French royal house and a Habsburg dynastic coalition. Secondly, there were the increased costs of maintaining an expanded landed frontier, vulnerable especially from the north and north-east. The Emperor Charles V provided a demonstration of this fact in 1544 when he set out from Luxembourg with his army and was only finally halted by Francis I at Meaux, the gateway to Paris. It would be repeated in 1557, 1596, 1636, 1708, 1814, 1870, 1940. In consequence, France had to retain a large standing army.

The French monarchy was compelled to maintain a standing officialdom too. France was uniquely the office-holding state of early modern Europe. Its officials held their posts through venality and in permanence. By the early seventeenth century, these posts were an hereditable commodity, as vital to the health of the French monarchy's finances as they were important to the disposition and transmission of wealth in early modern France. In 1515, it has been estimated that there were over 4 000 royal officers in the kingdom. If we include their clerks and *commis* there were probably more like 7–8 000.[58] This meant that there was one official for every 60 square kilometres or one for every 2 000 inhabitants. By 1665, a similar calculation provides a different result. There were at least 50 000 office-holders with an additional 20 000 or so tax farmers and 10 000 clerks. There was one official for every five square kilometres or one to every 200 inhabitants. Along with the increase in the size of the French army, the state's 'tertiary sector' had become very considerable by early modern standards. This is why French historians speak of the rise of an 'administrative' monarchy. The office-holders provided the backbone to the integration of the peripheral zones into the French domain in the fifteenth century. They would do so again in France's renewed expansionism in the seventeenth century.

The incorporation of Béarn into the French territories hardly counted as the most important of the acquisitions France would make in the seventeenth century. It was a small principality of about 100 000 inhabitants tucked in to the French-facing flanks of the Pyrenees close to a frontier which posed few serious problems – a kind of extinct volcano from which the existence of Béarn, a small part of the old kingdom of Navarre, was a surviving piece of debris. Its incorporation into France had already been extensively discussed before the edict of union of 1620. Yet that act was of considerable symbolic importance. Firstly, it represented the integrative intentions of the Bourbon monarchy, its willingness to incorporate its separate domains of Navarre and France into a unity. It also meant the eclipse of a Calvinist protestant stronghold and demonstrated the catholicizing intentions of the revived French monarchy.

The techniques which were applied to the integration of Béarn into France were traditional and they would be reapplied elsewhere during the seventeenth century. They included a willingness to work within the political and social institutions already in place alongside a progressive emasculation (where necessary) and adaptation (where politic) of them to suit the changed circumstances. The Estates of Béarn, the shrine of its custom or *for*, remained intact although they lost important aspects of their power. A sovereign court of office-holders or *parlement* was established in the provincial capital, Pau. Intendants, royal officers on commission to act as the eyes and ears of the ministers, were despatched to the province. The French monarchy has often been described as a 'centralizing' monarchy. Yet, as Christian Desplat indicates, centralization is not quite the *mot juste* to describe the integration of Béarn into the French kingdom. By accepting the customs of the province, Louis XIII formally accepted the constitutional myth of the province which held that princes were under the law and not absolute. What often appear at first sight as the centralizing activities of the state in economic and social policy turn out on closer inspection to be the initiatives of the local nobility in the estates acting ahead of and in advance of the state. The *parlement* of Pau became the protector of the political rights of the province in the eighteenth century whilst the intendants, provided with few troops in a province whose border was not threatened, were not noticeable for taking the initiative. 'Centralization', concludes Desplat, 'emerged more often than is generally realized from below . . .'.

The conquest of Flanders, by contrast, was essential to the security of the vulnerable French northern frontier. It was a key component in French royal strategy throughout the seventeenth century and only achieved piecemeal. Lille, its capital, only fell to the French in 1668. Although it was fortified according to the plans personally devised by Vauban, it was still recaptured by Prince Eugene in October 1708 and occupied by the Dutch. Only a military reverse, the 'miracle of Denain', allowed Louis XIV to reoccupy the 'Paris of the Pays-Bas', a reoccupation formally confirmed at the peace of Utrecht in 1713.[59]

Given its strategic importance, not to mention its wealth and resources, no effort was spared, as Alain Lottin describes, in bringing it within the *pré carré* of France.[60] Vauban's military frontier, with its centrepiece constructions at Lille and Douai, was elaborate and immensely expensive. A considerable French administrative presence was developed and a French-speaking university founded at Douai. The Catholic Church, including the regular orders, was required to play a part and seminaries were ordered to teach in French. Preferential customs duties were used to shift the focus of the regional economy from looking northwards to the commercial metropolises of the Low Countries towards looking southwards and westwards towards Dunkirk, Picardy and the Somme. Such efforts have to be set against a background of often passive hostility or muted resentment towards France, sentiments widely recognized by the French administrators: 'The Flemings despise the French'. Yet the achievement was a lasting one. As Lottin says, by the end of Louis XIV's reign, convictions had hardened in favour of a more willing acceptance of French rule by a generation which had known no other and, by the time of the French Revolution, Flanders would prove itself to be irreducibly and proudly French. Such was the integrative power of the administrative monarchies of Europe by the end of the seventeenth century.

Comparisons can often be misleading. It is tempting to compare the English and the French experience of state-making. Both states were broadly of a similar size around 1200. Both formed strong states at an early date. Both showed an early propensity to consolidate their territories and to grow. Yet this is to ignore the equally important differences. The expansion of the English state was determined by its island location. Despite the Anglo-Norman kingdoms and the Hundred Years War, the English state found it practically impossible to annex and integrate kingdoms abroad in the spectacular way that France did in the later Middle Ages. Much of its state-making resource was thus turned in on itself with the result that England's state, by the early sixteenth century, was highly integrated although within a compact territorial limit. Its ruling élites, particularly its nobility and gentry, played a far greater rôle in making state power more effective in England than elsewhere in Europe. This reliance upon local élites gave the English state an internal suppleness and flexibility of response to crisis which has been claimed as remarkable.[61]

Such a polity had both strengths and weaknesses when it came to the consolidation of power within the British Isles. In the case of Ireland, as Ciaran Brady explains, English aristocrats and administrators had an 'English' model for the governance of Ireland which involved some singularly optimistic 'English' assumptions as to how it would work out in practice.[62] A succession of Tudor governors believed that England's conquest of Ireland in the Middle Ages had been an initial success which had not been followed up. But Ireland could still be reshaped within the integrated constitutional framework operating in England. Gaelic lords and the Anglo-Irish could be persuaded to play the part of the English ruling élite, accepting its culture and institutions. Irish lordships would be transformed into English shires. A degree of coercion would be necessary and some lordships would have to be confiscated and regranted to English settlers. But persuasion would be essential and this was to be provided through the strategic use of 'composition'. The result, as Ciaran Brady says, was an almost unmitigated failure which was registered in a series of confrontations between the government and the native communities which were subsumed into a major and debilitating Irish war at the end of the sixteenth century. These conflicts should not be regarded as part of the Tudor 'conquest of Ireland', according to Brady, but rather as the defeat of the Tudor 'integration of Ireland'. The defeat left a fundamental mark upon future political developments in both Ireland and England. On the one side, it left the native communities of Ireland, the Gaelic lordships and the 'Old English' further divided one from another with both agreeing upon 'little other than the unreality of English aspirations for Ireland'. On the other hand, it encouraged English administrators, the settlers on confiscated estates and the soldiery, to rely more in practice upon their own resources to defend themselves and advance their own interests. At the same time, they proclaimed their theoretical loyalty to the English interest in Ireland; but they also criticized what they regarded as the failure to offer them more support and speculated in what authority the English interest could command in Ireland to their own benefit. Ireland's English governors in the seventeenth century became the leaders for a speculative, protestant settler interest whose piecemeal expropriation of England's influence in Ireland led to its longer-term fragmentation rather than its integration into English political culture.

Ireland became the nightmare of the English liberal state-making conscience, but Scotland was its quiet triumph. The integration of Scotland into the English polity appeared wholly successful. Yet, as Daniel Szechi argues, the success owed little to any co-ordinated effort of the kind which Louis XIV applied in Flanders, or to any preconceptions of the sort which Tudor governors had sought to bring to bear upon Ireland.[63] The Stuart dynasty largely failed in its formal attempts to build a more cohesive state on the basis of the Union of the English and Scottish crowns in the seventeenth century.[64] Informally, however, the processes of integration had proceeded through the anglicization of the Scottish monarchy, to be followed by that of the Scottish nobility.[65] This would be reflected in the party politics of the Scottish parliament prior to the Act of Union of 1707. The integration which was achieved after 1707 owed little, though, to conscious effort and co-ordinated planning on the part of English ministers. Instead it relied upon the maintenance of an English-orientated oligarchy through patronage and the longer-term social effects of the Union which were, in the context of the rapid evolution of English society, profound.

Bohemia's past did not dictate, in the way that it has done in the other case-studies so far, the dominant partner. The kingdom of Bohemia had, on the basis of its fertile agriculture and its mineral resources, been one of the strongest, most populous and largest states in central Europe in the early fourteenth century.[66] Its capital, Prague, was a wealthy, cultivated and cosmopolitan city. It was, in some ways, well placed to be the political heart of a broader-based Danubian polity which it occasionally became. Yet the kingdom of Bohemia had grown out of the Holy Roman Empire, of which it was a fief, and it remained historically and politically bound up within this Germanic heritage, something reinforced by the influential minority (in some of its provinces, majority) of Germans in its population. Bohemia also saw itself juxtaposed to the other political entities of the Danube region, such as Hungary. It even periodically conceived of its destiny in terms of confederacy with Buda and Vienna, and with Poland to the north. Vienna was far from being the automatic capital city for the Habsburgs in 1526 when Ferdinand I laid claim to Bohemia.

This may have assisted Ferdinand I in his energetic rule of Bohemia. In some respects he succeeded in just those ways in which Philip II and III would fail in Portugal. He made his sons learn Czech, ensured regular visits to the kingdom, and operated the patronage network to maintain a 'court' party there. He had advantages, however, which were not open to Philip II, in terms of the regional tensions in Bohemia which he was able to exploit.

However his achievements were not entirely permanent. The estates of Bohemia revived in the later sixteenth century and the geographically based tensions within the country increasingly took on the configuration of the religious divisions of the Reformation. A wider crisis within the Austrian Habsburg family and the Holy Roman Empire also fed through into Bohemia. The result was a revived attempt, chaotic and brief, on the part of the protestant nobility in the Bohemian estates to establish a Bohemian-centred confederacy. It ended in civil war and the famous fiasco of the Battle of the White Mountain in 1620.[67]

Unlike the Spanish Habsburgs in Portugal, the Austrian Habsburgs held on to Bohemia militarily in 1620. The religious motivations which had penetrated its civil war led to the temporary effacement of an entire political grouping in Bohemia, the confiscation of its estates, the execution of some of its number, and its replacement with an assorted bunch of newcomers. Some have seen this as the beginnings of an Austrian Habsburg absolutism based on Vienna but, as Robert Evans indicates, that is an oversimplification. Bohemia temporarily lost its political élite and eventually became provincialized. But, in the process, a sizeable contingent of the newcomers (along with a selection of the traditional Bohemian noble families who managed to work their way back) gained influence in Vienna and gave a 'Bohemian' dimension to Austrian politics even into the nineteenth century.

Europe's patterns of integration have to be interpreted in the light of the national myths which have had such an effect upon the historiography of their states. Spain's sense of national decline, especially noticeable at the end of the nineteenth century, permeated its interpretations of the Portuguese secession. Nineteenth-century English liberalism provided the context in which English historians interpreted its relations with Ireland and Scotland. The continuing debate over Frederick the Great's annexation of Silesia also has to be seen, according to Peter Baumgart, in the context of nineteenth-century debates over German unification.[68] Some advocated a broad confederal perspective and others a more teleological, Prussian, 'annexationist' unification.

To many contemporaries, the invasion of Silesia was an act of folly. How would it be possible for a German statelet, vulnerable in its geography, scattered in its dynastic possessions, surrounded by stronger neighbours and poorish in its natural resources, to incorporate a substantial part of the Austrian monarchy's domain into its territories against Habsburg wishes?[69] Like many German statelets, Brandenburg-Prussia had interpreted its survival after the Thirty Years War in terms of the establishment of a standing army. In Prussia, however, this went further and faster than elsewhere. By the beginning of the eighteenth century, Prussia had some of the characteristics of a 'military state'; 70–80 per cent of its heavy taxation went towards its armies. Its military organization provided the backbone to the state's growing administrative apparatus.[70] The nobility, particularly the Junkers of Prussia, were dragooned into providing the army's officer corps.[71] In 1730, the regimental cantonment arrangements were announced which linked the recruitment needs of the army with the estates of the nobility and the agrarian social structure of much of its domains. By this date, the horizons of the Hohenzollerns were wider than those of a lesser German dynastic house. They had annexed and incorporated other regions, had established primogeniture in the succession (1692) and the indivisibility and inalienability of their domains (1713). In 1701, Frederick the Great's father, Frederick William, had crowned himself king *in* Prussia at Königsberg.

The annexation of Silesia was a culmination of the reality of the 'military state' and Hohenzollern ambitions. Silesia became the Flanders of the Prussian state. It required sustained defence and absorbed Prussian administrative energies. But whereas Flanders did not provide the financial resources with which Vauban's fortresses had been constructed or their garrisons paid, Silesia bore the brunt of succeeding military campaigns, funded its own defence, and also provided a surplus to Frederick the Great which went directly to his treasury. In addition, since it was ruled in a direct fashion by Frederick the Great, by-passing the aristocracy of Prussian officialdom, it provides a test-case for the direction and scale of reforms envisaged by an 'enlightened absolutist' monarch like Frederick the Great. His religious tolerance, the shape of the legal reforms in Silesia, the more uncertain direction of his economic policies provide a context in which to explain the degree to which Silesians appeared to accept their new identity by the end of Frederick the Great's reign. The incorporation of Silesia foreshadows the annexations which would be undertaken by revolutionary and Napoleonic France in the last decade of the century.[72]

At the frontier between the steppe and the sown, the question of integration was overlaid by the more fundamental matter of the extent to which political power should reflect the loose mutual defence of the kin, the horde, the marauding host of the steppes, or, alternatively, whether it should emulate the more stable state-patterns of the sown. Ukraine lay across the division of the steppe and the sown. To the east of the Dnieper river were some of the last uncolonized lands close to Europe in the early sixteenth century.[73] Here an assorted mixture of Ukrainians, Poles, Lithuanians and Serbs established communities of hunters and trappers, protecting themselves from steppe marauding by means of a military array known as the Cossack *Sitch*. In the course of the early modern period, the boundaries between the steppe and the sown changed. Under the stimulus of grain exports to the west, southern and eastern Ukraine became slowly and progressively transformed into estate-dominated agriculture, operated with serf labour. It was in this context that the integration of Ukraine to Muscovy took place.

In the sixteenth century, Ukraine owed allegiance to the Polish/Lithuanian condominium and accepted its legal traditions. Yet that allegiance was unstable and ill-formed. From Poland came magnates, 'little kings' or *krolewieta*, who colonized in Ukraine, exploited its peasantry and persecuted the Orthodox Church. Brought up within the Polish traditions of a formal state structure, they wanted those structures extended to Ukraine and closer ties with Poland. Ukrainians and Cossacks identified these grandees with the state of Poland and, by the end of the sixteenth century, Ukraine had become an unstable frontier society with endemic native unrest.

From this crucible emerged the remarkable Cossack Hetmanate of the left bank of the Dnieper. Khmel'nyts'sky was the military secretary of the Cossacks who became the leader of a successful anti-Polish uprising in the aftermath of which a Ukrainian polity was constructed, looking to Muscovy for protection. Zenon Kohut explains why its efforts to preserve its traditions within the framework of Russian autocracy were never likely to be completely successful. Yet the vagaries of the Hetmanate are an excellent counterpoint to the growth of the Russian state, through Peter the Great's unplanned and ill-prepared efforts at integration (shades of Olivares and Portugal) to Catherine the Great's more thorough-going 'institutional russification' at the end of the eighteenth century.

Coalescence

Historical tradition, state power, resources, geography and international conditions all played their part in determining the patterns of integration in Europe's states. Yet a common thread running through each of the case-studies is the degree to which integration involved the active engagement of the localities, and particularly their élites. The privileges of urban oligarchies had always to be treated gingerly; provincial capitals were of the utmost importance. So the Papal State tolerated the autonomies of the '16 reformers of liberty' in Bologna not because, *in extremis*, they could not have been crushed, but because such actions would in the long run have been counter-productive. So Louis XIV offered the magistrates of Lille his protection for their liberties *before* they declared their allegiance to him – acknowledging their pretensions whilst establishing his pre-eminence. It was important too, that regional nobilities did not feel ignored, isolated or endangered (Ireland; Portugal). The flows of patronage must not exclude them. The more sensitive issues remained language and religion rather than political forms and institutional survival.

We tend to interpret political identity in too exclusive a fashion, as though the adoption of one meant the automatic exclusion of another. In practice, political identities often survived, and may even have thrived, upon a plurality of identities, some local and regional, others broader or national, but each reinforcing the other in oppositional, but also complementary, ways. Louis XIV's propagandists claimed at the time of the edict of union in Béarn that the acceptance of French sovereignty meant not the loss of their privileges but rather their protection within a wider unit. English propagandists maintained that the Act of Union of 1707 invested the old identities of England and Scotland in a new state which would embrace them both. Whilst the Portuguese affected to disdain the haughty Castilians in the period of Spanish rule and were proud of their national identity, seeing it reinforced in their overseas empire, they were also content to accept the wider cultural Spanish influences which the union of the crowns brought with it as well as the economic advantages which accrued initially to their empire. Scottish aristocrats disliked the indifference of the English towards them but they became anglicized at the same time as sustaining an increasingly imaginary Scottish identity. The eighteenth-century Bohemian nobility retained their Bohemian sense of identity whilst simultaneously advising Austrian monarchs in Vienna. From these complementary and oppositional identities the nation-state of the nineteenth century finally emerged.

NOTES FOR CHAPTER 1

1 No effort has been made in this essay to indicate the full range of the bibliography relating to state-building in early modern Europe. The subject has been extensively treated and from many different angles and it would evidently require much more scope than this chapter can provide. A bibliography of over 700 historical and socioanalytic references in Charles Tilly (ed.), *The Formation of National States in Western Europe* (Princeton UP, 1975) provides a useful starting-point. The following footnotes attempt to provide a cross-section of more recent material, mainly in English, relating to the questions of territorial acquisition and integration in Europe from 1500 to 1800 along with some reference to recent materials on the development of the European state, in the light of which the essays in this volume may be read.

2 The example is taken from the excellent recent study by Peter Sahlins, *Boundaries. The making of France and Spain in the Pyrenees* (California UP, 1989).

3 See J. H. Herz, 'The rise and demise of the Territorial State' in *World Politics* ix (1956–7), pp. 473–93.

4 W. Weinart, *Die Anfänge der europäischen Staatensystems im späteren Mittelalter* (1936) was among the first to argue convincingly for the vitality of the European state system in the central Middle Ages.

5 R. Wesson, *State Systems: International Pluralism, Politics and Culture* (New York, 1978); figures also utilized in Tilly, *Formation of Nation States*, p. 15.

6 See R. Mousnier, *La monarchie absolue en Europe du Ve siècle à nos jours* (Paris, 1982) chs. ii–iv and, more recently, R. J. Bonney, *l'Absolutisme* (Paris, 1989), pp. 9–16. Also M. J. Wilks, *The Problem of Sovereignty in the Later Middle Ages: The Papal Monarchy with Augustinus Triumphus and the Publicists* (Cambridge UP, 1963).

7 G. Strauss, *Historian in an Age of Crisis; The Life and Works of Johannes Aventinus, 1477–1534* (Harvard UP, 1963), p. 56.

8 The debates are alluded to in Mousnier, *La monarchie absolue . . .* pp. 132–9.

9 See his *Entretiens de Philarète et d'Eugène sur le droit d'Ambassade* (in *Werke*, 6 vols., Hanover, 1864), iii, pp. 340–58.

10 *Oeuvres complètes de Jean-Jacques Rousseau* (3 vols., Paris, 1964), iii, p. 572.

11 B. Guenée, *States and Rulers in Later Medieval Europe* (1st edn, 1971; rev. edn, 1981; trans., Oxford, 1985) provides an excellent survey of the traditions surviving in Europe in around 1500 as well as a very full bibliography of works relating to the European state in the later Middle Ages.

12 Recreated for the French nobility in R. Mousnier, *The Institutions of France under the Absolute Monarchy, 1598–1789* (Chicago UP, 1974) i, ch. 3 and, more recently, in Arlette Jouanna, *Le devoir de révolte. La noblesse française et la gestation de l'état moderne, 1559–1661* (Fayard, 1989) parts 2 and 3.

13 N. Girard d'Albissin, *Genèse de la frontière franco-belge. Les variations des limites septentrionales de la France de 1659 à 1789* (1970), p. 26ff.

14 Quoted in A. Sorel, *L'Europe et la révolution française* (8 vols., 1885–1904), i, pp. 319–20.

15 M. S. Anderson, *Europe in the Eighteenth Century* (1961), pp. 214–15.

16 See ch. 9, below.

17 Cited in P. Sahlins, *Boundaries*, ch. 2.

18 N. Girard d'Albissin, *op. cit.*, p. 313.

19 See the suggestive remarks in F. Braudel, *The Mediterranean and the Mediterranean World* (2 vols. trans. 1973) ii, pp. 701–3. It should be noted that historical enquiry of European state-making has tended to concentrate upon the larger and more complex entities to the neglect of the smaller. That tendency has fortunately been resisted by some historians. H. G. Koenigsberger's studies of Sicily and Savoy are models for the detailed investigation of smaller early modern states. J. A. Vann, *The Making of a State. Württemberg, 1593–1793* (Cornell UP, 1984) is a distinguished example of a case-study of state-making in a smaller state over a longer period.

20 P. Tucoo-Chala and C. Desplat, *La principauté de Béarn* (2 vols., 1982), ii, chs. 1–2.

21 William John Wright, *Capitalism, the State, and the Lutheran Reformation: Sixteenth-Century Hesse* (Ohio UP, 1988). H. Schilling, *Konfessionskonflict und Staatsbildung. Eine Fallstudie über das Verhältnis von religiösen und sozialen Wandel in der Frühneuzeit am Beispiel der Grafschaft Lippe* (Gütersloh, 1981) argues the case for the rôle of 'confessionalization' in state-building strategies amongst the German territorial states. But the responsiveness to change is already apparent before the reformation in Henry J. Cohn, *The Government of the Rhine Palatinate in the Fifteenth Century* (1965).

22 See ch. 9, below.

23 E. Sieber, *Die Idee des Kleinstaats bei den Denkern des 18. Jahrhunderts in Frankreich und Deutschland* (Basel, 1920).

24 Figures in table 1.1 are accumulated from G. Parker, *Spain and the Netherlands* (1979), p. 96; J. R. Hale, *War and Society in Renaissance Europe (1450–1620)* (London, 1984), pp. 62–3; J. Childs, *Armies and Warfare in Europe, 1648–1789* (Manchester, 1989) pp. 42–3.

25 G. Parker, *The Military Revolution. Military innovation and the rise of the West, 1500–1800* (Cambridge UP, 1988) provides an excellent introduction to the extensive literature on this subject.

26 W. H. McNeill, *The Pursuit of Power. Technology, Armed Force and Society since AD1000* (Oxford, 1982), ch. 4 – McNeill concentrates upon the effects of European colonialism as a force which enlarges some of Europe's states and thus engenders a competition with others.

27 No survey has yet been undertaken to prove this contention. The most suggestive

general account in English is G. Aylmer, 'Bureaucracy' in *New Cambridge Modern History* xiii (Companion Volume) ch. 6.

28 For Hesse-Cassel and the comparable example of Jülich-Berg, see Childs, *Armies and Warfare*, pp. 56–7 and Charles W. Ingrao, *The Hessian Mercenary State; Ideas, Institutions and Reform under Frederick II, 1760–1785* (Cambridge UP, 1987). For Scotland's bankruptcy from its military engagements in the 1690s, see below, ch. 7. For Württemberg, see Vann, *Making of a State*, ch. 7.

29 The necessity for selection made the choices of case-study difficult, but not arbitrary. The choices were made in the light of other recent studies which were already available and the areas where research was currently active. This still leaves many areas where case-studies would still have been useful, particularly the interesting case of the Swedish imperial experience in the seventeenth century and the case of Savoy in the seventeenth and eighteenth centuries.

30 C. L. Stinger, *The Renaissance in Rome* (Indiana UP, 1985) ch. 5, esp. pp. 235–8.

31 Machiavelli, *The Prince* (London, 1961) Penguin edn, chs. i–vii, esp. pp. 47–8: 'When states newly acquired . . . have been accustomed to living freely under their own laws, there are three ways to hold them securely: first, by devastating them: next, by going and living there in person; thirdly, by letting them keep their own laws, exacting tribute, and setting up an oligarchy which will keep the state friendly to you'. Cf. *The Discourses* (London, 1970) Book 2, esp. chs. 19–23 which advise that no 'half-measures' should be taken when it came to administering conquered territories.

32 Anne-Marie Lecoq, *François Ier imaginaire. Symbolique & politique à l'aube de la Renaissance française* (Paris, 1987) ch. vii.

33 Robert P. Adams, *The Better Part of Valor: More, Erasmus, Colet and Vives on Humanism, War and Peace, 1496–1535* (Washington UP, 1962), esp. chs. iv–vi.

34 His biting satirical verses entitled *In tempora Julii* are in *Opera Hutteni*, 3 vols. (Munich, 1859–70) i, p. 267.

35 Thomas More, *Utopia* (London, 1965), Penguin edn, p. 42.

36 See J. E. Longhurst, *Alfonso de Valdés and the Sack of Rome* (Albuquerque, 1952) and his *Dialogo de Mercurio y Caron*, ed. J. P. Montesinos (Madrid, 1929).

37 See J. A. Fernandez-Santamaria, *The State, War and Peace. Spanish Political Thought in the Renaissance, 1516–59* (Cambridge UP, 1977).

38 F. Hotman, *Francogallia*, eds. R. E. Giesey and J. H. M. Salmon (Cambridge UP, 1972), ch. I.

39 *Ibid.*, ch. 3.

40 Beza, *Du droit des magistrats*, ed. R. M. Kingdon (Geneva, 1970) pp. 13–14, etc.

41 Hobbes, *Leviathan* (London, 1965), ch. 20.

42 M. Hawke in *Killing is Murder and No Murder* (London, 1657), cited in Quentin Skinner, 'The ideological context of Hobbes' political thought', *Historical Journal* ix (1966), p. 307.

43 Algernon Sidney, *Discourses concerning Government* (in *Works*, 1772 edn), p. 446.

44 Pufendorf, *Law of Nature and of Nations* (Oxford, 2nd edn, 1710), pp. 92–7; 144–50, etc.

45 Quentin Skinner, 'History and ideology in the English Revolution', *Historical Journal* viii (1965), pp. 151–78; cf. his 'Conquest and consent: Thomas Hobbes and the engagement controversy', in G. E. Aylmer, *The Interregnum* (1972) ch. 3.

46 L. Bernard, *The Emerging City* (Duke UP, 1970) pp. 12–30; cf. O. Ranum, *Paris in the Age of Absolutism* (1968) ch. xii.

47 G. Walton, *Louis XIV's Versailles* (1986) ch. viii.

48 Y-M. Bercé, 'Rome et l'Italie au XVIIe siècle. La dernière chance temporelle de l'état ecclésiastique, 1641–49' in *l'Europe, l'Alsace et la France, Etudes réunies en l'honneur du doyen Georges Livet* (Strasbourg, 1987), pp. 229–37.

49 See below, ch. 3.

50 They were also fundamental to the conception of the French monarchy more generally. For a good modern survey see H. Rowen, *The King's State: Proprietary Dynasticism in Early Modern France* (Rutgers UP, 1980).

51 Paula S. Fichtner, *Protestantism and Primogeniture in Early Modern Germany* (Yale UP, 1989) provides an excellent bibliography to the complex question of the evolution of the rules governing dynastic succession in Germany, and also more broadly in Europe.

52 See below, ch. 2.

53 J. Vicens Vives, 'The administrative structure of the state in the sixteenth and seventeenth centuries', reprinted in Henry J. Cohn, *Government in Reformation Europe* (1971), pp. 58–87.

54 F. Walser, *Die spanischen Zentralbehörden und der Staatrat Karls V* (Göttingen, 1948).

55 F. Mauro, 'Les frontières du pouvoir au Portugal' in A. Stegmann (ed.), *Pouvoir et institutions en Europe au XVIe siècle* (1987), pp. 107–15.

56 Figures compiled from R. Mousnier, *The Institutions of France under the Absolute Monarchy, 1598–1789* (2 vols. Chicago UP, 1974–8), i, ch. 16 and P. Chaunu, *La France* (Paris, 1982) chs. 12–17.

57 The revenues of the French crown towards the end of the thirteenth century are estimated to have been worth between 61.5 and 99 tons of silver at contemporary equivalents. P. Chaunu, *Histoire économique et sociale de la France* (Paris, 1977), i, p. 134. This compares with an average of *c*.210 tons in silver equivalent for the revenues of the French monarchy in the period 1547–59 although the purchasing power of silver in the intervening period had declined by a factor of 7 or 8 times (*ibid.*, p. 46).

58 R. Mousnier, *Le conseil du roi de Louis XII à la Révolution* (Paris, 1970), p. 193ff.

59 The phrase was used by a traveller in 1714; see Louis Trenard (ed.), *Histoire d'une métropole. Lille, Roubaix, Tourcoing* (Toulouse, 1977) chs. 6 and 7.

60 See below, ch. 5.

61 These remarks are based upon P. Corrigan and D. Sayer, *The Great Arch* (Oxford, 1985). Remarkably, this work (by two sociologists) is almost the only broad study of the English state over a long chronological span. See also K. H. F. Dyson, *The State Tradition in Western Europe* (Oxford, 1980) pp. 36–44 who argues that there was an 'absence of the idea of the state in England' and that, 'As regards territorial politics within the United Kingdom, the informal collaborative arrangements of indirect rule were preferred to the formal controls associated with the idea of the unitary state' (p. 41).

62 See below, ch. 6.

63 See below, ch. 7.

64 B. P. Levack, *The Formation of the British State* (Oxford UP, 1987) provides a recent analysis of the varied ways in which it was proposed to integrate the two kingdoms more closely together in the seventeenth century.

65 These are matters which are imperfectly understood and actively the subject for further research by Dr K. M. Brown of the University of Edinburgh.

66 See below, ch. 8. V. L. Tapié, *The Rise and Fall of the Habsburg Monarchy* (trans. 1971) is still, however, of use.

67 See below, ch. 8. R. J. W. Evans, *The Making of the Habsburg Monarchy (1550–1700)* (Oxford, 1979) is essential to the comprehension of the wider perspectives of the Bohemian crisis of 1618. Cf. Robert A. Kann and Zdenek V. David, *The Peoples of the Eastern Habsburg Lands, 1526–1918)* (Washington UP, 1984).

68 See below, ch. 9.

69 H. W. Koch, *A History of Prussia* (1978) for a recent synoptic account of Prussia's history.

70 See H. Rosenberg, *Bureaucracy, Aristocracy and Autocracy: the Prussian experience (1660–1815)* (Boston, 1966).

71 *Ibid.* Cf. F. L. Carsten, *A History of the Prussian Junkers* (1989) chs. 2–3.

72 See O. Connelly, *Napoleon's Satellite Kingdoms* (Toronto, 1965); S. Schama, *Patriots and Liberators* (1977).

73 See W. McNeill, *Europe's Steppe Frontier* (1962) and the fundamental introduction to Ukrainian history, Nicholas L. Fr.-Chirovsky, *An Introduction to Ukrainian History* (1919), ii.

2

The Papal State: 1417–1600

PETER PARTNER*

A state of diverse foundations

Rome – Christendom's capital and regional metropolis

The Papal State occupied an economic and political arena which was simultaneously broad and restricted, European in scope on the one hand and more narrowly Italian on the other.[1] The only other state in Italy in a comparable geopolitical situation was Venice. Rome had provided (with the Holy Roman Empire) one of the two 'universal' political models of the Middle Ages. Yet in many cultural and social respects Rome had remained a provincial city, especially during the bleak periods of the Avignonese papacy and the Papal Schism, together lasting from 1309 to 1417. The re-projection of papal Rome and, with it, the growth of the Papal State, was a lengthy affair lasting several generations. The first Renaissance pope to fashion for the catholic world – or at least part of it – the image of the new Rome combining a restored classical splendour with a mystical Christian sense of destiny was Pope Julius II (1503–1513).

In the European context, the other cities of the papal dominions paled into insignificance beside Rome although a few, such as Bologna, Perugia and Ancona, had horizons which extended beyond the confines of the Papal State.[2] Rome stood at the centre of one of the most important communications networks. As soon as any great Latin bishopric became vacant, messengers were at once despatched to inform Rome, whilst other couriers hastened to inform the Holy See of any great changes in the policies of the catholic princes.

Rome's economic fortunes depended not only on the revenues of the Papal State but also on those drawn as 'spiritual' taxes and contributions from the catholic world in addition to the revenues of benefices held throughout the catholic world by clergymen resident in the city. From the mid-fifteenth century, Rome became a great centre for conspicuous consumption and its unfavourable trade balance with the outside world, especially with Tuscany, had to be supported by these papal revenues.

The most important port of the Papal State was Ancona, a city with oriental trading connections, and especially with Ragusa (Dubrovnik) and Istanbul. Venice was both a rival and a trading partner of Ancona, which had only partial

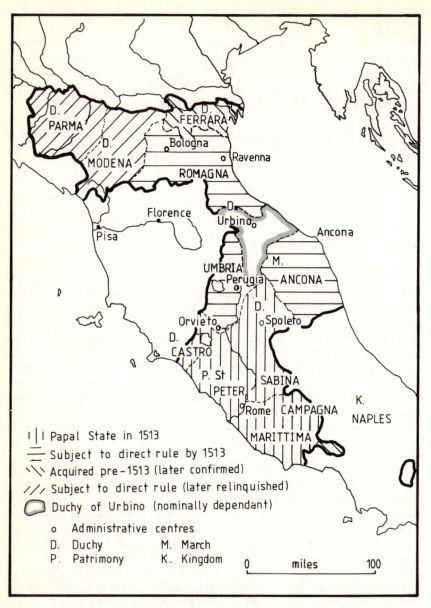

Fig. 2.1 The Papal State in the sixteenth century

success in resisting Venetian commercial pressures. Ancona's trade was connected with Florence and Rome along internal routes. Rome itself possessed a port which communicated with minor and major centres of the Tyrrhenian Sea and the islands, especially with Genoa, Pisa, Piombino, Gaeta, Sicily and Corsica. In the sixteenth century, Civitavecchia regained some of its former importance as a port whilst Corneto (Tarquinia) ceased to be one.

Perugia and Bologna remained larger commercial centres connected with trading partners outside Italy. Their universities, both more important than that at Rome, were frequented by students from northern and central Europe. Bologna's medieval manufacturing importance had declined, but it still possessed its silk and linen industries. However, the industrial and commercial activities of cities like Perugia, Viterbo and Orvieto had also decayed although they still retained commercial contacts outside the Papal State. The most important connections lay with Tuscany but the Lombard plain was also important, especially for the papal cities of Emilia and Romagna. Some cities, however, were less within the economic orbit of the Papal State than others. Ferrara was virtually independent of papal control until its 'devolution' to the Holy See in 1599. Parma, Piacenza and Reggio were never properly absorbed into the Papal State. They were assigned papal governors for a short period in the early sixteenth century; but Parma and Piacenza fell to the Farnese as fiefs under Pope Paul III (1534–49) whilst Reggio returned to the control of the Este family.

Romagna was less prosperous than it had been in the Middle Ages. The fairs of Senigaglia had declined and the timber exported from its shallow harbours was modest in value. Venice prevented these little ports from having any real maritime trade; the port of Rimini had silted up and that at Ravenna no longer existed. Cervia, which the popes had recovered from Venice in 1509, had a small port, and Pesaro was a market centre of limited range; but Ancona was the only port of real trading importance.

The March of Ancona also lost ground in economic terms. Here the most important trade lay with the Neapolitan Kingdom, theoretically a vassal-state of the Holy See. The Kingdom was subject in many ways to similar social and economic trends to those in the Papal State. The exchanges were mostly of livestock or agricultural products – imports of Neapolitan wine to Rome, of saffron through the east of the Papal State – or the movement of great flocks of sheep on the transhumance system from the Appenine highlands of the Kingdom to the lowlands on the west side of the Papal State.

Population change

The Papal State continued to suffer during the fifteenth century from the effects of the demographic crisis of the previous century.[3] Epidemics continued to recur. Viterbo, for example, a town of 10 000 inhabitants in 1400, lost 6 600 in the plague of that year and still had not made up these losses by mid-century. Other towns in the Patrimony of St Peter in Tuscia went through similar experiences; at Orvieto, the number of hearths in the city in 1449 was only half the figure of 1292. Rome may have contained 25 000 inhabitants in 1400 and no more than 35 000 by 1450. However the longer-term demographic trends in the city of Rome were upwards. Demographic decline was more evident in the small centres of population than in the larger. A significant number of villages in existence in the late thirteenth and early fourteenth centuries had disappeared by the fifteenth. Plague, the wars of the Avignonese popes and the Schism, population displacement in cultivated zones, especially in the transfer of agriculture to the alluvial plains, led to the decay and abandonment of hundreds of small villages.

The administrative District of Rome was an area bounded by Montalto di Castro in the north, Terni in the mid-Tiber area, and Terracina to the south, containing 366 towns, villages and fortified settlements. Its total population was about 150 000 with a density of about 10 to the square kilometre. Its population began to expand slowly in the sixteenth century. The population for the province of Umbria may be estimated to be at least 200 000 with a further 300 000 for the March of Ancona (including Urbino and Camerino). Further population increases for these provinces, and also for the District of Rome, seem to have been in the order of 20–25 per cent in the course of the sixteenth century. No reliable figures are available for Romagna.

Overall population estimates for the city of Rome are based on the census lists of 1526–7 which indicated about 54 000 'mouths' excluding unweaned babies. This census followed the plague of 1523 and the succeeding two years of war so that its population in the pontificate of Leo X (1513–22) may be supposed to have been higher. The Sack of Rome in 1527 and the flood of 1530 reduced Roman population to something approaching 32 000. Rome had always been a city of 'foreigners'; only 23.8 per cent of the inhabitants listed in the 1526–7 census had been born in Rome or its District. Recovery was not particularly rapid. Even in 1560, there were still probably fewer inhabitants than before the Sack of Rome in 1527. However the decade of 1580–90 saw the maximum growth of both Rome and Bologna. The population of the city of Rome reached a probably unprecedented 80 000 inhabitants in 1580 and further increased to 100 000 at the end of the century.

In Perugia, far more investment went into the surrounding rural areas than into the town. There were perhaps 15 000 inhabitants in the city and 30 000 in the neighbouring *contado*. In 1551, there were about 20 000 inhabitants in the city and a further 46 000 in the countryside. By 1588, the urban population was unchanged but rural population had risen to 57 000. For the same period, Ancona had a population of only about 12 000 inhabitants. In Bologna, after a decline in the fourteenth century, the rate of population recovery was faster. The city's population is estimated at about 45–50 000 in the late fifteenth century, thus exceeding that of Rome in that period. Bologna reached 62 000 in 1570, and a maximum of 72 000 around 1580, a peak which reflected the impulse given to the economy of the area by the Bolognese pope, Gregory XIII (1572–85). According to A. Bellettini, the number of children baptized in Bologna remained at a fairly constant level in the second half of the fifteenth century, rose in the sixteenth and, in the period 1570–90, reached a median rate about double that of the preceding century.[4]

Population increase in the sixteenth-century Papal State may have been lower than contemporary demographic trends in the Neapolitan Kingdom which seems to have received a certain amount of immigration from the Papal State in the second half of the century. Internal migration within the Papal State was chiefly into the main cities, especially Bologna and Rome. Many minor towns promoted immigration, especially in the fifteenth century, by means of local ordinances granting tax and other privileges to qualified immigrants.

Papal absolutism

The Apostolic Chamber was the main organ of government of the Papal State. The Chamber also had functions in the drafting and engrossing of papal letters and in the general running of papal finances. The Apostolic Chamberlain stood at its head. He was the supreme judge in spiritual and temporal cases relating to his office and was also responsible for the nomination of central and provincial officials. Oaths were sworn by papal officers between his hands and the 'apostolic vicars', or lords to whom delegated powers had been given were also sworn in before him. Unlike other major papal officials, he had powers which were not suspended during the interregnum which followed a pope's death.

Under the Chamberlain's authority were the Vice-Chamberlain and Apostolic Treasurer. The latter was responsible for auditing and approving the accounts of the Chamber and answered directly to the pope on questions of financial policy. From the Chamber clerks, the pope drew a good proportion of his main papal state officials (about a third of Chamber clerks might expect to be employed in this way). They were particularly employed as governors, treasurers and 'commissioners'. The duty Chamber clerk (*mensarius*) sorted the incoming Papal-State correspondence and law suits, and directed them to the appropriate officer or tribunal: often, the appropriate tribunal was that of the Apostolic Chamber or its Auditor. The clerks could be given commissions for the supervision of papal armies, and, in the sixteenth century, they were also despatched on circuit in the Papal State as commissioners with supervisory duties.

The main lines of the system of temporal government remained as had been laid down in the *Constitutiones Aegidianae* of Cardinal Gil Albornoz in 1357. The Rector – more often the Governor or President towards the latter part of this period – had full delegated powers, though these were modified in the early fifteenth century by powers granted to the Treasurer, and in the sixteenth century by various measures of control imposed directly by the Apostolic Chamber. The provincial finances were managed by the Treasurer, who also was assigned appropriate judicial powers. However, in the later sixteenth century, the provincial treasuries were auctioned to lay tax farmers, and the 'triennial subsidy' (a direct tax imposed by Paul III in 1543 and increased by Gregory XIII in 1572) was run by its own commissioners. Under the Rector or Governor, there were judges in spiritual and temporal cases, and there could be a provincial appeal court where there was no provincial *Rota* for appeals.[5] The provincial judges were part of a *curia generalis* which included a fiscal proctor and other judicial officers. In the March of Ancona, the local communes continued to send representatives to a provincial parliament which was regularly convoked by the Rector or Governor. The central governing organisms required little modification in order to unify the Papal State's dominions.

The most important post within the temporal sphere was that of Apostolic Legate, an officer who was usually of cardinal's rank. In the early fifteenth century, the Legate was normally the temporal head of a substantial region of the Papal State such as the March of Ancona or Romagna and he enjoyed very extensive temporal and spiritual powers. But, by the end of this period, the Legate had become a dignified officer who seldom exercised his theoretically wide powers, and had become an absentee administrator resident in Rome. The effective head of a province of the Papal State by this time was normally the governor or vice-legate. Separate governors were, by the sixteenth century, normally appointed to certain towns, which were thus, in effect, ruled separately from the main body of the province. Such city governors would normally also rule the territory round the city. Perugia, Viterbo, Ascoli Piceno, Ancona, Fermo, Loreto, Iesi, Matelica and Montalto all developed separate governmental units in this manner in the late sixteenth century and this had the effect of partially dismantling the old governing patterns, especially in the March of Ancona.

The Patrimony of St Peter in Tuscia, the oldest provincial unit, extended north of Rome as far as Montalto di Castro. South and east of the city, the province of Campagna (which included Marittima and Sabina) went as far south as Terracina. Perugia and its surrounding countryside were ruled by a governor, and the region of Umbria (which had thus been detached from Perugia) was sometimes subject to a cardinal-legate. Romagna was ruled by a president and the March of Ancona by a governor. Rome was, to some extent, directly controlled by the Apostolic Chamber. The city was ruled in the earlier period by the vice-chamberlain, then by a governor. In the sixteenth century, the *Presidente delle Strade* and the *Presidente dell'Annona* (both Chamber clerks) both had important duties in running Rome. The papal enclaves of Benevento, in the Neapolitan Kingdom, and Avignon, with its associated Comtat Venaissin, both had their own separate administrations.

At the end of the period, *Consulte* or 'congregations' of cardinals were set up to report on various aspects of curial government. Eventually, under Sixtus V (1585–90) and Clement VIII (1592–1605), permanent standing committees of cardinals were established to supervise some of the main functions of government in the temporal sphere, including grain supply, aspects of defence, taxation and communications. The main congregation, *De Bono Regimine*, had its jurisdiction excluded from the 'Legations' but it nevertheless acted as an extra tier of government for the Papal State. The *visite economiche* or tours of areas of the Papal State by specially appointed central agents, were a further occasional measure taken in the last decade of the sixteenth century to ensure central control.

Papal centralization was a powerful feature in the striking integration of this diverse inheritance. Yet not all papal policies led directly towards papal central-ization. In this period, some popes continued to make major feudal grants, either for nepotistic or for other political ends. The main result was the creation of new duchies which were exempt from the jurisdiction of governors and legates. The creation of the duchy of Ferrara in 1471 failed to influence temporal policy in a radical fashion. Ferrara had long been on the periphery of papal power. The marquis of Este had already been created duke of Modena and Reggio by the Holy Roman Emperor Frederick III in 1452. But the creation of the duchy of Urbino by Sixtus IV in 1474 had, on the other hand, important effects on provincial organization. When the Delle Rovera family inherited Urbino, adding Pesaro and Senigaglia to it in 1508–12, the result was the creation of the *stato d'Urbino*. This new unit incorporated extensive territories in the March of Ancona in addition to the original nucleus formed by the counts of Montefeltro.

Pope Leo X (1513–21) tried to create a new family fief for the benefit of the Medici after the lands in Emilia had fallen in to the Holy See but his attempt failed. Giovanni Maria da Varano was made duke of Camerino by Leo X after the failure to create a Medici duchy of Urbino. However, the devolution of the duchy of Camerino to the Holy See in 1539 avoided a new feudal problem in this area. On the other hand, the creation of the duchies of Castro, Parma and Piacenza for the sons of Pope Paul III (1534–49) imposed new and important limits on the papacy's temporal power. In the sixteenth century, the popes created other new ducal titles but these usually avoided the error of exempting the territories of their dukedoms from the jurisdiction of papal officers.[6]

Paul III made nepotism a recognized part of the papal administrative system by placing much of the diplomatic and territorial policy in the hands of the cardinal-nephew. This practice was not followed by all his successors but both Paul IV (1555–59) and Gregory XIII (1572–85) created a cardinal-nephew as 'superintendent' of their affairs, thus ensuring them a key position in the Papal State. Therefore, in the midst of the period in which the College of Cardinals was becoming more bureaucratic, the Counter-Reformation popes set up a new and long-lived institution in the cardinal-nephew which, by implication, was directly inimical to bureaucracy (at least in the sense in which we now understand that term). Centralization was thus tempered by papal willingness to reward the local aristocracy, just as the bureaucratic trends of the Papal State were modified by papal willingness to rely on family and patronage in the government of the patrimony of the Holy See.

Authority and law

The canon law tradition of the Roman Curia and the communal traditions of the cities both had a rôle in the formation of Papal State law which was, in its basic form, administered in the courts of the provincial governors and rectors. The existence of a coherent body of pontifical common law, a *diritto comune pontificio*, has been asserted by some historians and denied by others.[7]

The supreme courts of the temporal power, the court of the Auditor of the Apostolic Chamber and the courts of the Holy Roman Auditors of the Apostolic Palace (*Sacra Romana Rota*) were also among the most important courts of the papacy as a religious institution. Civil and criminal cases went in appeal from the Papal State to the Auditor of the Chamber. From there, with papal approval, there was a further appeal possible to the *Rota*. In the sixteenth century, major civil cases (*causae majores*) could be taken directly before the *Rota*.

The Auditor's jurisdiction was 'ordinary' and not 'delegated', i.e. inherent to the office and not delegated by a higher judicial authority. The Auditor was also the judge of first instance in criminal and civil cases involving clerics. This produced numerous conflicts of jurisdiction between his court and the communal courts of Rome about cases between laymen and ecclesiastics. Towards the close of the sixteenth century, the new congregations began to restrict the jurisdiction of the *Rota* in cases coming before it from the Papal State. The Chamberlain and Vice-Chamberlain also possessed judicial powers affecting cases arising in the temporal sphere; their intervention was especially frequent in cases involving the Roman communal courts.

The rector or governor was supreme head of the province committed to his charge. He had powers of 'mere and mixed empire and the power of the sword' as well as ordinary jurisdiction in civil and criminal cases. However, where the commune had obtained a grant of rights of 'mere empire', or where the commune and the rector both had the concurrent jurisdiction known as *preventio* (or precedence in first hearing), the rector's jurisdiction was limited to the first hearing.

The most important jurisdiction belonging to the rector rested in the appeals which he had rights to hear, rights which the communal courts tried to diminish. The popes conceded the right to hear appeals only to a small number of important towns, chiefly Bologna and Perugia where, in the sixteenth century, the new tribunals, or *rota*, were authorized to hear cases in appeal. Similar though less important courts of appeal, also termed *rota*, were established at Urbino and Macerata.

The lands directly ruled by the papacy, those 'immediately subject to the Holy See' (*terrae immediate subjectae*), were sharply distinguished in law from those granted out in apostolic vicariates or quasi-autonomous fiefs. The apostolic vicariate was a kind of legitimization of the powers exercised over the communes by the *signori*. The grant sought at the same time to preserve as much as possible of papal sovereign rights. Normally the apostolic vicars were granted 'mere and mixed empire with temporal jurisdiction' for a term of years. In practice, this gave them the right to appoint the judges, to authorize trials, and to have sentences issued. Following a decision of the Council of Constance (1414–18), a vicariate usually lasted after 1417 for three years though this restriction did not last very long. From the pontificate of Pius II (1458–64), and through the sixteenth century, the popes either conceded perpetual vicariates, or granted fiefs with legal powers similar to those of the older vicariates.

According to Cardinal Albornoz in the *Constitutiones Aegidianae* (*lib.v, cap.26*), the tribunals of the Rector's Court were supposed to follow, in order of precedence, first papal constitutions, then those of papal legates, and then finally the judicial custom of the province (i.e. the communal statutes). Canon law was thus to have precedence over Roman law, though Rome, where the contrary law was observed, remained an exception. The *Constitutiones Aegidianae* were only applied at Rome in the sixteenth century and, during that century, they were issued generally throughout the Papal State in two versions, of which the second and definitive one appeared during the pontificate of Sixtus V (1585–90). In practice, communal status continued to be extremely important throughout the Papal State. Yet the government often changed communal statutes, either through the process of approving them when they were submitted for re-enactment, or through the use of papal edicts. Law was, therefore, less of an instrument for the integration of the Papal State than might superficially have been thought.

Social structure and local autonomy

Communes: vicariates: feudatories

Papal State communes were classified either as *mediate* or *immediate subjectae*.[8] In the former category were all places conceded either in fief or in vicariate. The remainder were subject to the direct rule of the church. But this did not mean that the latter class all had a uniform legal status which applied to every place under direct rule. Relations between the church and its subject communes were infinitely variable, dependant in many cases on agreements which had, at some stage, been made between the papal government and the town concerned. For example, the whole history of subsequent relations between the church and Bologna was governed by the capitulations signed between the city and the Holy See in 1447, and the same applies to Perugia, which had signed a comparable agreement in 1424.

Papal power was exercised in different ways, depending on the economic and military power of the town involved, on its civil liberties and its location. At Perugia, the agreement reached in 1424 gave the pope 'full rule' (*governo pieno*) in the city. The legate or governor named the magistrate (*podestà*) but other municipal officials continued to be elected under the communal statutes. An agreement of this nature tended to create a mixed régime or dyarchy run jointly by the communal authorities and the governor, although the last word was with the pope or his representative. In the sixteenth century, the government of Perugia was modified after the military suppression of the 'salt war' revolt of 1540, and the construction of the papal fortress. However, there was a partial return to mixed rule after the restoration of communal magistracies in 1545.

The agreement just referred to between Bologna and Pope Nicholas V in 1447 was the last in a series of such agreements which stretched back to the preceding century. It allowed that commune to be governed by the '16 reformers of the state of liberty' (*sedici riformatori dello stato della libertà*), an arrangement which had been the subject of bitter quarrels between pope and commune in the earlier period, and it also permitted a considerable degree of autonomy in fiscal matters. The pope was well aware that the 1447 agreement might open the door to the rule (*signoria*) of some powerful native families in the city but the political circumstances gave him no alternative. After the expulsion of the Bentivoglio rulers of Bologna by Julius II in 1506, the 16 reformers were abolished, and replaced by a different form of government which was firmly controlled by the papal legate. Yet the local autonomy of this rich and powerful commune was not over and papal governments continued to court the Bolognese oligarchy.[9]

Even in less important towns such as Orvieto, Todi, Città di Castello or Ascoli Piceno, papal government had to be cautious in its dealings with the municipality, usually conceding some local autonomy by means of specific capitulations, and following a prudent policy which allowed a lot of room to the local magnates and oligarchs. In the fifteenth century, this meant coming to terms with powerful families such as the Monaldeschi of Orvieto, the Vitelli of Città di Castello and the Baglioni of Perugia. The relationship between these over-powerful families and the church often reached a critical point, and might even lead to their temporary or permanent expulsion from their native city.

In other ways, too, the papacy had means of cajoling the towns. In all major cities, the question of the subjection of the surrounding countryside (the *comitatus*) to the commune was an important element in municipal politics. The papal régime implicitly recognized the legal concept of the *comitatus*, and papal documents frequently refer to *civitas et comitatus*. The multitude of submissions made at various times by the little rural centres to the dominant towns were often

– though not invariably – recognized by the papal government. The taxes which a commune had to pay for the whole territory subject to it were paid by the minor communes on behalf of the dominant town, and eventually were agglomerated into the revenues of the latter. However, papal government did not always favour this process of 'territoriality' (*comitatitanza*), and a certain number of rural units, for example, the little commune of Baschi, in the mid-Tiber area between Orvieto and Todi (and still visible today from the motorway) managed to acquire a degree of local autonomy in respect both of the more powerful communes and of the local lords.

At Rome itself, local autonomy was least in evidence. The free commune of Rome had ended in 1398 when Pope Boniface IX abolished the magistracy of the *banderesi* and imposed a new and permanent reorganization upon communal government. From that date, the officials of the Roman commune were nominated by the pope. The Roman Senator, also a papal nominee, was in effect the executive of papal power. There were some anti-papal risings and the last major disturbance in Rome occurred in the abortive movement against Julius II in 1511. Yet these disturbances, even the serious Porcari rising of 1453, were short and had no lasting effects on government.

Papal power was for a long time circumscribed by an institution unique to the Papal State. In the first half of the fifteenth century a considerable proportion of the area of the state was granted out in 'apostolic vicariates' which exempted it from the effective rule of rectors and legates. The gradual decay of the apostolic vicariate was one of the major trends of the period which extended from the pontificate of Pius II (1458–64) to that of Paul III (1534–9). The vicar, granted 'mere and mixed' empire and temporal jurisdiction, could collect the taxes due to the church in the territory granted him and use them as he pleased. He appointed and could deprive officials of their posts and controlled the communal magistrates.

Even at the height of the authority of the apostolic vicariates, there were important limitations to a vicar's power. Papal sovereignty was expressly protected by clauses which obliged the vicar to recognize it, and to swear an oath of loyalty and obedience. He also undertook to display the arms of the church in his territory. Until Pius II, the vicar was normally appointed for a fixed term, at the end of which he was bound to restore the territory to the Holy See. He was also made to pay an annual rent which, in the case of the more significant vicariates, was a large sum.

In the latter half of the fifteenth century, the number of vicariates fell sharply. The move to diminish their number had begun as early as Pope Martin V (1417–31) and it received an important impulse from Pius II. The tyrants and *signori* of Romagna and the March of Ancona gradually lost their vicariates, until their virtual extinction was brought about by Cesare Borgia at the turn of the century. As a legal form the vicariate was far from at an end, and in the sixteenth century the number of small vicariates was still appreciable. But, apart from the grand vicariates which had been transformed into feudal duchies, the apostolic vicariate was, as an instrument of the princely *signoria*, extinct by the mid sixteenth century.

To describe the lords of the Papal State as 'barons' may be misleading. A large number of lords commonly described as such were, in reality, allodial landowners, whose tenure was in no way feudal. Feudalism did, of course, exist in the Papal State in a technical and legal sense. In the sixteenth century it could also be said that the papal government had a 'baronial policy' in the sense that it had a desire to stop tax evasion on the part of feudal landholders and also to prevent improper alienations of lands to these lords, especially alienations of church property.

At the same time, however, the papal government continued to issue a large number of feudal grants, the most important of which were of duchies or equivalent large landholdings. Many of these new feudal grants were to nobles or patricians who had not previously had any feudal status. The jurisdiction which accompanied the new grants was far from negligible, although only rights normally termed *signorili* accompanied the smaller ones. Meanwhile, for the extensive duchies such as those granted to the Della Rovere, the Varano and the Farnese families, the jurisdiction which went with the fief was very extensive, even to the point of establishing (in the case of the duchies of Parma and Piacenza) what was virtually a new independent state. It may be observed that, amidst the period in which some historians have recently claimed to see the emergence of a papal 'anti-feudal' policy, Pius V granted the duchy of Bracciano in 1560 to Paolo Giordano Orsini on the same terms as those fixed by Paul III for the duchies of Castro and Parma a generation earlier. The political effects of such a grant, of a region in the vicinity of Rome, were less than those of the Emilian duchies, but they were still far from negligible.

Barons, noblemen and gentlemen

Among the 'gentlemen who live idly on the plentiful income derived from their estates, without having anything to do with either their cultivation or the other efforts necessary for life' whom Machiavelli mentions in the *Discourses*, one species was still more pestiferous than the rest, namely, those who '. . . besides these aforesaid resources, have castles at their disposal and subjects under their obedience.[10] Of this sort, the Neapolitan Kingdom, the Roman District, Romagna and Lombardy are all full'. It is of little surprise that Machiavelli should have included two papal provinces in this list and he might well have added the Appenine regions of Umbria and the March of Ancona.[11]

Few of the 'lords' who exercised authority over papal cities possessed ancient feudal titles. In the countryside, there were feudal families such as the Montefeltro counts of Urbino; but such families were few in comparison with the powerful clans which dominated substantial territories without possessing specific feudal titles. Such families included the Atti of Sassoferrato, the Varano of Camerino, the Brancaleone of Castel Durante. The most impeccably ancient nobility of the Papal State, the Orsini, Colonna or Savelli of the Roman Campagna was composed of allodial collective groups (*consorterie*) which, in the fifteenth century, possessed no feudal titles except those which they had acquired in the *Regno*, though in the sixteenth and seventeenth centuries they added feudal titles which popes had granted them.

The idea of nobility was widely recognized in the social life of the urban communes, in which it was to play an increasingly important part. But it could not be used to describe a legally defined class in the fifteenth century. In Rome, for example, families were described as noble because they were rich and powerful, rather than because they belonged to any 'barony'. Nobility was a term of social distinction in Rome but not yet one of strict social status. In the Papal State communes, the old communal oligarchies were gradually transformed in the course of the fifteenth and sixteenth centuries into a new, permanent, hereditary caste which gradually began to call itself 'noble'. The origins of the change were complex. On the one hand, the richer groups in the towns made increasingly large investments in the rural areas under urban jurisdiction, a process which could, on occasion, create a new non-noble class such as the *bovattieri* of the Roman countryside. There was another social movement in the reverse direction, in the course of which many rural landowners moved into the towns, buying real estate there and acquiring citizenship. This urbanization of the rural landowners, taking place at the same time as the purchase of rural investments by the old urban ruling class, led in the long term to the appearance of a new ruling class of 'gentry' in the city. It would be inexact to term this new class a *noblesse de robe*, although numerous notaries, lawyers and physicians were involved in it. It was rather a fusion of merchants, country gentry and lawyers.

We may refer instead to a new ruling class in the towns, based on the closure of the municipal magistracies in favour, in any one city, of a specific group of families. This was not a new class in the Marxist sense. It contained both bourgeois and feudal elements. Rather, it was a modification of the old social order although, in the present state of our knowledge, it is difficult to identify the phases by which it came into existence. The urbanization of the rich country landowners already referred to caused the older urban ruling class to form a common front with elements of the older rural landowning groups. Examples of the process may be cited from Perugia, Bologna and elsewhere. From 1416, the nobles were no longer shut out from the Perugian guilds. In the early fifteenth century, the ruling group of the city were styled *gentiluomini*. However, the real emergence of a new noble class in Perugia in the sense of the customary right of certain families to monopolize the chief city magistrates did not take place until the late sixteenth century. At Bologna, the formation of a senatorial class, the group of families which, by right, formed the magistracy of the Council of 40 (later 50) occurred after the expulsion of the Bentivoglio in 1506. In the cities of the March of Ancona, the lines of demarcation are harder to fix. At Macerata, for example, the *Consiglio di Credenza*, the principal town council, was closed in favour of certain 'noble' families in the late fifteenth century, but membership of the *Consiglio Generale*, which continued to be important, still required only 30 years' residence and an income of 500 florins annually. At Ascoli Piceno, the closure of the communal offices in favour of a small group happened only late in the sixteenth century. When the Statutes of the city were printed in 1496, they continued to be in the fourteenth-century version which gave substantial power to the *popolo*. On the other hand, at Cesena, and even before the Malatesta family was finally ejected in 1466, it was customary to attribute the post of a communal councillor who died in office to the brother or son of the dead man. The idea of hereditary succession to communal office was a widely diffused one which had profound results on communal law in the Papal State generally.

Factional strife between Guelph and Ghibelline, which was still a common feature in the fifteenth-century Papal State, waned only slowly. Its decline was due partly to seignorial, princely rule, partly to the control imposed by papal governors. But even in the mid sixteenth century, the problem was still there, especially in Romagna and the March of Ancona. Factional clashes (the *lotta di parte*) could still be ferocious in Faenza, Cesena, Rimini, Forlì, Ascoli Piceno. Occasionally, papal governors themselves suffered the consequences, for example, the vice-legate of Perugia, killed by the Baglioni in 1533, the governor of Ascoli Piceno, murdered in the city's cathedral with all his followers in 1555, and the governor of Fano, who was also massacred with his people in 1561. In the late sixteenth century, the exiles and bandits of the factional conflicts were often transformed into 'brigands', as occurred at Ascoli Piceno and also at Ancona.

The clergy

'The freedom of the church is nowhere better respected than where the Roman Church exercises full power in matters both temporal and spiritual.' This remark of Pope Innocent III would have seemed merely ironical to a sixteenth-century clergyman. Almost all bishoprics in the Papal State were directly subject to the Holy See, and all were subject to papal reservation, so that their incumbents could be nominated in the papal consistory. Papal State bishops were, in theory, supervised by the appropriate legate.[12]

In reality, however, clerical life in the Papal State closely resembled its counterpart in other parts of Italy. It was neither more nor less rigorously regimented than elsewhere. The top clerical positions were all occupied by an élite which was recruited either in the Roman court or among members of the local oligarchies. The career curialists at Rome were mostly Italian, though some hailed from elsewhere. The remainder of the major Papal State clergy were local magnates, the *gentiluomini*. Major families were everywhere in Italy using their clerical patronage to consolidate local power and reinforce family wealth. They treated church benefices as part of their own patrimony, transferring them from one family member to another by means of 'resignation'.

In the Papal State, such families were legion. Some, such as the Geraldini and Ferratini (of Amelia), the Capranica (of Lazio and the March) and the Staccoli (of Urbino) used the Papal State episcopate as a springboard to establish themselves locally. Others, such as the Spiriti (of Viterbo), the Eroli (at Narni), the Numai (at Forlì), used the church to reinforce an already strong social position. The ruling families naturally found patronage, though the popes resisted appointing members of the seignorial families to their native sees in the fifteenth century, and only one Malatesta was bishop of Rimini. On the other hand, there were two Baglioni bishops of Perugia, and, in the first half of the sixteenth century, Ippolito and Ludovico d'Este were both bishops of Ferrara.

The College of Cardinals itself set a none too shining example. Cardinals obtained Papal State bishoprics, usually in administration, though there were some examples of flagrant corruption in the cases of cardinals who actually occupied such bishoprics such as, for example, Benedetto Accolti's episcopate at Ravenna (whilst, concurrently controlling another see at Ancona). More frequently, a cardinal resigned such a bishopric to a relative or client. For example, Cardinal Niccolo Ridolfi bestowed the sees of Forlì, Orvieto and Viterbo on various Florentine clients in 1520–38. Cardinal Alessandro Farnese behaved in much the same way with Ancona and Spoleto; and Cardinal Domenico de Cupis similarly with the sees of Camerino and Recanati.

Such a clergy was none too easy to control. Even in the Counter-Reformed environment of the late sixteenth century, Gabriele Paleotti found it immensely hard to reform the Papal State bishopric of Bologna, although he came to it as a cardinal and with the highest possible connections in the Curia. Like many bishoprics, Bologna was so burdened with pensions that Paleotti found the economic backing for his task to be lacking. Like most chapters, that of Bologna was staffed by a privileged body drawn from local magnate families, which resisted reform stubbornly.

Another important category of bishops was that of bishops in the Papal State who also exercised the office of governor or vice-legate or rector. Usually (though there were exceptions) the city acting as their administrative centre was not the one where they were appointed to pastoral duties. But a governor of Rome could be bishop of Ascoli or Fossombrone; a vice-legate of Perugia was (at various points in time) bishop of Terracina, Veroli and Forlì. In fact, and as in other sixteenth-century states, a bishop in the Papal State should often be viewed as a servant of the state rather than a pastor of souls, an ambivalent representative of a more integrated Papal State and its patronage structures. At the end of the sixteenth century the application of Tridentine rules of residence made the civil servant-bishop a much rarer animal in the Papal State.

Politics, finance and public policy

Priestly politics and princely objectives

All papal policy was eventually the policy of the *sacerdotium*. Nineteenth-century historians who referred to a 'secularized' papacy or to popes who were above all 'Renaissance princes' failed to understand the continuity of the papal institution. On the other hand, more recent historians have underlined the more subtle ways in which the institutions of the Papal State and the concept of the papal principate influenced the way in which papal spiritual power perceived itself and was organized.[13]

Four main objectives may be identified in the policies of the Renaissance popes. Firstly, there was opposition to ideas and tendencies harmful to the papal primacy, which had become manifest during the Schism and the Council of Constance. Secondly came the repression of heresy – at first mainly the Hussites in Bohemia but there were others too. Thirdly, the maintenance of the direct dependence of the states of the church on the pope was of importance. Finally, taking account of the importance of papal relations with the eastern churches, there was the prosecution of the crusade against the Muslim powers.

The Papal State played an important rôle in the furtherance of these objectives. Papal finances had emerged after the Schism and the Council of Constance in a weakened condition. 'Spiritual' revenues had been reduced by a third in comparison with their fourteenth-century levels. Giving the popes an income which would finance military defences, diplomacy and propaganda could be achieved only by a substantial increase in Papal State revenues, and these in fact doubled between the pontificates of Martin V (1417–31) and Sixtus IV

(1471–84). 'Spiritual' revenues continued to decline as a proportion of total papal income so that, by the sixteenth century, papal finances as a whole came to depend overwhelmingly on the Papal State.

Military defences, diplomacy, propaganda and the crusade were all important in the maintenance of priestly power. Recent research has emphasized, for example, the rhetorical and propagandist functions of the humanists in Rome in papal service. Burckhardt's hypothesis that the Papal State was a 'complete anomaly' ('eine völlige Anomalie') may now be refuted.[14] Burckhardt had argued the case not on the grounds of the priestly nature of the state but the persistence of its many disorderly *signorotti* and the decay of its free communes. What Burckhardt overlooked was the manner in which the Papal State conformed to the trends observable in other contemporary Italian states, and particularly that the smaller lordships were disappearing and making way for large-scale government, while at the same time local life was being taken over by new or transformed oligarchies. The decay of the free commune was not peculiar to the Papal State, but occurred everywhere.

It is true that the impression of the Papal State as an anomaly may be drawn from the ironic judgement expressed by Machiavelli that the popes alone 'have states which they do not defend and subjects whom they do not govern. And though their states are not defended they are not for that reason taken from them, and though their subjects are not governed, they pay no attention to that fact, and neither wish to break away from church rule nor have they the power to do so. Only these [papal] principalities are secure and happy'.[15]

Machiavelli wanted to emphasize in this passage the disparity between the ineffectiveness of fifteenth-century papal temporal rule and its emergence under Julius II as a real power in his own times. According to him, the earlier popes had been impotent in their own state and, at that time, 'not only powerful outside powers but any minor lord or baron, however modest, took a low view of papal temporal power'. Machiavelli's view was very influential, especially on Ranke and Burckhardt. Yet essentially Machiavelli was not offering a historical judgement but rather a literary *topos* in order to emphasize the political and moral importance of the wars of Julius II.

Territorial change and centralization

After the disorder of the final period of the Schism, the Papal State continued to be fragmented into small lordships, and to be threatened by the ambitions of big mercenary leaders like Fortebraccio da Montone, Francesco Sforza, Niccolò Piccinino. The popes found it the harder to defend themselves against the aggression of *condottieri* and the insubordination of *signorotti* because their spiritual policies were still being opposed by the Conciliar party in the church. Only after the definitive defeat of the Council of Basle in 1449 was the way open for a more active rôle in temporal politics. The Papal State had found that there were other problems occasioned by the struggle for power in the Neapolitan Kingdom, theoretically the vassal-state of the Holy See. The abandonment by the popes of the Angevin cause in the Kingdom of Naples in 1443 allowed the papacy more latitude to pursue its own ends in temporal affairs, and also to lend its weight to the search for an equilibrium among the Italian states after the Peace of Lodi in 1455.

Between the Peace of Lodi and the War of Ferrara (1482), a more successful method was identified for the defence of papal interests in its state. The popes did not seek all-out war with the *signorotti*. Rather, they sought to exact obedience from lords and vassals but were always ready to tolerate, and even to legitimize, the lordship of those who were willing to obey. Take, for example, the action initiated against the turbulent Sigismondo Malatesta da Rimini by Pius II (1458–64), a long military campaign which ended the lordship of the Malatesta of Rimini. Pius II's instrument was Sigismondo Malatesta's great rival and fellow-*condottiere*, Federigo da Montefeltro. Federigo was afterwards hand-somely rewarded, culminating in the bestowal of the duchy of Urbino upon him by Sixus IV in 1474. This was not without long-standing result for the Papal State. The Montefeltro family only lasted a few years in the duchy but the latter was a factor in papal politics until the seventeenth century.

The French invasion of 1494 was a watershed for the Papal State as for the other Italian states. The political prestige of the papacy, and its diplomatic expertise, enabled the popes and their servants to use foreign military and political help to impose a much tighter control on their dominions. The military campaigns of Cesare Borgia in Romagna and the March of Ancona, with the subsequent reorganization of papal rule in the re-conquered areas, eliminated many 'vicars' and petty tyrants in these territories, and laid the basis for a newer régime less cluttered by minor lordships. Julius II (1503–13) achieved the recovery of Bologna and the expulsion thence of the Bentivolgio family. The defeat of Venice in 1510 freed a large area in the north-east of the Papal State from the direct or indirect rule of the Venetians. Julius II made only minor changes in the way the Papal State was governed and, even in Bologna, preserved a good deal of the former municipal autonomy.

The period between the death of Julius II in 1513 and the Sack of Rome in 1527 was as unfortunate for the Papal State as it was unpropitious for the church in general. Leo X (1513–21) contributed nothing to the Papal State but a useless and expensive war which was intended to wrest the duchy of Urbino from the peaceful rule of Francesco Maria della Rovere in favour of Lorenzo de' Medici. Parma, Piacenza and Reggio were occupied by papal authorities but not re-organized in a way that made the conquests permanent.

In this period, the great Italian wars of France and Spain gradually changed political conditions, thus rendering obsolete the old ways in which papal subjects could also be *raccomandati*, *collegati*, and *aderenti* of other Italian powers. When military mercenaries (or *condottieri*), natives of the Papal State, behaved in a way politically unacceptable to the pope, their own towns would refuse to admit them, as happened to Gianpaolo and Malatesta Baglioni of Perugia. In the fifteenth century, the main lords of the Papal State outside Rome had been able to pursue, providing that they did so with prudence, virtually independent foreign policies relative to those of their papal masters. This became impossible early in the following century.

The 'liberty of Italy' – i.e. the policy which aimed at excluding French and Spanish forces from the peninsula – was a noble ideal, but one which was far above the modest military resources of the Papal State. After the battle of Pavia in

1525, the political and military potential of the Papal State was sharply eroded. The last effort of papal policy at the time of the League of Cognac (1526) made little headway against the enormous power of the Holy Roman Emperor, Charles V. In 1527, Rome was occupied and sacked by imperial troops.

The later period of the Italian wars ran from the surrender of Florence to papal-imperial forces in 1530 until 1559, the year of Pius IV's election and of the treaty of Cateau-Cambrésis (1559). This was a period of overwhelming but not uncontested Habsburg hegemony, in which the popes often managed to negotiate understandings with the emperor which gave them a measure of quiet and protection in their state. Paul III was thus in a position to discipline the cities and social groups which resisted a more severe fiscal régime in the Papal State. Thus Perugia was subdued (1540) and Ascania Colonna defeated (1542). Yet real resistance to Habsburg power was beyond papal capacity. Julius III (1550–5) sought in vain for a territorial settlement which would exclude the Habsburgs from central Italy, and the Spanish war of Paul IV (1555–9) brought the papacy in 1557 to the verge of political collapse and Rome to the brink of being ransacked by imperial troops, as it had been in the great Sack of Rome of 1527.

In the last four decades of the century, Habsburg dominance was uncontested by the popes. In the Papal State, the two main governmental trends were the increase in taxation, and the attempt to police the state more effectively in order to subdue the dissident movements in the countryside known as 'brigandage'. Brigandage was connected on one side with the factional struggles in the towns, struggles which were carried into the countryside by rebellious gentry, and on the other with fiscal pressure, peasant misery, and the drift of the population from one area to another.[16] In the last decade of the century, papal rule was, to some extent, reorganized through the new tier of government supplied by the congregations. Finally, in 1599, the devolution of Ferrara to the Holy See brought under direct rule one of the most important territories which had hitherto been effectively autonomous – though the duchies of Parma, Piacenza, Urbino and Castro all retained a substantial degree of independence.

Government, communal and seignorial finances[17]

In the first half of the fifteenth century, the popes had access to the capital market mainly through their bankers, especially the banking official known as the 'Apostolic Depositary'. Through him, they obtained short-term loans, backed by assignments on the various revenues of the Apostolic Chamber. It is unlikely that interest was charged on these loans; the Depositary made small percentage charges (*retentiones*) on the money he handled. Papal State income doubled in the half-century beginning with Martin V in 1417, but there is no indication of a further large rise in temporal revenues in the last part of the fifteenth century. The popes made one or two rather unsuccessful attempts (especially under Innocent VIII (1484–92)) to farm parts of the spiritual revenues but found the best way to raise money was to sell the curial offices in a more systematic manner than had been practised hitherto. The main class of venal office was that of the short-term *vacabili*, transferable to a third party after payment of a fee and recoverable by the papal *Dataria* either on the death of the occupant or on his promotion to an 'incompatible' benefice. There were also new 'colleges' of venal offices, with mainly honorific or no duties, which paid a lower rate of interest and were, in effect, investments in a long-term public debt.

From the late fifteenth century onwards, the papal budget was in deficit. From 1526 onwards, the popes returned to the capital market and obtained both long- and short-term loans through a system of *Monti*, the interest varying between 6 and 10 per cent.[18] At the time of the Sack of Rome (1527), the popes were spending a third of their gross revenues on repayment of interest to the *Monti* and office-holders. Half-way through the century, the proportion had risen to 40 per cent and, by the end of the century, it stood at around 53 per cent.

The only other way in which the popes raised fresh income was from the profits on the alum mines at Tolfa. These were opened in the mid fifteenth century and remained an appreciable source of revenue until the end of the period. Gross papal revenue rose in the early sixteenth century, in part because of the acquisition of the Emilian duchies. In 1565, papal gross revenue was double that of 1525; by the end of the century, it had trebled. This was based largely, however, on the increase in Papal State revenues which, in 1599, had quadrupled in respect of their amount in 1525. Papal fiscality in the temporal power became much more burdensome, especially from the imposition of a tax on landed property by Paul III in 1543 which was exacted from feudal landowners as well as from the remaining population. The clergy were at first exempt from this 'triennial subsidy' but, in 1557, the subsidy of 'a scudo or a half' was exacted from church as well as from other lands. Paul III and his successors also increased indirect taxation (by taxes on flour, meat, etc.), and revived earlier direct taxes such as the *tassa dei cavalli morti* (in theory a tax to replace the horses of the papal army). The tax burden on the Papal State reached its peak under Sixtus V (1585–90), but then tended to relax slightly with the agricultural crisis of the last decade of the century. To some extent, the increased tax burden reflected the contemporary rise in prices. At Rome, nominal prices doubled in the course of the sixteenth century but taxes had quadrupled during the same period.

The partial fiscal autonomy of the communes was reflected in the separate debt burden which they had to shoulder. Their responsibility for payment of public officials and the financing of local public works (the maintenance of town walls, local town-planning schemes, and the support of a local university where there was one) was systemized at the end of the sixteenth century in an annual *tavola*, or schedule of payments, issued by the Apostolic Depositary in Rome. The debts of the communes also covered local grain purchases and agrarian credit schemes. The amounts were large. Rome and Bologna each owed approaching a million silver *scudi* by 1600, which together came to about 15 per cent of the amount owed at that time by the central papal administration.

Finally, it should not be forgotten that in the sixteenth century, the princely autonomous or semi-autonomous courts of Ferrara, Parma-Piacenza and Urbino each had budgets of far from negligible proportions. They each spent large sums on princely ostentation and also financed quite important agricultural improvement programmes. The increased fiscal authority of the Apostolic Chamber was far from removing other fiscally active and autonomous units within the Papal State.

Power, culture and propaganda

The court and the city and representations of power[19]

The papal court was both the administrative centre of Christendom and the ruler's household, his 'palatine family'. The household grew by leaps and bounds from the mid fifteenth century. Under Pius II (1458–64) there were 150 papal familiars in the Vatican palace divided between 'lords' and 'ministers', and a subordinate staff of about 80. Under Leo X (1513–21), the total household rose to about 700 people to reach a maximum of about 1 000 in 1562. There were some cut-backs in the Tridentine period but the proportionate cost of the court rose to its maximum at the end of the sixteenth century under Clement VIII (1592–1605).

The papal court was the centre of a great propagandist enterprise, the symbolic representation of papal power. The early traditional forms of this were the Roman liturgies and ceremonies at the various principal churches, and the institutions of the pilgrimage and the Jubilee. Its princely side was the papal consistory, the main papal council in which major benefices were conferred, judicial decisions pronounced, court sermons heard, and diplomatic audience accorded.

The reconstruction and embellishment of the Vatican palaces and the urban renewal of Rome were major papal aims from the time of Nicholas V (1447–55). From the latter part of the century, the Vatican palace was extended in the direction of the Belvedere, originally a villa for relaxation, but under Julius II the scene for the most grandiose exercise in building and landscaping which Rome had known since ancient times. The functions of the Belvedere *cortili* (court-yards) were essentially profane: they contained gardens, ancient statues, fountains, and even an area for tournaments and bullfights. The papal palaces were not only rebuilt but then were decorated according to the most elaborate artistic plans executed in any court in Europe, all designed to impress the beholder with the might and particular policies of the Holy See. As in other princely courts, the achievements of the dynasty of the ruler were emphasized as well as the power of the institution.

Restoring and improving the churches of Rome was the natural objective of the bishop of Rome, and the great project to rebuilt St Peter's engaged papal energies for over a century. The renewal of Rome was encouraged by a mechanism of tax concessions and town-planning legislation. By slow and tortuous stages, culminating in the great projects of Sixtus V at the end of this period, Rome became a centre where the greatest architects and planners exercised their powers.

The achievement was not merely one of decoration. The scenic wonders of Rome had been revived in new forms to display the ceremonial functions of the head of Christendom. Meanwhile defence and water supply, housing and charitable endeavour were not forgotten. The place of the ancient city and of the early Christian monuments in the imagination of Christian Europe was reinforced, and Rome became a 'cabinet' of ancient and Christian antiquities, as well as a model for the town-planning of an early modern capital.

Oligarchs, bankers and 'modernization'[20]

The effect of the decay of older municipal autonomies and the accompanying growth of power of the Roman Court was the creation of a new oligarchy of clerks and financiers. In the sixteenth century, families of bankers and tax-farmers inserted their own members in the clerical hierarchy of the Roman Court and the Papal State administration. This process amounted to the creation of a new ruling class in Rome and the Papal State. Its origins lay in the fifteenth-century control exerted over papal finances by Tuscan and Ligurian merchant-bankers, and it was encouraged by the Medici popes and by the activities of the great tax-farmers of the pontificate of Paul III (1534–49). The great bankers – the Altoviti, Strozzi, Salviati, Olgiati, Odeschalchi, Sauli, Chigi, Ubaldini, etc. – became, alongside the cardinals (to whose ranks they contributed) and the great Roman barons, leaders in Roman society. Even the second-rank merchants were often relatives of the Chamber clerks and other managers of the Roman Court so that, when the tax-farming contracts were auctioned 'by the candle' (the bidding process being conventionally governed by the time it took for a lighted candle to reach the end of the candlewick), many financiers enjoyed decisive advantages over the others. In Italy, the financiers enjoyed a much higher social status than their contemporaries in France and the comparison is an instructive one.

The dominant place of the Roman baronies in its society ended towards the close of the fifteenth century. After the defeat of the Roman magnates by Julius II in 1511, few Romans were employed in the papal court at all until the accession of Paul III in 1534. By the late sixteenth century, the great Roman baronial families such as the Savelli, Colonna and Orsini were in decline and in debt, though their possessions and social prestige were still substantial. Other elements of the Roman patriciate, former minor houses such as the Massimi, the Leni or the Mattei, occupied a far more prominent place than hitherto. A new class of Roman nobles began to make its presence felt, composed of Tuscan, Ligurian and Lombard bankers who often claimed (like the Borghese family from which Paul V was descended) to be 'Romans', of patrician but earlier non-noble Romans and other Papal State magnates. It was a society dominated by tax-farmers and investors in debt to the papacy. Government aims remained those of the *sacerdotium* but Roman society was becoming a clerical plutocracy.

The unpopularity among liberals and protestants of what remained of Roman-papal society by the nineteenth century made it very difficult for historians of that period to pass level-headed judgements on its earlier history. Not all nineteenth-century historians were blind to the realities of the Papal State, and Ranke himself drew attention to the fact that the early modern papacy was far less of a static, fossilized organization than had been commonly imagined. But the view that a traditional society is supposed, under certain circumstances, to develop into something modern, and thereby to shed its former traditional learnings, presents considerable difficulties when applied to the Papal State.

For sociologists of Max Weber's generation, it was difficult to think that a society as supposedly traditional as that of the Roman Court should also have been precociously modern, even though it was recognized that papal bureaucracy was very advanced for its period.[21] The institutionalization of nepotism, however, points in a different direction, and Weber drew attention to the 'patrimonialism' in the Papal State which enabled it to be managed, from the late sixteenth century onwards, by the cardinal-nephew.

Fifty years ago, Clemens Bauer remarked that, without papal finance, there would have been no early European capitalism.[22] The implications of this observation for a Papal State which could be said to have been modernizing both in its bureaucracy and in its financial system, even though powered by traditional religious forces, were lost on sociologists then, and continue to be overlooked now. The early modern Papal State therefore remains something of an enigma for those theorists of modernization who imagine an integrated, secular, modern state as emerging in Europe in a linear progression from traditional to more modern societies.

NOTES FOR CHAPTER 2

* Dr Peter Partner taught at Winchester College until 1986. He is an associate Fellow of the *Deputazione di Storia Patria per l'Umbria*.

1 General surveys of the Papal States in this period include M. Caravale and A. Caracciolo, *Lo stato pontificio da Martino V a Pio X* (Turin, 1978); P. Prodi, *Papal Prince – One Body and Two Souls: The Papal Monarchy in Early Modern Europe* (Cambridge UP, 1988; Italian edn, 1982); P. Partner, *The Lands of St Peter: The Papal State in the Middle Ages and the Early Renaissance* (California UP, 1972). J-C. Maire Viguer, 'Comuni e signori in Umbria, Marche e Lazio', in G. Arnaldi, P. Toubert, D. Waley, J-C. Maire Viguer and R. Manselli, *Comuni e signorie nell'Italia nordorientale e centrale: Lazio, Umbria e Marche, Lucca* (Turin, 1987).

2 For the following paragraphs, see J. Delumeau, *Vie économique et sociale de Rome dans la seconde moitié du XVIe siècle* (2 vols., Paris, 1957–9). A. Esch, 'Importe in das Rom der Frührenaissance' in *Studi in memoria di Federigo Melis* (3 vols., Naples, 1978) iii, pp. 381–452. P. Earle, 'The commercial development of Ancona, 1479–1551', *Economic History Review* xxii (1969), pp. 28–44. E. Ashtor, 'Il commercio levantino di Ancona nel basso Medioevo' in *Rivista Storica Italiana* xlviii (1976), pp. 213–53. S. Anselmi, 'Venezia, Ragusa, Ancona tra Cinque e Seicento', *Atti e Memorie della Deputazione di Storia Patria per le Marche*, 8th Series, vi (1968–70), pp. 1–76; C. Calisse, *Storia di Civitavecchia* (Florence, 1936). C. F. Black, 'Politics and society in Perugia, 1488–1540' (B. Litt. Thesis, University of Oxford, 1966); *Storia di Bologna* (Bologna, 1978). *Storia dell'Emilia-Romagna* (3 vols., Imola, 1977) ii. T. Dean, 'Venetian economic hegemony; the case of Ferrara', *Studi Veneziani*, xii (1986), pp. 45–99.

3 K. J. Beloch, *Bevölkerungsgeschichte Italiens*, (Berlin and Leipzig, 1939) ii. A. Bellettini, *La populazione di Bologna dal secolo XV all'unificazione italiana* (Bologna, 1961). E. Lee, *Descriptio Urbis: il censimento di Roma del 1526* (Rome, 1986). P. Partner, *Renaissance Rome, 1500–1559: A Portrait of a Society* (California UP, 1976). M. Mallett and D. Whitehouse, 'Castel Porciano: an abandoned medieval village of the Roman Campagna', *Papers of the British School at Rome* xxxv (1967), pp. 113–46.

4 Bellettini, *Populazione di Bologna*, p. 103.

5 For the *Sacra Rota* see below, p. 31.

6 New dukedoms were created for the Colonna, Orsini and the newer Cesi families in the regions of Rome and Umbria.

7 G. Ermini, *Guida bibliographica per lo studio del diritto comune pontificio* (Bologna, 1934). *Idem*, 'Validità della legislazione albornoziana nelle terre della chiesa dal Trecento alla codificazione del secolo XIX', *Studia Albornotiana* xxxv (1979), pp. 81–102. F. E. Scheider, *Die Römische Rota; nach geltendem Recht auf geschichtlichen Grundlage* (1914); E.

Cerchiari, *Capellani papae et apostolicae sedis auditores causarum sacri palatii apostici* (4 vols., Rome, 1919–21). B. Frattegiani, 'Il tribunale della Rota perugina', *Bollettino della Deputazione di Storia Patria per l'Umbria* xlvi (1949), pp. 5–117.

8 C. F. Black, 'The Baglioni as tyrants of Perugia, 1488–1540', *English Historical Review* lxxxv (1970), pp. 245–81. *Idem*, 'Perugia and papal absolutism in the sixteenth century', *Ibid*, xcvi (1981), pp. 509–39. G. Orlandelli, 'Considerazioni sui capitoli di Niccolo V coi bolognesi', *Rendiconti della Accademia nazionale dei Lincei: Classi di scienze morali, storiche e filologiche*, 8th Series, iv (1949), pp. 457–73; M. Bartolotti, 'Sui capitoli di Niccolo V per la citta di Bologna', *Annali della Facoltà di Lettere e Filosofia dell'Università di Macerata*, ii–iv (1970–1), pp. 511–38. P. Partner, 'L'Umbria durante i pontificati di Martino V e di Eugenio IV', *Atti del settimo convegno di Studi Umbri, 18–22 maggio 1969: Storia e Cultura nell'Umbria nell'età moderna* (Perugia, 1972), pp. 89–98. A. Esch, 'Al fine del libero comune di Roma nel giudizio dei mercanti fiorentini', *Bollettino dell'Istituto Storico Italiano per Il Medio Evo* (1976–7), pp. 235–77. P. J. Jones, *Malatesta of Rimini and the Papal State* (Cambridge UP, 1974). C. M. Ady, *The Bentivoglio of Bologna* (Oxford UP, 1937). M. Mallett, *The Borgias* (London, 1937). *Idem, Mercenaries and their Masters; Warfare in Renaissance Italy* (London, 1974). L. Martini, G. Tocci, C. Mozzarelli, A. Stella, *I ducati padani, Trento e Trieste* (Turin, 1979).

9 E. g. Pius V's help given to the University of Bologna in 1562.

10 Machiavelli, *Discorsi*, i, ch. 55.

11 Larner, The Lords of the Romagna (London, 1965). L. Chiappini, *Gli Estensi* (Varese, 1967). W. Tommasoli, *La vita di Federico da Montefeltro (1422–1482)* (Urbino, 1978). P. Partner, 'Federico e il governo pontificio', in *Federico di Montefeltro: lo stato, le arti, la cultura*, i (Rome, 1986). G. Franceschini, *I Montefeltro* (Varese, 1970). I. Robertson, in *Storia de Cesena* ii (Rimini, 1985) pp. 5–90. M. Troscé, 'Governanti e possidenti nel XVI e nel XVII secolo a Macerata', *Quaderni Storici*, xxi (1972), pp. 827–48. G. Chittolini, 'Signorie rurali e feudi alla fine del medioevo', in *Storia d'Italia*, iv (Turin, 1981), pp. 589–676. P. J. Jones, 'Economia e Società nell'Italia medievale: la leggenda della borghesia', in *Storia d'Italia, Annali*, i (Turin, 1978), pp. 187–372. A. Esch, 'Tre sante e il loro ambiente sociale a Roma', in *Atti del Simposio Internazionale Cateriniano-Bernardiniano* (Siena, 1982), pp. 89–120. W. L. Gundersheimer, *Ferrara: the Style of a Renaissance Despotism* (Princeton UP, 1973). C. Gennaro, 'Mercanti e Bovattieri nella Roma della seconda metà dal Trecento', *Bull. Ist. Stor. Ital. Medio Evo*, lxxviii (1967), pp. 155–203. T. Dean, 'Lords, vassals and clients in Renaissance Ferrara', *English Historical Review*, c (1985), pp. 106–19.

12 D. Hay, *The Church in Italy in the Fifteenth Century* (Cambridge UP, 1977). S. McClung Hallmann, *Italian Cardinals. Reform and the Church as Property, 1492–1563* (California UP, 1985). M. Meriam Bullard, *Filippo Strozzi and the Medici: Favor and Finance in Sixteenth-Century Florence and Rome* (Cambridge UP, 1980). C. Eubel, *Hierarchia Catholica* Rev. edn 7 vols. [vol. 8, 1979] (Munster, 1913–35) i–ii. N. del Re, *La Curia Romana: Lineamenti storico-giuridici* (Rome, 1970). *Idem, Monsignor Governatore di Roma* (Rome, 1972). J. F. D'Amico, *Renaissance Humanism in Papal Rome. Humanists and Churchmen on the Eve of the Reformation* (Johns Hopkins UP, 1983). C. L. Stinger, *The Renaissance in Rome* (Indiana UP, 1985). P. Prodi, *Il Cardinale Gabriele Paleotti (1522–1597)*, 2 vols. (Rome, 1959–67). P. Hurtubise, *Une famille témoin: les Salviati* (Rome, 1985).

13 Besides the works by Caravale and Caracciolo, Prodi and Partner already cited, see also M. Monaco, *Lo stato della Chiesa*, 2 vols. (Pescara, 1971) i. G. Carocci, *Lo stato della chiesa nella seconda metà del secolo XVI* (Milan, 1961). B. Barbiche, 'La politique de Clément VII à l'égard de Ferrare en novembre et décembre 1597', *Mélanges d'archéologie et d'histoire*, lxxiv (1962) pp. 289–328. R. Elze (ed.), *Rom in der Neuzeit* (Rome and Vienna, 1976). J. Delumeau, 'Rome; political and administrative centralisation in the Papal State in the sixteenth century' in E. Cochrane (ed.), *The Late Italian Renaissance, 1525–1630* (London, 1970), pp. 287–304.

14 J. Burckhardt, *Die Kultur der Renaissance in Italien* (Leipzig, 1925) p. 95.

15 Machiavelli, *The Prince*, ch. xi.

16 I. Polverini Fosi, *La società violenta; il banditismo nello Statopontificio nella seconda metà del Cinquecento* (Rome, 1985).

17 P. Partner, 'Papal financial policy in the Renaissance and Counter-Reformation', *Past and Present* 88 (1980), pp. 17–62. F. Piola Caselli, 'Aspetti del debito pubblico nello stato pontificio; gli Uffici Vacabili', *Università degli Studi di Perugia; Annali della Facoltà di Scienze Politiche*, anni academici 1970–2, 11 (n.s. 1973), pp. 99–199. M. Caravale, *La financa pontificia nel Cinquecento: le provincie del Lazio* (Naples, 1974). *Idem*, 'Entrate e Uscite dello stato della chiesa in un bilancio della metà del Quattrocento', in *Per Francesco Calasso: Scritti degli Allievi* (Rome, 1978), pp. 169–90. C. Rotelli, 'La finanza locale pontificia nel cinquecento: il caso di Imola', *Studi Storici*, ix (1968), pp. 107–44. G. Moschetti, *Il catasto di Macerata dell'anno 1560 e la bolla 'Ubique terrarum' di Paolo IV del 18 maggio 1557* (Naples, 1978). P. J. A. N. Rietbergen, 'Problems of government: some observations upon a sixteenth-century "Istruzzione per il governatori delle città e luoghi dello stato ecclesiastico",' *Mededelingen van het Nederlands Instituut te Rome*, n.s., vi (1979), pp. 173–201. C. Penuti, 'Aspetti della politica economica nello stato pontificio sul finire del '500: le "visite economiche" di Sisto V', *Annali dell'Istituto Storico Italo-Germanico in Trento*, ii (1976), pp. 183–202. K. Stow, *Taxation, Community and State* (Stuttgart, 1982). G. Orlandelli, 'Note di storia economica sulla signoria del Bentivoglio', *Atti e Memorie della Dep. di Storia Patria per le provincie di Romagna*, n.s. iii (1953). E. Manenti, 'Lo spazio amministrativo centrale: un'indagine sulla struttura della camera marchionale poi ducale Estense a Ferrara', in G. Papagno and A. Quondam (eds.), *La Corte e lo spazio: Ferrara estense* i (Rome, 1982), pp. 107–16. G. Contini, 'Contributo documentario per uno studio delle condizioni finanziarie del comune di Perugia alla vigilia della "guerra del sale"', *Rassegna degli Archivi di Stato*, xxx (1970), pp. 365–76. E. Stumpo, *Il capitale finanziario a Roma fra Cinque e Seicento* (Milan, 1985).

18 The *Monti di pietà* were municipal Christian banks and pawn-shops.

19 The literature on Roman urbanism and the papal palaces is enormous. Some brief indications may be found in Partner, *Renaissance Rome* and Partner, 'Finanze e urbanistica a Roma (1420–1623)', *Cheiron*, i (1983), pp. 59–71.

20 For the general question, see J. H. Elliott, 'Revolution and continuity in early modern Europe'. *Past and Present*, 42 (1969), pp. 35–56. For some trenchant remarks about oversimplified and inappropriate theories of modernization, see G. Stokes, 'How is nationalism related to capitalism?', *Comparative Studies in Society and History*, xxvii (1986), esp. p. 592 and also Q. Skinner's review of R. Bendix, *Kings or People: Power and the Mandate to Rule* (California UP, 1978) in *New York Review of Books*, xxii (March 1979).

21 M. Weber, *Economy and Society: An Outline of Interpretive Sociology* (eds. G. Roth and C. Wittich. 3 vols., New York, 1968) iii, esp. p. 1033. For the question of papal bureaucracy, see P. Partner, *The Pope's Men: the Papal Civil Service in the Renaissance* (Oxford, 1990).

22 C. Bauer, 'Die Epochen der Papstfinanz: ein Versuch', *Historische Zeitschrift*, cxxxviii (1927), p. 475 – 'Ohne Papstfinanz kein Frühkapitalismus'.

3

The Spanish Monarchy and the Kingdom of Portugal, 1580–1640

J. H. ELLIOTT[*]

Portugal was united to the crown of Castile in the shadow of a great disaster. On 4 August 1578 the Portuguese army, under the leadership of the 24-year-old King Sebastian, was crushingly defeated by the Moors on the Moroccan battlefield of El-Ksar-el-Kebir. Sebastian himself was killed, along with the cream of the Portuguese nobility, and thousands of prisoners were taken. Of the estimated 16 000 men in the Portuguese expeditionary force, only a few hundred succeeded in struggling back to the coast. What had begun as the dream of a half-crazed king, obsessed with visions of crusading glory, had ended in the shattering of a ruling class, and, with it, of a nation.[1]

As the country reeled beneath the shock of the disaster, one painful fact immediately impinged on the national consciousness: a succession crisis was imminent. Sebastian's heir and successor was his great-uncle Henry, the cardinal-archbishop of Lisbon, now 66 and visibly senile. Even if he lived long enough to secure a papal dispensation and a wife, there seemed little prospect of his being able to perpetuate the royal line of Avis. Political manoeuvres therefore began at once, both inside and outside Portugal, with an eye to the succession. A number of candidates could trace back their descent to Manuel I the Fortunate (1495–1521). Among these were António, Prior of Crato, the only living son of one of Manuel's sons, but unfortunately illegitimate, and, in addition, anathema to the Cardinal-King Henry; Catharine, duchess of Bragança, the daughter of Manuel's son, Duarte; her nephew, the nine-year-old Ranuccio Farnese, the son of Alexander Farnese, duke of Parma, Spain's governor in the Netherlands; and – on the female side, descending from Manuel's daughters – the duke of Savoy and Philip II of Spain. Of these, Philip of Spain did not have the strongest claims, but, as the ruler of Portugal's neighbour and the most powerful monarch in Christendom, he held the strongest cards. In the months that followed the news of El-Ksar-el-Kebir he took all the necessary steps to ensure that the succession would be his.

These steps included the despatch to Lisbon of a native Portuguese, Don Cristóbal de Moura, who had risen to favour at the Spanish court. Moura proved to be a skilled negotiator, adept at pressing Philip's claims. He came well provided with Spanish silver, urgently required for the ransom of Portuguese nobles held captive by the Moors. Even without this pressing requirement, silver could be expected to speak loudly in the Portugal of the 1570s, where it was badly needed by the Lisbon merchants to sustain their Far Eastern trade. Moura also made a special bid to win the support of the influential Portuguese Jesuits, including the Jesuit confessor of the cardinal-king, whose initial opposition to the succession of his Spanish nephew began to weaken under pressure. He summoned a meeting of the Portuguese Cortes to help settle the question, but died on 31 January 1580 with the problem still unsolved, leaving five governors to act as a regency council.

In Madrid, Cardinal Granvelle, at this moment Philip II's most influential minister, urged speed and decisiveness on his congenitally cautious royal master. Popular sentiment in Portugal was rising in favour of the Prior of Crato, who had escaped from his Moroccan captivity, and could be expected to make a bid for the throne. It was essential to forestall a major move by either of the local candidates. Of these, the duchess of Bragança was bought off by Philip, but on 19 June, from his stronghold at Santarém, the Prior of Crato proclaimed himself king. It was, however, a hopeless gesture. During the preceding months a Spanish army of some 40 000 men had been assembled on the frontier, and the veteran duke of Alba placed at its head. In late June, Alba's army moved into Portugal, and embarked, against little resistance, on its long, hot march towards the capital. With the assistance of a supporting fleet the invading army approached Lisbon from the west, and, after defeating a motley force of the Prior of Crato's supporters, entered the capital on 24 August. The Prior himself escaped to northern Portugal, and eventually fled the country to take refuge in France. No one now remained in a position to contest the king of Spain's accession to the throne, and, when the news reached them, Portugal's overseas territories, India and Brazil, also rallied to Philip as their king. Only the Azores refused to follow suit, and it was not until 1583 that the Prior of Crato's last outpost in the Azores, the island of Terceira, abandoned its resistance. Thereafter, the Prior was a phantom king in exile, his pretensions kept alive by the courts of France and England, both of whom saw him as a useful pawn in their struggle against an over-mighty Spanish Monarchy.[2]

To all intents and purposes, therefore, the accession of Philip II of Spain to the throne of Portugal was the result of the invasion and military occupation of a temporarily enfeebled kingdom by its more powerful neighbour. But this was not how it was represented by Madrid to the world, and whatever may have been the popular view inside Portugal – or indeed the view of Europe as a whole – Philip's own subsequent actions make it clear that he himself never saw the events of 1580 in this light. As the oldest male descendant of Manuel the Fortunate, he had no doubt of his legitimate right to the Portuguese succession, and he had despatched an army to Portugal only to secure what the jurists had told him was rightfully his. The acquisition of Portugal, in other words, was to him an essentially legal and dynastic event, occurring within a complex juridical framework of historical rights and inherited obligations, which made careful provision for just such an occurrence.

The Spanish Monarchy of which the kingdom of Portugal now found itself a part was itself in large measure woven out of comparable dynastic occurrences in the past. Essentially it consisted of a variety of kingdoms and provinces, almost all of which owed allegiance to the same ruler as the result either of dynastic accident or dynastic design. Addressing Philip II's grandson, Philip IV, in 1624, his principal minister, the count of Olivares, explained that 'all [the kingdoms] that Your Majesty possesses today, with the exception of a few small parts that it is not necessary to mention, you possess by right of succession; only Navarre and the empire of the Indies are conquests.'[3] The heart of Philip II's Monarchy, Spain itself, was the outcome of the Union of the Crowns of Castile-León and Aragon, following the marriage of Ferdinand of Aragon and Isabella of Castile in 1469. To this had been added the Habsburg and Burgundian inheritance brought by their grandson, the Emperor Charles V, of which the Netherlands and the Franche-Comté had descended to Philip II. Philip's rights to his Italian possessions of Sicily and Naples had devolved upon him through his Aragonese inheritance. Navarre and the Indies, as Olivares explained, fell legally into a different category. Both, as 'conquests', were juridically incorporated into the crown of Castile.

Technically, a ruler could do what he liked with a territory that he, or his ancestors, had conquered. In practice, Navarre, which had been occupied by Spanish forces in 1512, was allowed to retain the customs and institutions that it had possessed as an independent kingdom. This concession effectively gave it comparable status to the other European realms and provinces constituting the so-called 'Spanish Monarchy'. These were nominally subject to the king on an equal footing. Legally they retained their traditional institutions, rights and privileges, and each succeeding monarch was under oath to preserve their laws and liberties intact. Since these kingdoms differed widely among themselves, the Spanish Monarchy of Philip II and his successors was an extraordinary patchwork of variegated subject territories, with a wide diversity of laws and institutions. But the monarch had sworn to respect this diversity. In the formulation of a seventeenth-century jurist, 'the kingdoms must be ruled and governed as if the king who holds them all together were king only of each one of them.'[4]

Portugal in 1580 fell easily and logically into this flexible, pre-existing system of union by association. Indeed, its incorporation within a wider Hispanic grouping had long been contemplated, and could well have occurred a century earlier if events had taken a slightly different turn. Although Portugal emerged as an independent kingdom from the struggle against the Moors during the twelfth century, and had secured its definitive boundaries by the middle of the thirteenth, there was no preordained reason for it to remain permanently separate from the other parts of the Iberian peninsula. By the later Middle Ages this was divided into three large territorial groupings: Portugal, Castile-León, and the Catalan-Aragonese federation, consisting of the kingdoms of Aragon and Valencia and the principality of Catalonia. Memories of the Roman *Hispania* helped to nourish aspirations for a revived Iberian unity, and the dynastic ambitions and matrimonial alliances of the Portuguese, Aragonese and Castilian ruling houses made an eventual union of the three crowns a distinct possibility. In 1469 Isabella, as heiress of Castile, could as well have married the king of Portugal as the heir to the throne of Aragon, and 'Spain' would then have consisted of Castile-Portugal, rather than Castile-Aragon. Similarly, there seemed every prospect of an eventual Portuguese succession to the throne of Castile after the death in 1497 of

Prince Juan, the only son of Ferdinand and Isabella. This left his sister, Isabella, the wife of King Manuel of Portugal, as the Castilian heiress; but the possibility had hardly arisen before it was dashed by her death, followed by that of her son, Prince Michael, in 1500. Portuguese-Castilian marriages continued into the next generation with the marriage of Charles V to Manuel's daughter, so that the extinction of either line was likely to lead to its replacement by the other. Thanks to the folly of Sebastian it was the Portuguese line that came to an end in 1580, with the consequent devolution of his inheritance on Philip of Spain, the son of a Portuguese mother.

Philip II regarded this as the providential conclusion in his own lifetime to the reconstruction of the old Hispania, and chose to take over his new inheritance on terms similar to those on which his predecessors had in earlier generations taken over newly inherited kingdoms and provinces – namely, by guaranteeing their distinctive rights and forms of government. But not all those around him approved of this approach. Cardinal Granvelle, in particular, wanted the king to exploit the opportunity provided by the annexation to reorganize Portugal's system of government.[5] This in effect meant treating it as a conquered kingdom. Granvelle's attitude was that of a man with first-hand experience of the revolt of the Netherlands, who knew what it was to govern a country in which the royal authority was severely curbed by well-entrenched constitutional liberties. But Philip, either out of caution, or more probably because of his natural inclination to think along conservative and traditional lines, preferred to act as if the conquest had not been a conquest. The crown of Portugal was simply to be one more crown added to the many that he already held, and his new Portuguese subjects would experience no change in their status.

He therefore convoked a session of the Portuguese Cortes, which opened in his presence at Tomar in April 1581. Here he was sworn in and acclaimed as King of Portugal under the title of Philip I. In return, he agreed to abide by a series of articles which, significantly, constituted a repetition of the terms of dynastic union agreed by Manuel the Fortunate in 1499 when it seemed that a Portuguese prince would succeed to the throne of Castile.[6] These articles in effect guaranteed the independent identity of the crown of Portugal and its overseas possessions within Philip's Monarchy. The government of Portugal and its empire was to remain in the hands of native Portuguese. Castilians, therefore, were firmly excluded from office in the royal administration, just as they were excluded from office in the kingdoms of the crown of Aragon below the level of viceroy. If the king himself were not present in Portugal, his governors or viceroys must be native Portuguese, unless they were members of the royal family. The laws of Castile were not to be introduced into Portugal; the language of government was to remain Portuguese; and all sessions of the Cortes were to be held inside the kingdom. The control of trade with Portugal's overseas territories would remain in Portuguese hands, but the king's Portuguese subjects would be free to travel in the Spanish Monarchy. The practical effect of this provision would be to enable Portuguese to move not only into Castile, but also into Castile's American empire, where Portuguese merchants would begin to play an active rôle. As an act of favour Philip had already abolished the customs posts between Castile and Portugal, but these were reinstituted 12 years later, in 1592, presumably because of the loss of royal revenues.[7]

These were generous conditions, which confirmed Philip's intention to treat the union of the crowns on the same lines as those adopted for the union of the crowns of Castile and Aragon a century earlier – as a purely personal union. In the short term at least, this generosity made good political sense. The Portuguese governing class, depleted and traumatized by the defeat of El-Ksar-el-Kebir, was anyhow in no condition to put up serious resistance to Philip's incorporation of their kingdom into his Monarchy, but the terms of union made it easier to reconcile themselves to a change which at this moment could be construed as offering many positive advantages.

It was true that, traditionally, there was no love lost between Portuguese and Castilians, any more than there was love lost between Castilians and Catalans. After the arrival of the news of the death of King Sebastian, the Portuguese ambassador in Madrid remarked melodramatically to his Venetian counterpart that 'we would rather be French, English, even Turks, than Spaniards.'[8] This attitude was in part a reflection of the traditional hostility between neighbours with a long history of conflict and rivalry. But it had been aggravated on both sides over the course of recent generations by the experience of empire. The arrogance of the Castilians was legendary. According to a Catalan writing in the 1550s, they 'want to be so absolute, and put so high a value on their own achievements and so low a value on everyone else's, that they give the impression that they alone are descended from heaven, and the rest of mankind are mud.'[9] The Portuguese, for their part, were no less proud of their imperial achievements, which had reinforced their sense of national loyalty and national identity. But this sense of national identity had not prevented a growing Castilian influence on Portuguese cultural life during the course of the sixteenth century. While it was true that royal marriages had involved a constant cultural interchange between the two courts, and that Philip II's palace-monastery of the Escorial owed a good deal to the Portuguese 'plain style' of architecture,[10] the dominant influence was that of Castile. Educated sixteenth-century Portuguese were either bilingual or spoke some Castilian, and leading Portuguese authors often chose to publish in Castilian in preference to their native tongue.[11] Castilian cultural infiltration was therefore extensive even before the Union of the Crowns. It was also beginning to percolate down to the lower classes of Portuguese society, without, however, diminishing their antipathy to Castilians.

To the upper levels of society, therefore, the union, if not necessarily a welcome development, was one to which they were to some extent acclimatized by personal and cultural contacts. Beyond this, many of them saw important opportunities and advantages to be gained by a formal association with the Spanish crown at this particular juncture. Philip II was powerful, and an impoverished nobility glimpsed the possibility of lucrative rewards from employment in his service. Both his silver and his army served as salutary reminders of Portugal's own weaknesses. The annual treasure-fleets arriving in Seville from the Indies had made Castile a silver-rich empire, with increasingly large resources at its command. Portugal's own overseas empire in East Asia and India, by contrast, was becoming less profitable as trading problems multiplied and the costs of administration and defence began to escalate.[12] With neither the manpower nor the financial reserves to sustain indefinitely its distant Asian outposts, it seemed that Portugal could only stand to gain from Spanish military and naval assistance, and from the new influx of silver that could be expected to follow from a Union of the Crowns. Only later would it become apparent that the package deal was rather less attractive than appeared at first sight, since Spain's enemies would automatically become Portugal's enemies once the two crowns were united.

Spain, for its part, could welcome the incorporation of Portugal into its Monarchy as providing a valuable accession of strength. At the very least, by bringing the entire peninsula under a single ruler, it put an end to Castile's vulnerability to foreign attack from an exposed western flank. But there were other and more positive gains, of which Philip II and his north European enemies were equally aware. Vast new areas of overseas territory, not only in Asia, but also in Africa and Brazil, were now added to the already extensive overseas dominions of Philip, to make his monarchy an empire on which, literally as well as metaphorically, the sun never set. Even if Portugal retained its own trading monopoly, and Castilians were excluded from office in its imperial possessions, the sheer wealth and expanse of the two combined empires constituted an impressive aggrandizement of Spain's already great power. It also brought to Spain a new and valuable stretch of Atlantic seaboard at a moment when there were increasing signs that its struggle with the northern Protestants, the English and the Dutch, was shifting to the waters of the Atlantic; and with the new stretch of seaboard came a welcome accretion of naval power, in the form of dockyards, skilled seamen, a large merchant fleet, and 12 fighting galleons.[13]

The shift of Spain's strategic interests away from the Mediterranean to the Atlantic – a shift that was itself reinforced by Philip's acquisition of Portugal – made Lisbon a vital observation-post and potential command point for the impending Atlantic battle. After concluding the Cortes of Tomar Philip moved to Lisbon, where he remained until 1583. Cardinal Granvelle, with his acute eye for strategic realities, wanted the king to take up permanent residence in the city, instead of isolating himself from the great events of the day in the heartland of Castile.[14] The choice of Lisbon, in place of Madrid, as the capital of the Monarchy would have had a profound impact on its future development, and might well have reconciled the Portuguese to the permanency of union, although no doubt at the price of alienating the Castilians. But Philip chose instead to return to Madrid in February 1583, and would never again set foot in Portugal.

From 1583, therefore, the Portuguese would be ruled by an absentee monarch. The Cortes of Tomar had asked that the elder of the king's two surviving sons, Prince Diego, should be brought up in Portugal, but the young prince died in 1582, leaving his two-year-old brother Philip as heir to the throne. This meant that there was no prospect of government by a prince of the immediate royal line, but Philip did his best to meet Portuguese sensibilities by leaving as his viceroy his 23-year-old nephew, the Cardinal Archduke Albert, who would govern the country until 1593. But nothing could alter the fact that Portugal now became one more among the several kingdoms of the Spanish Monarchy which no longer enjoyed the presence of a resident king. In the crown of Aragon, more or less permanent royal absenteeism during the course of the sixteenth century had created considerable problems of adjustment. Not only did government seem alien and remote when conducted by a monarch who resided in Castile, but regional nobilities felt themselves deeply deprived by the absence of a king who in principle was expected to be well acquainted with them and their needs, rewarding the deserving with offices, honours and posts about his royal person.[15] To make matters worse, he lived surrounded by Castilians, who had exploited their privileged position to occupy one after another of the commanding heights in the Monarchy. With their native dynasty extinguished, it was now the turn of the Portuguese, who could soon be expected to join the ranks of the permanently disgruntled.

Philip had promised to preserve Portugal's system of government, but the sheer fact of his non-residence reinforced a process of institutional change that was already under way from the moment of his accession. During the sixteenth century the Spanish Monarchy had developed an institutional structure designed to satisfy the criterion that 'the kingdoms must be ruled and governed as if the king who holds them all together were king only of each one of them.' This took the form of a conciliar system, whereby the king was advised by a series of councils, some of which had a territorial character, with native councillors of the respective kingdoms or territories handling their governmental business, and acting as the intermediaries between king and viceroy. In conformity with this model, a Council of Portugal, consisting of six councillors, was established in 1582, and duly took its place in Madrid alongside the Councils of Castile, Aragon, Italy and the Indies. The old Council of State of the kings of Portugal remained in being in Lisbon as an advisory council to the viceroys or governors, but lost all real influence and co-ordinating functions. On the other hand, new institutions appeared in the two decades following the Union of the Crowns, notably a Council of Finance, created in 1591, comparable to Castile's Council of Finance, but with wider jurisdiction, since it was also responsible for the financial oversight of the overseas territories. A Council of India, comparable to Spain's Council of the Indies, was set up in 1604, but abolished 10 years later after a series of clashes with other administrative tribunals.[16]

In general, the changes introduced by Philip II in the years following the union seem to have been welcomed as improvements on the somewhat antiquated administrative and judicial machinery by which the kingdom had been governed under the last kings of the House of Avis. But, by bringing the Portuguese model of government into closer conformity with the model prevailing in Madrid, they also tended to subject it to the same long-term processes, as the crown sought for ways of improving administrative efficiency. Councils, by their nature, were slow-moving institutions with an essentially juridical approach to administrative questions, and Portugal under the government of Philip III and Philip IV of Spain (1598–1621; 1621–40), would experience the same kind of administrative pressures as were being felt elsewhere in the Monarchy, as *ad hoc* juntas were created to deal with specific aspects of governmental business, and secretaries enhanced their powers at the expense of the councils. The jurists, in effect, were being elbowed aside by professional administrators, and, also, on occasions, by unqualified royal favourites.

This tendency towards a more centralized system of government, with power increasingly concentrated in the hands of a select group of ministers and officials enjoying the special confidence of the king or his principal minister, widened the distance between the governors and the governed, and added to the opportunities for abuses of bureaucratic authority. The uneasiness would be compounded, where Portugal was concerned, by the inability of the crown to find a satisfactory long-term answer to the institutional problems of government in Lisbon in the absence of the king. On the departure of Archduke Albert in 1593 to assume the government of the Netherlands, Philip replaced him by a regency council of five governors, who were native Portuguese. This collective system of government did not work well, and Philip III (II of Portugal) returned to the appointment of individual viceroys, among them Don Cristóbal de Moura (now marquis of Castel Rodrigo), who was viceroy from 1600 to 1603, and again from 1608 to 1612. The viceregal system, however, gave rise to loud complaints, and Philip IV (III of Portugal) on his accession in 1621 returned to the old collective formula of a council of governors, which proved no more satisfactory, or acceptable to the Portuguese than when his grandfather had tried it in the 1590s.

In spite of the problems and tensions inevitably consequent on the incorporation of a formerly independent kingdom into a wider political grouping, the first decades of the union were a time of political stability and relative prosperity for Portugal, especially in comparison with the last years of rule by the House of Avis. Improved government certainly helped to reconcile the country to its new situation, and, as expected, significant material benefits followed in the wake of union. For Portugal, the 60 years of the Union of the Crowns seem to have been a period of modest population growth after a period of losses at the turn of the century. If the total population, including some 100 000 Portuguese overseas, stood at about 1 300 000 in 1580, it may have reached or passed 1 500 000 by the time the country recovered its independence in 1640.[17] This is all the more striking when contrasted with the experience of neighbouring Castile, which proved unable to make up the loss of some 600 000 inhabitants in the great plague at the end of the sixteenth century, and entered a long period of demographic stagnation or decline, with its population hovering around the seven million mark.[18]

Early seventeenth-century Portugal also contrasted strikingly with Castile in its capacity to maintain a stable coinage. The Portuguese monetary system was unaffected by the Union of the Crowns, and the first 40 years of the century, which for Castile were characterized by a depreciation of the coinage and sharp oscillations in prices, were for Portugal a period of notable monetary stability.[19] The lack of any serious need to resort to the Castilian practice of minting large quantities of copper coins was a reflection of its capacity to capitalize, as its merchants had hoped to capitalize, on the silver resources of the Spanish Monarchy. They managed to achieve this through vigorous entrepreneurship at a moment when changing patterns of global trade threatened Portugal's overseas empire with a major dislocation, while also holding out opportunities of spectacular growth, if they could once be seized.

The crisis of Portugal's Far Eastern empire was exacerbated in the final years of the sixteenth century by the growing penetration of the English, and even more of the Dutch, into waters and regions which until then had been regarded as an essentially Portuguese preserve. As part of the Spanish Monarchy, the Portuguese empire was fair game to Spain's north European enemies, and from the 1590s they had broken the Portuguese monopoly of the Cape route and were competing directly with Portuguese merchants in the Spice Islands. The 1609 truce between Spain and the Dutch proved to be no truce where the Indian

Ocean and the Far East were concerned, and by 1621, when Spain resumed hostilities with the Dutch, Portugal had effectively lost its Far Eastern spice empire, although there were still substantial profits to be made in the Goa–Lisbon trade. But even as one Portuguese empire was in process of disappearing, another was emerging. This was a new Atlantic empire, based on the possession of Angola and Brazil. After a tussle with the Genoese, Portuguese merchants acquired in 1601 monopoly rights to furnish the Spanish Indies with African slaves, and retained them until the dissolution of the union in 1640. The silver that came from this and other services was used for capital investment in the rapidly expanding sugar economy of Brazil. The emergence in the opening decades of the seventeenth century of a great Brazilian sugar empire removed some of the bitterness associated with the decline and fall of the Far Eastern pepper empire, and brought new opportunities to an aggressive generation of merchants both in Lisbon and in the lesser port towns of the Atlantic seaboard.[20]

In their quest for new markets and for Spanish silver to finance their overseas activities, some of these merchants and their agents began to infiltrate into Spain's American possessions, taking up residence in Lima or the mining city of Potosí, while others moved into Spain, to be at the receiving end of the American silver, in Seville. Many of them were members of a highly prominent minority, the Portuguese community of converted Jews. Where Spain had expelled its Jews in 1492, the Portuguese crown had chosen instead to have them forcibly baptized, and forbade their departure from the country, where they were subject both to popular hostility and the attentions of the Inquisition, from which they would procure temporary reprieves by offering large subsidies to the crown. This community of nominal Jewish converts, or *marranos*, as they came to be called, proved to be among the principal beneficiaries of the Union of the Crowns. Having for so long been claustrophobically confined to Portugal, many of them made use of the freedom of movement offered by the union to leave their national ghetto and settle in some of the major Spanish cities, including Seville and Madrid. This migratory movement within the peninsula was to have unfortunate consequences for their kinsmen, the *conversos*, or New Christians, of Castile, where it sparked a revival of the Inquisition's interest in their beliefs and behaviour at a time when Castile's Jewish question seemed to be losing some of the urgency of earlier years. But, at least in the short run, it gave enormous new scope to the Portuguese *marranos*. They worked their way into the Castilian financial system as revenue collectors and administrators, and began, in their rôle as merchants and businessmen, to challenge the Genoese for domination of the Castilian economy.[21]

The success of the Portuguese in penetrating the Spanish and Spanish-Atlantic economy and exploiting the deficiencies in Castile's economic and financial structures serves as a reminder that in a union imposed by a stronger on a weaker power, the weaker need not necessarily be the loser all along the line. But the economic benefits accruing to Portugal from its union with Spain were neither uniformly distributed nor universally enjoyed. For many members of the Portuguese upper classes, the first two decades of the seventeenth century were a period of mounting disillusionment. Government by a viceroy whose hands were tied by Madrid proved to be a poor exchange for government by a native king resident in Lisbon. The Portuguese nobility, like its fellow-nobility in the crown of Aragon, resented the Castilian monopoly of offices in the royal household. Nor did Madrid's tolerance of the New Christians sit well with a profoundly conservative Catholic society. Among the lower orders, continuing hostility to Spanish rule found a bizarre outlet in the strange phenomenon of 'Sebastianism'. Although the corpse of King Sebastian had been found on the battlefield of El-Ksar-el-Kebir, and was later returned for burial in Lisbon, many refused to believe that the body interred with such pomp at Santa María de Belém was in fact the body of their king. Rumours began to circulate that Sebastian still lived and would come back in due time to reclaim his own; and in 1584 there appeared on the scene the first in a series of false Sebastians. The myth of the hidden king, which was nurtured by some of the lower clergy and members of the religious orders, rapidly acquired messianic and millenarian overtones. By fostering the belief that Spanish rule was a Babylonian captivity which would one day end in a providential liberation, Sebastianism helped delay the process of Portuguese accommodation to the Union of the Crowns.[22] It was to tranquillize troubled spirits and calm the discontents that Philip III of Spain made his one and only visit to Portugal in 1619, convoking a session of the Cortes in Lisbon in order to obtain formal Portuguese acceptance of his son, Prince Philip, as heir to the throne. Apart from the Cortes of Tomar in 1581 this was the only meeting of the Portuguese Cortes to be held in the 60 years of Spanish rule. From the standpoint of Madrid, royal visits, whether to Portugal or the crown of Aragon, were costly affairs for which it was never easy to scrape up the funds. But the rarity of sessions of their Cortes was an understandable source of grievance to peoples who looked on them, not only as the proper forum for legislation and the voting of taxes, but also as occasions for a solemn reaffirmation of the unity of king and kingdom as an organic whole.

When Philip III, who had fallen ill while returning from Lisbon to Madrid, died on 31 March 1621, he therefore left an uneasy Portuguese legacy to his young son, Philip IV of Spain (III of Portugal). A few weeks after the opening of the reign, Dr Mendo da Mota, a member of the Council of Portugal, prepared an analysis of Portuguese discontents for the new administration.[23] Portugal, he argued, was being badly governed; corruption was rife and the Portuguese royal patrimony had been dissipated. The Portuguese claimed, with reason, that they were exposed to the enemies of Castile, and that the defence of their overseas empire had been neglected. They also complained of the infringement of their privileges, and of the lack of royal favours. This analysis came at a moment when, both inside and outside the administration, the whole character and structure of the Spanish Monarchy were coming under scrutiny. The growing economic weakness of Castile would in any event have forced a general reappraisal, but this was given fresh urgency by Spanish military intervention in Central Europe from 1618, and the expiry of the Twelve Years' Truce with the Dutch in the spring of 1621. The costs of war and imperial defence were mounting dramatically, and Castile, increasingly drained of men and money, was looking for greater assistance from its partners in the Spanish Monarchy in shouldering the burden. They, for their part, were unhappy with a system in which the benefits of empire, and of the royal presence, accrued almost exclusively to the dominant partner, Castile.[24]

It fell to the count (later count-duke) of Olivares, who emerged as the principal minister in the new administration, to formulate a programme of action for the revival and salvation of the Spanish Monarchy. In any such programme of renewal, Portugal would have an important part to play. The Great Memorial, or secret instruction, which he presented to Philip IV at the end of 1624, contained a section on Portugal which went to the heart of his plans.[25] 'The kingdoms of Portugal', it began, 'are without doubt among the best in Spain, both for the fertility of the soil in some regions and for the commercial disposition of others, with their excellent ports. They abound in people, some of them of great wealth because of their trading capacity, and they are difficult to govern.' He went on to discuss the different estates of the realm. The church, as far as he knew, was in a satisfactory state. Among the nobles, whom he described as having a high opinion of their own worth, he noted the special status of the dukes of Bragança for their closeness to the throne. He spoke of a general demoralization in Portuguese society, which he ascribed to royal absenteeism, and he recommended that Philip should satisfy legitimate aspirations by moving his court to Lisbon for a lengthy residence. He also recommended the appointment of Portuguese to the government in Madrid and the royal household, and their employment as viceroys and ambassadors. 'And I would regard it as expedient to do the same with Aragonese, Flemings and Italians . . . impressing upon Your Majesty that this is the most important action that can be taken to ensure the security, stability, conservation and expansion of this Monarchy. This mingling of vassals currently treated as if they were foreigners, and their admission to the offices mentioned above, is the only way to achieve its unity.'

This aspiration towards a closer integration of the different parts of the Spanish Monarchy, and in particular of the different kingdoms within the Iberian peninsula itself, was to be a dominant political theme of the 1620s and 1630s, the Olivares years. As applied to Portugal, it reflected a third and final stage in the uneasy relationship of the united crowns. The first phase, covering the nearly 20 years of Philip II's government in Portugal, had been a reformist phase, as a conscious effort was made to modernize institutions and raise the standards of administration and justice. The second, covering the reign of Philip III of Spain, from 1598–1621, was in general for Portugal, as for much of the monarchy, a period of benign neglect. The third phase would be interventionist and integrationist, as the government of Olivares attempted to move away from the recognition of diversity which had for so long been the governing principle of the Spanish monarchy, towards the creation of a new-style Monarchy characterized by a greater degree of uniformity between the different kingdoms – uniformity, in particular, of laws and institutions – and a closer collaboration of its various parts, particularly in the military and economic spheres.

This proposed change of direction for the Spanish Monarchy reflected the thinking of a new generation of European statesmen, who had come to see order, discipline and a greater concentration of authority in the hands of the crown as the only means of enhancing the power and efficiency of their states in a ruthlessly competitive world. These statesmen – a Richelieu in France, an Olivares in Spain, a Strafford in England – were looking to a more rational organization of resources as an answer to their problems, and were impatient with archaic rights and corporate privileges when they stood in the way of modernizing change.[26] The pressures for political and institutional change were all the stronger in Madrid because of the crippling weaknesses of the Castilian economy, weaknesses which, unless corrected, could alter the balance of forces within the monarchy and the peninsula itself. The Castile of the 1620s, although politically the preponderant partner, no longer possessed the overwhelming reserves of strength which made its dominance uncontestable in the 1580s. It was therefore natural for it to seek compensation for its weaknesses in a more systematic exploitation of the Iberian periphery, which could be regarded as fiscally privileged in relation to Castile.

The programme of Olivares for a unified peninsula, summarized in his famous statement that the most important task facing Philip IV was to make himself 'King of Spain', instead of being merely 'King of Portugal, Aragon and Valencia, and Count of Barcelona',[27] was his answer to the perceived problem of the decline of Castile. By coupling it with a programme designed to reduce royal absenteeism and open offices more widely to non-Castilians, he was addressing simultaneously the demands of the peripheral kingdoms, which also, like Castile, had their legitimate grievances. Through this offer of wider participation in the benefits of the Monarchy, he could hope, in addition, to blunt the opposition of the governing classes in the non-Castilian kingdoms to any attempt by Madrid to raise their levels of taxation and modify traditional laws and liberties – an exercise which he knew would be highly sensitive.

Portugal, although profoundly jealous of its autonomous rights and liberties, stood to gain more than many kingdoms of the Monarchy from a greater degree of openness and collaboration between its various parts. Having all but lost one empire, in the Far East, it was desperately anxious for the military and naval assistance which would prevent a repetition of the same story with Angola and Brazil. Such assistance could only be provided by a more powerful, and more united, Monarchy. Anything, too, that would reduce anti-Portuguese discrimination at court and in the Monarchy as a whole would facilitate the process of Portuguese infiltration that was already under way. It is not therefore surprising to find a coincidence of views, accompanied by an increasingly close co-operation, between sections of the Portuguese merchant community and the Olivares régime. Indeed, the mercantilist and integrationist policies of Olivares may themselves owe something to the lobbying of Portuguese merchants and financiers. In particular, there are striking parallels between Olivares's programme, and the proposals advocated by a Lisbon merchant, Duarte Gomes Solis, in a book published in 1622, and dedicated to the king.[28] Gomes Solis argued, as Olivares would argue, that it was to the advantage of Spain that the Italian, Aragonese and Portuguese vassals of the king should unite and become friends; that the Castilian and Portuguese crowns should join forces; that trading companies should be established, and customs barriers removed.

The pressures for a greater measure of integration, therefore, did not come solely from Madrid, and in some respects the 1620s were a period of more intense Castilian-Portuguese association than any other decade in the 60 years of union. This association was particularly striking in the field of imperial defence. In response to the Dutch capture of the Brazilian port of Bahia in 1624, a joint Spanish-Portuguese expeditionary force of 52 ships and over 12 000 men left Lisbon in the following year for the reconquest of Brazil.[29] The success of this expeditionary force, under the command of a Castilian general, Don Fadrique de Toledo, encouraged Olivares to move a step closer to military co-operation between the various kingdoms of the Spanish Monarchy, by launching at the end of 1625 his scheme for a 'Union of Arms'. Under this scheme, each kingdom would guarantee a fixed quota of paid men, a proportion of whom would be called to service whenever some part of the Monarchy was subjected to enemy attack. Out of this total reserve force of 140 000 men, Portugal's quota was 16 000, the same as that of Catalonia, while 44 000 men would be furnished by Castile and the Indies.[30]

While planning for military co-operation as a prelude to the unification of the Monarchy, the crown also devised schemes for its economic revival through the regulation and encouragement of trade and industry, in accordance with the mercantilist principles of the day. One key to this revival was to be a series of interlocking trading companies, one of them an India Company with its head-quarters at Lisbon. Although appeals to private and municipal subscribers generated little enthusiasm, the India Company was officially launched in August 1628. But the company was dogged by failure from the start, partly because its economic basis was regarded as unsound, but also because it was tainted by the original sin of its association with the government in Madrid, whose supervision of the project could be construed as an infringement of the guarantees given in the Cortes of Tomar.[31]

The India Company suffered, too, from its association with the New Christians, who unexpectedly found themselves in demand in the Madrid of Olivares. The count-duke had consistently shown himself sympathetic to the aspirations of those whose Jewish ancestry had barred them from important positions in Castilian society because of their 'tainted blood'. He was also determined to free the crown's finances from the suffocating grasp of the Genoese bankers, who had for so long dominated the Spanish financial scene. The emergence of a group of wealthy Portuguese merchants and businessmen with financial expertise and international connections offered an unparalleled opportunity to replace the Genoese with bankers who were subjects of the Spanish crown. But many of these were of Jewish blood, and in some instances their orthodoxy was suspect. They needed Olivares's protection, therefore, just as he needed their services.

The emergence in the mid 1620s of a consortium of Portuguese businessmen at the Spanish court, willing and able to act as crown bankers, gave Olivares valuable leverage in his dealings with the Genoese, and was to make a major contribution to Spanish war finance throughout the 1630s.[32] But it had other, and less positive, consequences for the Portuguese-Castilian relationship. In patro-nizing and protecting a group of men widely regarded as crypto-Jews, Olivares made new enemies for himself in Castile without significantly adding to the number of his friends in Portugal. The high visibility of these Portuguese New Christians at the court of Philip IV was a source of scandal to the faithful, whose worst forebodings were confirmed by the discovery in Madrid of a group of Judaizing Portuguese, subsequently the victims of a spectacular *auto de fe* in 1632.[33] Anti-semitic sentiments gave fresh impetus to a rising tide of hostility, both in the Spanish peninsula and in Spain's American possessions, to the apparently ubiquitous Portuguese. This anti-Portuguese backlash, reflected in an order issued in 1631 to the Audiencia of Charcas to 'move against the Portuguese who have entered the Indies through Buenos Aires, of whom many are to be found in Potosí,'[34] showed that the limits of tolerance were being reached. Olivares had hoped, through familiarizing the peoples of the Monarchy with each other, to break down what he called 'the dryness and separation of hearts'[35] that kept it disunited. But there were mounting indications during the 1630s that, where Castilians and Portuguese were concerned, increased familiarity served only to breed hatred and contempt.

Growing Castilian resentment of the Portuguese during the years of Olivares's ministry was paralleled by growing Portuguese suspicions of Castilian intentions. Nothing came of the count-duke's proposals for a temporary transfer of the court to Lisbon, and his thoughts of appointing a prince of the blood royal as governor of Portugal were frustrated by the unexpected death in 1632 of Philip IV's brother, Don Carlos, as he was being groomed for the post. In the absence of any spectacular gesture flattering to Portuguese sensibilities, the old resentments festered, while new ones were added. The Dutch had returned to Brazil in 1630, and this time, unlike 1625, the projected relief expedition was postponed from one year to the next. Olivares felt with some justice that Castile had borne the lion's share of the 1625 expedition, and that the Portuguese, who were grossly undertaxed in relation to Castilians, should be doing more on their own behalf. Castile could not afford to subsidize indefinitely the defence of Portugal and its overseas possessions, and from 1631 he was therefore looking for ways of securing from the Portuguese a fixed annual revenue of 500 000 *cruzados*, to be used to meet the costs of imperial defence, including the fitting out of a permanent fleet of 30 ships for the recovery and subsequent protection of Brazil. Once this was achieved, Portugal would become a real partner in the Union of Arms. In the meantime, the extension to Portugal of new fiscal devices, like the *media anata* on the first year's income from offices, only confirmed Portuguese suspicions that they were to be reduced little by little to conformity with Castile. Arbitrary taxation, imposed without a convocation of the Cortes, was seen as further evidence of a great and growing threat to the terms of the Tomar agreement and to national liberties.

Although the count-duke was aware of the dangers, the peremptory demands of war left him with little room for manoeuvre. When Princess Margaret of Savoy, the widowed duchess of Mantua, was chosen to govern Portugal in 1634, she was expected to make an intensive effort to obtain from the Portuguese the fixed annual appropriation of 500 000 *cruzados*.[36] The outcome of her efforts was a popular revolt, which began in the city of Évora in the summer of 1637 as a protest against the payment of new taxes that had not been voted by the Cortes, and rapidly spread to the Alentejo and the Algarve. 'If our lord the king cannot punish a sedition, riot or rebellion extending over three whole provinces', wrote Olivares in January 1638, 'he is not King of Portugal and cannot be regarded as such.' An army was assembled on the frontier, and as it entered the country, the rebellions collapsed. The count-duke would later propose to the British ambassador in Madrid his successful handling of the Évora revolt as a model for Charles I to follow in his dealings with the Scots.[37]

Although the revolts of 1637–8 collapsed with scarcely a shot being fired, they contained a number of disturbing features which might have suggested to a percipient eye the growing fragility of the union between Castile and Portugal. Anti-tax revolts were common enough in the seventeenth century – as Olivares himself remarked, 'popular tumults occur daily without giving cause for concern.'

But these betrayed a deep and continuing hostility among the Portuguese populace to the association with Spain. It was also noteworthy that the rioters had received open or covert encouragement not only from the priests, but also from the Jesuits, who in 1580 had been partisans of the Union of the Crowns. It seems clear that a shift in attitudes was under way that has still to be explained. Although not unrelated to the spread of messianism and Sebastianism among the Portuguese Jesuits, it may have had more to do with the sense of grievance in the Order at the failure of the Spanish crown to protect Portuguese interests overseas, where Jesuit missions were active.[38] But Olivares, although concerned by the behaviour of individual Jesuits, was most worried by the impotence, or impassivity, of the Portuguese ruling class in the face of popular disorder. Why, he wanted to know, had the nobles done nothing to crush the popular revolts?

The count-duke's worry points to a critical weakness in the Castilian-Portuguese association, apparent from an early stage, but now becoming glaringly so. This was the failure of the Spanish crown to secure any deep sense of commitment from the aristocracy and nobility. One or two Portuguese nobles, like Francisco de Melo, had attracted favourable attention in Madrid and been rewarded by the count-duke's patronage. But in general the Portuguese nobility had continued to feel excluded, and this sense of alienation was reflected in their notable reluctance to rally on the crown's behalf to the cause of public order in 1637. The alienation derived not only from an awareness of their marginal position in relation to the Spanish court, but also from the malfunctioning of the patronage system essential in any early modern European society to the smooth operation of government. The appointment of the duchess of Mantua proved to be no improvement on what had gone before. Her only qualification for the viceroyalty was the possession of some Portuguese blood as the great-grand-daughter of Philip II, and she proved incapable of controlling an administration torn by rivalries and faction feuds. In an attempt to remedy the weaknesses of the Council of Portugal as an instrument of government, the count-duke had placed increasing reliance on its secretary, Diogo Soarez, whom he had appointed to the post in 1631. During the 1630s Soarez gathered the strings of patronage into his own hands, acting in collaboration with Miguel de Vasconcelos (his father-in-law and brother-in-law) who was secretary of state in the administration in Lisbon. The two secretaries, manipulating the patronage system between them, and pocketing substantial profits for themselves along the way, completed the task of alienating the Portuguese ruling class from Madrid.

The count-duke, who was complaining bitterly that for 60 years Portugal had lived in a 'state of separation and division from the rest of the Monarchy',[39] possessed neither the time nor the local knowledge to set the system straight. Instead, he preferred to neutralize potential opposition by depriving it of its leaders. He summoned Portuguese notables to Madrid, nominally for consultation, in 1638, and he continued his efforts to lure the duke of Bragança out of the country, rightly suspecting that Bragança, although cautious to the point of invisibility, was the obvious figurehead for any general movement of political protest. But he seems to have retained an unswerving faith in what he had described in his Great Memorial of 1624 as the 'essential' loyalty of the Portuguese[40] – a faith rudely shattered when news reached Madrid that on 1 December 1640 the viceregal government of the duchess of Mantua had been overthrown, Vasconcelos murdered, and the duke of Bragança proclaimed as King John IV of an independent Portugal.

The Portuguese Revolution – or, more accurately, *coup d'état* – of December 1640 was precipitated by an order to the Portuguese nobility to join Philip IV on campaign against his Catalan vassals, who had revolted against his government in the summer of 1640. If they obeyed the order, the country would find itself without leadership at a critical moment. While the summons from Madrid determined the timing, it was the revolt of Catalonia that provided the opportunity. Faced with one insurrection inside the peninsula, it would be difficult for Madrid to turn its attention simultaneously to the suppression of another, and Portugal at the time of the revolt was in fact denuded of Spanish troops – a fact which helped to make it an almost bloodless revolution. But if it was the conjunction of immediate circumstances that provoked the revolution and made it feasible, it was a revolution that had been waiting to happen, at least since 1637. For the events of 1637 had demonstrated that the government in Madrid had no natural body of supporters inside Portugal, and that the Union of the Crowns had become a hollow sham, sustained only by the fear of Castile's military might.

The dissolution of the Castilian-Portuguese union, and Portugal's recovery of independence after the 60 years of its 'Babylonian captivity', therefore provides an unusual example of the total failure, even at the most formal level, of an early modern merger of two neighbouring states. Olivares, looking back defensively on the history of his ministry after his fall from power in 1643, characteristically attributed the failure to the mistakes of Philip II. It was, he argued, impossible to maintain indefinitely a Monarchy 'composed of such disproportionate parts, without union and conformity between each other', and the only solution was to reduce them to 'union and equality in laws, customs and forms of government'. Philip II should have realized this and adopted appropriate measures. He should, for instance, have taken the duke of Bragança back to Spain with him, 'because men of such eminent lineage and with pretensions to kingship should never be left in conquered provinces'. He should have abolished the customs posts between Castile and Portugal, 'for the preservation of this Monarchy was worth more than 200 000 ducats', while trade helped cement the bond of friendship between different kingdoms. He should have given Portuguese nobles 'viceroyalties and administrative positions in Castile and its dominions', and conferred bishoprics and abbacies on Portuguese ecclesiastics, 'and by the same token introduced Castilians into Portugal, and Portuguese into those parts of Europe that Your Majesty rules'.[41]

Perhaps the most unconsciously revealing words in this sustained critique of Philip II's policies were the words 'conquered provinces'. For Portugal had never officially been a 'conquered province', and Olivares himself had not included it among the conquered kingdoms in his Great Memorial of 1624. It was precisely because Portugal had been treated from the moment of the union as an inherited rather than a conquered kingdom that Madrid's room for manoeuvre had been so limited. Philip's decision to treat it in this way was no doubt a personal decision, but it also reflected the traditional approach to 'state-building' in Habsburg Spain. It was against this whole tradition of state-building by accretion, rather than by integration, that Olivares had rebelled, on the grounds that an unintegrated Monarchy was incapable of defending itself from its enemies in the changed world of the seventeenth century. In this he may well have been correct, but his attitude reflected the sensibilities of the 1620s more than those of the 1580s, even though the reactions of Cardinal Granvelle to Philip's Portuguese policies make it clear that the Habsburg accretionist tradition had its sixteenth-century critics. In particular, since the time of Ferdinand and Isabella there had been Castilian hardliners at court who advocated the 'Castilianization' of the non-Castilian kingdoms by reducing them to conformity with the laws of Castile.[42] The count-duke owed something to this Castilian tradition, as his dismissive reference to Portugal as a Castilian conquest made clear. But he was influenced, too, by the counter-tradition, which also had its sixteenth-century advocates, of a genuinely participatory monarchy, in which offices were open to Castilians and non-Castilians on an equal basis. As a man of the seventeenth-century, however, he brought to the problems of a diversified and fragmented Monarchy a more self-conscious approach than his predecessors to the whole process of 'state-building' – an approach reflecting the contemporary fascination with system and order.

But even if Portugal had been treated from the first as a conquered kingdom, there is no guarantee that this would have succeeded in holding the union together, any more than the adoption of Philip II's methods – in spite of Olivares's criticisms – can be regarded as guaranteeing its eventual dissolution. Drastic change imposed by the new rulers in 1580 might simply have increased Portu-guese antipathy to the Castilians, and consequently have brought forward the day of revolt. On the other hand, the kind of policies advocated by Olivares for the employment of Portuguese throughout the Monarchy might, if skilfully pursued from the start, have mitigated one of the greatest defects of the union, its failure to win the full allegiance of the Portuguese ruling class. Little was done to make it feel that the union was any more than a marriage of convenience, and by the 1630s even the convenience was ceasing to be obvious. The union had failed to provide an effective focus of loyalty to replace the old loyalty to the native House of Avis. It had failed to save Portugal's overseas possessions, including even Brazil, from conquest by its enemies; and, by the 1630s, even the group that had gained most from it, the merchants of Lisbon and the outports, were finding that previously open doors in Castile and the Spanish Indies were being barred against them. Add to this the growing fears of Madrid's intentions, and the concern expressed by Portuguese jurists that the government of Philip IV was systematically undermining the ancient Portuguese constitution, and it was clear that the time had come to terminate the marriage.

There could, however, be no question of divorce by mutual consent. Portugal was only able to make a unilateral announcement of the dissolution of the marriage because the stronger partner, Castile, was, for the time at least, no longer what it was, and its attention was distracted. In ordinary circumstances Castile would have had no great difficulty in subjugating the rebellious kingdom, but the circumstances of 1640 were far from ordinary. At this moment, following a series of setbacks and defeats in the war with the Dutch and the French, the balance of forces in Europe was tilting against the Spanish Monarchy. The weakness of Castile, already flagging under the strain, was compounded when the revolt of Catalonia opened a new military front inside the peninsula itself. If

Portugal were ever to revolt, there could be no more opportune moment than this, and the conspirators of 1640 used the occasion to brilliant effect. But even then, there was no certainty of long-term success. Madrid had been taken by surprise, but sooner or later it was likely to rally its forces and return to the attack. It did this in Catalonia, which, after 12 years of increasingly difficult separation from Castile, was forced to return to allegiance to Philip IV in 1652, although retaining the liberties that the count-duke had sought to undermine. Having won back Catalonia, Philip was no less determined to see his rebellious Portuguese subjects brought back into the fold.

In this he was unsuccessful, in spite of all the efforts of an undeniably enfeebled Castile, which was eventually compelled to recognize Portuguese independence in 1668. There were a number of reasons why Portugal succeeded where Catalonia failed, and not the least of them was the greater internal cohesion of Portuguese society under pressure, although Portugal, like Catalonia, could not escape the strains that came from divided loyalties, especially among nobles, ecclesiastics and businessmen still benefiting from the Spanish connection. But if there was any one outstanding reason for Portugal's ability to retain its independence, this is to be found not so much in the domestic situation, which was often less than promising, as in the international conjuncture. At one moment or another the Dutch, the French and the English all had their own reasons for abetting the survival of an independent Portugal, and it was the foreign assistance given at critical moments during the 28 years of conflict that enabled the restored kingdom of Portugal to retain its liberty.

Foreign states rightly saw in Portugal's survival as an independent entity a decisive opportunity to reduce the power of Spain. The same could be said of their attitude towards Catalonia during the years of its rebellion, but to a lesser degree. For Portugal possessed a major asset denied to the Catalans – a large and potentially rich overseas empire. This Luso-Brazilian empire, with its African and Asian extensions, held out the promise of a rich future, not only for Portugal itself, but also for its friends. Catalonia, on the other hand, had no such glittering prospects to offer. It had long since been shorn of its Mediterranean empire, and the Mediterranean itself was no longer the principal focus of interest of the states of western Europe. It was Portugal's Atlantic location, and its Atlantic future, which did more than anything else to tilt the balance in favour of its survival.

It is Portugal's possession of overseas empire – an empire, moreover, in an expanding Atlantic world – which makes it a special case in the history of state-building by the larger European monarchies at the expense of lesser powers. It has sometimes been argued that the union of Castile and Portugal came too late, in the sense that Portugal already had a long and proud tradition of independence, and a firm sense of national identity. But the same could be said of Scotland, incorporated even later into the crown of Great Britain. National identity of itself is not enough to prevent the incorporation of an independent kingdom by a more powerful neighbour, although its strength may well help determine the terms on which the incorporation is arranged. There must be viable alternatives to incorporation when the moment comes. Portugal in 1580 had no real choice; but by 1640, when incorporation threatened to turn into integration, an alternative future was once again a realizable possibility, thanks to a perhaps unrepeatable combination of favourable geographical and international circumstances. A kingdom that had lost its independence on the sands of North Africa won it back on the waters of a Portuguese Atlantic.

NOTES FOR CHAPTER 3

* Regius Professor of Modern History, University of Oxford.

1 For a vivid account of the Portuguese expedition and its fate, see E. W. Bovill, *The Battle of Alcazar* (London, 1952).

2 Alfonso Danvila, *Felipe II y la sucesión de Portugal* (Madrid, 1956) provides a narrative account of the succession crisis. The Spanish invasion is described in ch. 14 of William S. Maltby, *Alba. A Biography of Fernando Alvarez de Toledo, Third Duke of Alba, 1507–1582* (California UP, 1983).

3 John H. Elliott and José F. de la Peña, *Memoriales y cartas del Conde Duque de Olivares* (2 vols., Madrid, 1978–80) i, p. 93 ('Gran Memorial').

4 Cited J. H. Elliott, *The Revolt of the Catalans* (Cambridge UP, 1963; paperback edn 1984), p. 8.

5 M. Van Durme, *El Cardenal Granvela* (Barcelona, 1957), p. 352.

6 Joel Serrão (ed.), *Dicionário de História de Portugal* (6 vols., Oporto, 1981), entry on 'Restauracao'.

7 Modesto Ulloa, *La hacienda real de Castilla en el reinado de Felipe II* (Madrid, 1977), p. 259 where no explanation of the change of policy is given.

8 Cited M. Philippson, *Ein Ministerium unter Philipp II. Kardinal Granvella am Spanischen Hofe, 1579–1586* (Berlin, 1895), p. 89.

9 Cited Elliott, *Revolt of the Catalans*, p. 13.

10 See G. Kubler, *Building the Escorial* (Princeton UP, 1982), pp. 126–8.

11 A. H. De Oliveira Marques, *A History of Portugal* (2 vols., Columbia UP, 1972) i, pp. 309–10.

12 The growing problems of Portugal's Asian empire from the 1550s are summarized by Vitorino Magalhães Godinho, 'Crises et changements géographiques et structuraux au XVIe siècle', *Studi in Onore di Armando Sapori* (2 vols., Milan, 1957) ii, pp. 979–98. For an excellent general survey of Portugal's empire, see C. R. Boxer, *The Portuguese Seaborne Empire, 1415–1825* (London, 1969).

13 R. B. Wernham, *Before the Armada* (London, 1966), pp. 356–7; Abbott Payton Usher, 'Spanish Ships and Shipping in the Sixteenth and Seventeenth Centuries', *Facts and Factors in Economic History. Articles by Former Students of E. F. Gay* (Harvard UP, 1932), pp. 189–213.

14 Philippson, *Ein Ministerium*, p. 612. See also Fernand Braudel, *The Mediterranean and the Mediterranean World in the Age of Philip II*, trans. Siân Reynolds (2 vols., London, 1972–3) ii, pp. 1184–5, for Lisbon as an Atlantic observatory in 1580.

15 For royal absenteeism as it affected the nobility of seventeenth-century Catalonia, see Elliott, *Revolt of the Catalans*, esp. pp. 73–4.

16 Joaquim Veríssimo Serrão, *Historia de Portugal* (6 vols., Lisbon, 1978–82) iv, pp. 251–6. A. M. Hespanha, *As vésperas do Leviathan* (2 vols., Lisbon, 1986) is a recent and massive study of seventeenth-century Portuguese institutions, set into the context of the character and limits of state power.

17 Serrão, *História de Portugal* iv, pp. 267–75. The *Dicionário de História de Portugal* v ('Restauração'), p. 312 suggests a figure of nearly two million by 1640.

18 See Vicente Pérez Moreda, *Las crisis de mortalidad en la España interior, siglos XVI–XIX* (Madrid, 1980), p. 280, and the rather higher figures given in Manuel Tunon de Lara (ed.), *Historia de España* (Madrid, 1982) v, pp. 95–6.

19 Frédéric Mauro, *Le Portugal et L'Atlantique au XVIIe siècle, 1570–1670* (Paris, 1960), p. 417.

20 These developments are discussed in greater detail in Mauro, *Le Portugal et l'Atlantique*, Godhino, 'Crises et changements géographiques', and the Introduction to James C. Boyajian, *Portuguese Bankers and the Court of Spain, 1626–1650* (Rutgers UP, 1983).

21 Antonio Domínguez Ortiz, *Los judeoconversos en España y America* (Madrid, 1971), ch. 4. provides a convenient introduction to a subject on which there is a rapidly growing literature.

22 Raymon Cantel, *Prophétisme et Messianisme dans l'oeuvre Antoine Vieira* (Paris, 1960), ch. 2.

23 British Library, Egerton MSS. 1133, fo. 268–268v, letter of Mendo da Mota, 4 May 1621, and fos. 270–275, undated memorandum.

24 For a discussion of the Castilian crisis and of the reform proposals of the 1620s, see J. H. Elliott, *The Count-Duke of Olivares. The Statesman in an Age of Decline* (Yale UP, 1986), chs. 3–5.

25 Elliott and La Peña, *Memoriales y cartas*, i, pp. 89–92.

26 For certain common themes in the approaches of Olivares and his nearest rival among the statesmen of the 1620s, see J. H. Elliott, *Richelieu and Olivares* (Cambridge UP, 1984).

27 Elliott and La Peña, *Memoriales y cartas*, i, p. 96.

28 *Discursos sobre los comercios de las dos Indias* [Madrid, 1622], ed. Moses Bensabat Amzalak (Lisbon, 1943).

29 C. R. Boxer, *Salvador de Sá and the Struggle for Brazil and Angola, 1602–1686* (London, 1952), p. 60.

30 For the Union of Arms, see Elliott, *Count-Duke of Olivares*, ch. 7.

31 For the India Company and its fate, see A. R. Disney, *Twilight of the Pepper Empire. Portuguese Trade in Southwest India in the Early Seventeenth Century* (Harvard UP, 1978), esp. ch. 6.

32 See Boyajian, *Portuguese Bankers*, for these bankers and their activities.

33 Yosef Hayim Yerushalmi, *From Spanish Court to Italian Ghetto* (Columbia UP, 1971), pp. 105–22; and Julio Caro Baroja, *Inquisicioñ, brujería y criptojudaísmo*, 2nd edn (Barcelona, 1972), pp. 11–180 for the New Christian community at the court of Philip IV.

34 *Selected Writings of Lewis Hanke on the History of Latin America* (Arizona State UP, 1979), p. 149 ('The Portuguese in Spanish America').

35 Elliott and La Peña, *Memoriales y cartas*, i, p. 187.

36 For the duchess of Mantua's appointment and subsequent developments, see Elliott, *Count-Duke of Olivares*, pp. 526–32, and the sources there cited.

37 *Op. cit.* p. 530.

38 Boxer, *Salvador de Sa*, p. 143; H. and P. Chaunu, 'Autour de 1640: politiques et économiques atlantiques', *Annales* ix (1954), pp. 44–52.

39 Quoted Elliott, *Count-Duke of Olivares*, p. 531.

40 Elliott and La Pena, *Memoriales y cartas*, i, p. 92.

41 Elliott and La Pena, *Memoriales y cartas*, ii, pp. 251–2 ('El Nicandro').

42 See Elliott, *Revolt of the Catalans*, pp. 14–20.

4

Louis XIII and the Union of Béarn to France

CHRISTIAN DESPLAT*

A contemporary engraving of the events of 1620 in Béarn depicts the royal army under the walls of the citadel at Navarrenx, a large number of canon bombarding the stronghold, half-destroyed by fire, whilst serried ranks of French troops besiege it. Through this image and its accompanying text, royal propaganda did its utmost to convey the impression that Louis XIII had achieved a great victory in Béarn and that the principality's annexation was the result of a hard-won conflict. This somewhat tendentious presentation of the facts was doubtless inspired by the wish to emphasize the martial function of the king as well as a desire to inculcate some wholesome fear into subjects who had been tempted to rebel.

The reality, however, was less glorious and a good deal less dramatic. What passed for a violent invasion had, in reality, been no more than a military excursion. No town was taken by force and the only attempt at resistance had been delayed and irresolute. The expedition to Béarn in 1620 is thus a good example of the dramatization of historical fact in order to demonstrate royal authority. It also constitutes a test-case of the way in which the French monarchy undertook the annexation of a territory which, although never entirely independent, nevertheless had pretensions to its own sovereignty. Beyond the discrepancy between fact and fiction lie questions concerning the real consequences of this demonstration of royal power, in particular whether the edict of union between France and Béarn signed at Pau in October 1620 really did remove from this principality all the trappings of its past sovereignty and replaced them with an immediate and fully-developed centralization of authority.

It would have come as no surprise to contemporaries to learn that the union of 1620 had not been the result of brute force, for the question of uniting the principality of Béarn to the kingdom of France had been a matter under discussion for some time. The process had begun in April 1599 when Henri IV had granted the Catholics of Béarn an edict of toleration which was the mirror image of the edict of Nantes, granted the year previously to French Protestants. On 18 August 1599 the new bishops of Béarn arrived to celebrate a mass intended to symbolize the spiritual unification of the principality with the realm of the Most Christian king. The reinstitution of Catholicism proceeded apace although not to the extent of challenging the Calvinist establishment; spiritual reunification did not bring in its train an equivalent move towards political unification. In 1590, and again in 1607, Henri IV partially incorporated his patrimonial lands into the French crown; but the principality of Béarn and the kingdom of Navarre retained their status as sovereign states.[1]

The political and religious decisions of the Protestants overturned the fragile status quo. At the protestant political assembly at Saumur in 1611, Béarn's protestant deputies proposed the unification of their churches to those of France, while the regent Marie de Médicis promptly declared her readiness to reunite Béarn with France. Those favourable to this union at the French court received further encouragement in 1614 for although Béarn refused to send deputies to the French Estates General, its two bishops decided to attend on their own initiative. The Estates took advantage of their presence to declare that Béarn was 'territory owing allegiance to the crown (*terre mouvante de la couronne*)' and proposed its annexation. The Estates recalled, moreover, that the French kings had always refused to issue letters of naturalization to Béarnais because 'they had always held them to be indigenous subjects (*regnicoles*)'. French policy remained consistently faithful to this traditional doctrine: Béarn possessed the attributes of sovereignty but was not an independent state.

Far from standing aside during the civil war which threatened to engulf France once more, the deputies of Béarn offered their support to Rohan and Candale, the princes leading the revolt. They accepted a memorandum drafted by the syndic of the Estates of Béarn entitled: 'Disappointments of Béarn at the threats to unite it with France, containing the origin of the Béarnais . . . '. In reality, this political debate was confined to the aristocracy; the people were just their pawns, having no independent means of expressing their own preferences. Each side defended its own privileges and particular liberties, its religion. In no way did it do so in terms of a sense of national identity which would have been incomprehensible to the majority of the population. The Calvinists continued to demand the union of their churches with those of France, whilst the Catholics insisted upon rights comparable to those of the Protestants. All this placed the French monarchy in the position of being arbiter and it lost no time in taking advantage of this fact by enacting the reunion of Béarn with France on 31 December 1616.

The Estates of Béarn perceived the danger their disunion had placed them in, and hastened to express their own position; 'Béarn was a sovereign entity, separate from any other sovereignty and realm; its inhabitants had elected its sovereigns to maintain its laws and these could only be changed or reformed with the consent of the Estates of the principality . . . '. The Béarn deputies were reviving here a medieval constitutional legend – that of the election of the prince and the separation of powers. As it turned out, however, the edict of 1616 was not enforced and the strongest supporters of union quickly recognized the necessity of preserving Béarn's own judicial arrangements, its laws (as set out in its law codes (or *Fors*) and its customs. But if the political issues were capable of being resolved to everyone's satisfaction, this was far from being the case in matters of religion.

After the death of Concino Concini, marquis d'Ancre, Louis XIII took a vow to 'work towards the ruin of the Huguenots, if given the opportunity'; Béarn provided him with just that opportunity. Under pressure from the bishops of

Lescar and Oloron, the 1617 assembly of French clergy pressed the king to re-establish catholic worship in Béarn in its entirety and agreed to the restitution of all the ecclesiastical wealth which had been confiscated in the sixteenth century by Jeanne d'Albret. Louis XIII issued the edict of 'restitution' on 25 June 1617 which authorized the re-establishment of the Catholic Church to the property it had possessed prior to 1569. With considerable lucidity, the duc de Rohan realized that this edict was the beginning of the Calvinists' misfortunes for, ignoring the advice of Duplessis Mornay, France's Portestants pledged their support to their co-religionists in Béarn.

In the principality, the resistance to the edict of 1617 was overt, and when the councillor of state Renard arrived to enregister the edict before its Sovereign Council, he was jeered at by students at the protestant Academy of Orthez and, his mission unaccomplished, he was forced to leave Béarn. The moment to intervene which the French king had been waiting for had arrived; the Béarnais stood accused of rebellion and were openly allying with the Protestants of the French Midi who, in turn, were preparing a revolt against the king.

Unfortunately for Béarn, France's Protestants signed the peace of Loudun with Louis XIII who, reconciled once more with his mother after the 'diversion at the Ponts-de-Cé', had his hands free once more to intervene in Béarn. From 1617 onwards, Protestants and Catholics, defenders and adversaries of union with France, engaged in virulent propaganda campaigns; would this war of nerves be succeeded by real military conflict?

Louis XIII left Paris in July 1620 at the head of a rather inferior army; a few hundred soldiers without any artillery, all the companies 'badly armed and incomplete'. The contingents were at best a show of force rather than a military expedition. Whilst the king traversed Normandy, Poitou and Anjou, the French Protestants abandoned their co-religionists of Béarn. On 8 September, two protestant emissaries met the king at Poitiers and attempted to negotiate with him over the crucial issue of the lay abbeys, that is to say, the ecclesiastical wealth which had passed into lay hands since 1569. The Béarn delegates cleverly stressed that numerous families, both catholic and protestant, had acquired these abbeys and that the restitution of this property to the church risked provoking a social revolution. With the advice of Bérulle and, perhaps, Pierre de Marca, Louis XIII refused to listen to the deputies so long as the edict remained unregistered. Sending some of his troops back to Paris, the king reached Blaye on 17 September and Bordeaux on the 18th. The king still appeared to entertain some hopes that his subjects in Béarn would submit and thus spare him a long and tiresome journey. But the Estates and Sovereign Council of the principality adamantly refused to enregister the edict and, on 13 October, the king resumed his march southwards; since the protestant governor of Béarn, the duc de la Force, had prudently declared his loyalty to the king, the principality was defenceless.[2]

The king had clearly determined upon military intervention and 'neither the fear of famine nor of any peril could deflect him from his military resolve'. Yet he had his apprehensions. The beginning of October, with winter closing in, was no time for military operations and the royal forces were not strong. Crossing the river Garonne and the wooded wilderness of the Landes would not be easy. On the eve of the royal expedition, passions were running at fever pitch on both sides and amongst the élite groups of the province there were extremists and fanatics. Jean Paul de Lescun, the Protestants' chief spokesman and his various catholic adversaries continued to launch slanderous pamphlets at each other and the possibility that this war of words helped to prevent the outbreak of a real civil war cannot be ruled out. The President of the Sovereign Council was accused of being a 'downright weasel, a so-called gentleman, a narrow-shouldered, spineless creep with a dire crest'.[3] Following the earthquake of July 1618, the catholic pamphleteers declared: 'It should be noted that these tremors coincided particularly with the arrival of the king's commissioner. . . . The Lord has taken to heart the hostility shown to his Annointed in the person of the King's commissioner and he threatens those responsible with retribution'. Other signs from heaven confirmed the anger of the Almighty; many people saw 'a great cross in the sky about seven or eight o'clock in the morning, shining with a rosy glow . . .'. Others noticed 'a tomb in the cemetery covered with blood because of the disorders'. Some trees dropped tears of blood and a rich protestant draper of Oloron 'went one fine morning and threw himself in the [river] Gave de Sainte-Marie, satiated with the spoils and pillage of poor catholics'!

On 10 October, the small royal expeditionary force set out, accompanied only by the cavalry and the guards. The Béarn Protestants came to their senses rather late in the day and the edicts were registered in great haste on the 11th and even back-dated to the 8th. On the 14th the king arrived at Arzacq and on the 15th he entered Pau leaving the bulk of his army at the gates of the Béarn capital. It was immediately evident that the French king was hoping to avoid a military confrontation if at all possible. Some of the more committed protestant gentry assembled in the woods under cover of nightfall but they hardly mustered more than 60 men. Without military resistance, there was to be no war in Béarn. The catholic Pierre de Marca knew how to present the case for the principality before the king and Louis XIII had the tact to invite the local nobility to a banquet and they turned out in force . . . On 17 October it was back to serious business. Loménie de Brienne made sure that the edicts were verified without difficulty by the Sovereign Council of Béarn and the catholic clergy were reinstituted at St Martin, 'the great church in Pau, after 50 years of desecration'.

No one, however, could predict what might be the response of Monsieur de Sales, since 1570 the protestant governor of the citadel at Navarrenx, the Thebez on Mount Ephraim of the Béarn Calvinists. He had taken his precautions and his nephew had been warmly welcomed by the king of Bordeaux, but the king had his doubts and he decided to lead a march on the stronghold which could no longer be allowed to remain the possible redoubt of a rebel party. On Saturday 17 October, after mass, the king set out for Navarrenx, preceded by Schomberg and Créqui who sufficiently ordered the garrison of around 250 men to line up on the slopes outside the walls. Before the royal army had reached the walls of the place, the king had received the keys from the hands of the governor himself. The siege was over before it had even begun and 'it did not cost so much as a canon-fuse'. On the 18th the king celebrated the catholic religion in the church at Navarrenx and returned to Pau where he was greeted enthusiastically by the Catholics; 'The young clamoured to see him; children replied with shouts of "There he is" whilst

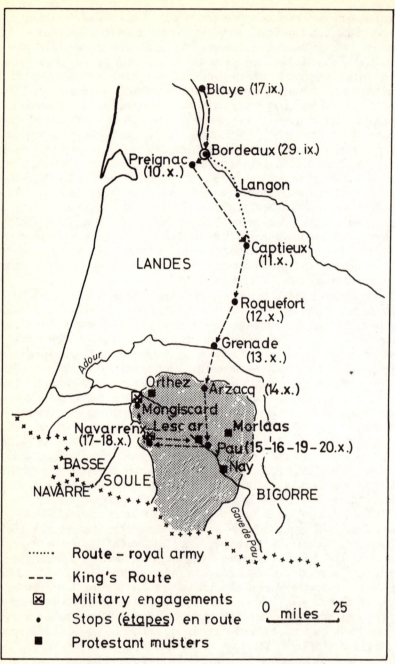

Fig. 4.1 The Béarn Campaign of Louis XIII (1620)

their elders looked upon him with admiration. The sick were brought to their windows to catch a glimpse of him . . .'.

On 20 October the king went to St Martin's church to attend a catholic mass and a procession of the Holy Sacrament, the first introduction of baroque ceremony to Béarn. The following day, Louis XIII left for Paris. Shortly after the king's departure, a small protestant force attempted to seize Navarrenx by force but it was a complete fiasco. The rebels retreated to the towers of Mongiscard and quickly surrendered. After some hesitation, the duc de La Force in turn submitted his resignation. Royal authority was re-established in Béarn without bloodshed, the catholic religion was restored and an edict united 'the realm of Navarre and the sovereignty of Béarn to the crown of France, with the express condition that their customs, rights, privileges and immunities would be protected and observed inviolably'.

Despite their relative insignificance, the military events of Béarn in 1620 had a considerable impact. Royal propaganda provided the account and images of it which justified and completed the process of annexation as the monarchy wished to present it. The weakness of the royal forces, the dangers of the expedition, real or imagined, served as the pretext for a dramatization of the event. With one exception alone, all the authors presented the king as besieged in Paris by rebel provinces; they all evoked the 'great conflagration which was a threat to all your provinces'. There was no glory in a success that was devoid of risk, which meant that Louis XIII could have enjoyed no glory in his triumph, and all were concerned to stress the lack of strength in the royal army and the unpropitious lateness of the season for military operations. Navarrenx was described as a formidable fortress, powerfully armed and well provisioned. In such conditions, it is not surprising that the papal nuncio, Bentivoglio, presented the success of the promenade as a sign of divine benediction; 'God wished to work all these miracles through the agency of His Majesty in such evident and mysterious circumstances that they vie one with another in their marvellousness'.

Lay writers were not slow to exploit this kind of Christian incredulity and their writings on the subject closely resembled popular chapbook literature. They all drew on the signs and symbols which surrounded the events. Some noted how the king's entry to Nararrenx undid that of the protestant army of Mongomery 50 years earlier to the very day. Others discovered that the readings for the office on the day of the conquest concerned the story of Maccabees and the re-establishment of the temple in Jerusalem by Antiochus. There was little hesitation about calling the Calvinists 'old witches' and presenting the royal expedition as 'a powerful exorcism of evil spirits'. Through these accounts, the military excursion of Louis XIII became an edifying story, a nursery tale.

The pamphleteers of 1620 did not intend consciously to mislead public opinion or ignore historical truth. Of mediocre value, their publications represent a kind of contemporary flotsam left by the high tide of historicist renewal between 1560 and 1620. They were the work of clerics and, more importantly, of men of the law, who set their skills to work on behalf of the royal state. The significance of their publications should not be belittled by comparison with the great names such as Etienne Pasquier or Jean Bodin; without them, the definition and functioning of the divine right absolute monarchy would not have been as it was.

The crown was the prime beneficiary of their efforts, eclipsing all others by the year 1620. The monarchy was, of course, still a military one but this traditional aspect of its function was on the retreat; the actual presence of the king's majesty could achieve more than mere military might; 'his presence alone making a greater impression on the hearts of his subjects than anything else whatsoever . . . it was imperative for these mountain peoples that the king be someone feared and respected'. Soon even the physical presence of the sovereign had become dispensable, with royal virtue being conveyed henceforth through other channels than those of fidelity and personal relationships.

Louis XIII was above all the king of Paris, 'the true temple of the Muses and of Themis'. The expedition against Béarn was a sacred reaction of the centre against the periphery, of unity against division. But this 'centralism' was not exactly what was portrayed by his critics. King of Paris, Louis XIII was also the defender of French liberty, threatened by local privileges and powers. He went to Pau 'to save the said town from manifest oppression'. His intentions were not to crush Béarn's liberties, rather the reverse. To the deputies from the Estates of Béarn, sent to the king upon his arrival, he declared that he would enter the principality as 'sovereign of Béarn', and not as king of France, and would restore its prosperity and its liberty. No text spoke of the unification of the realm and instead they evoked a union based upon a kind of reciprocity and a political contract. Louis XIII embodied these propositions in the oath which he swore on 9 October before the Estates to respect Béarn's liberties.

The pamphleteers of 1620 constructed a portrait of the worthy king and his virtues, the concomitant of his absolute authority. Louis XIII had pardoned the vanquished and had only resorted to force when the paths of conciliation had been exhausted. His intervention stemmed from his paternal sense of justice 'regulated and moderated by love towards inconsiderate children'. The absolute monarchy should also be a paternalist monarchy. Amongst the kingly virtues, two in particular caught the attention of the pamphleteers; the heroic lineage which made Louis XIII the descendant of St Louis and Henri IV, and the personal election of the king by the Almighty, the 'miracle of monarchs'.

The king of France was not only, by historical fortune, a descendant of a dynasty, but he was also imbued with 'a powerful innocence which forced the heavens, against the apparent logic of human affairs, to signal their favour by showering on your head numerous crowns'. Attributed to Jean de Limoges, a 15-year-old student, the *Speech before the king* upon his return from his expeditions to Béarn and Calais was a veritable declamation of divine right royal absolutism. Kings should no longer be distinguished from tyrants because 'the glory of kings is absolute authority . . . God requires that both good and bad kings should be obeyed . . . such obedience is due even to the worst kings, for God did not establish them without good cause'. Uncertainty had surrounded the notion of divine right until it gained precision in the climate of religious and noble revolts. The expedition to Béarn became an example for all those who were opposed to the monarchical state: 'What divine punishment awaits those who rise up in rebellion against God's Anointed'. The main elements of the cult of monarchy were thus in place by 1620; 'The King is the veritable image of God . . . You are Gods, and the only difference between Kings and Gods remains immortality'. To such sentiments Bossuet would add little beyond his rhetorical talents.

The defence against these absolutist propositions was singularly feeble and only one work appeared, *Calamity of Béarn*, published anonymously in Orthez in 1620. Written by a Protestant, who was definitely a Béarnais, this publication recycled the democratic ideas which had been developed by the supporters of the Catholic League as well as by French Calvinists and implicit in the preamble to the Custom (*For*) of Béarn: 'In the beginning, the inhabitants of the Seigneurie and Sovereignty of Béarn governed themselves by *Fors* and Customs. To retain their liberty, many knights are elected successively as sovereigns'. This 'republican' writer was the only one to express disquiet over the institutional consequences of the Edict of Union. He imagined that the principality had hitherto enjoyed two kinds of law; the law of the sovereign ruler which could be altered without changing the state, and the law of the principality by which the prince enjoyed sovereignty and which could only be modified with the consent of the Estates General of Béarn. The author of the *Calamity* had no difficulty in demonstrating that, in uniting the principality to the French crown, the Prince destroyed Béarn sovereignty and violated the 'constitution'. His thesis was not without merit; but how could a Protestant reconcile this view with the desire of the Calvinists to unite their churches to those of their co-religionists in France?

The events of 1620 demonstrated, therefore, two complementary trends. The first was to confront a state and a young dynasty with disunited provinces and privileges which were seen on the one hand as the fomenters of disorder by the former and as constitutional liberties by the latter. The state acted, of course, as a centralizing force, but it offered in exchange a 'French' liberty, and the principles of a certain equality, as a consequence of unity. The second trend was the rise of monarchical absolutism in opposition to contractual perceptions of political authority, the division of powers and the existence of intermediary territorial principalities.

The union of 1620, a complete success from the monarchy's point of view, entailed no immediate revolution in the political and social institutions of Béarn. Although victorious, the king was sufficiently astute to maintain the traditional structures in place before progressively superimposing on top of them those of the French state.

The preamble to the Edict of Union stated the royal intentions perfectly; it announced that Béarn would retain its customs, its rights, liberties and privileges. In a brief statement, the edict then laid down the reasons for the king's decision. Union with France meant ensuring that Béarn was no longer a prey to aggression from its Spanish neighbours and the introduction of the Salic Law into the Principality in order to forestall any succession crisis which might arise over the lack of a male heir.[4] The edict found further justification in the fact that since the Peace of Loudun in 1616 the Calvinist churches of Béarn were united to those of France. The union satisfied the wish that Henri IV had expressed shortly before his death. The institutional consequences of the Act signed at Pau were limited to the creation of a new sovereign law-court, the *Parlement* of Navarre with its seat at Pau, itself the result of the amalgamation of the Sovereign Councils of Béarn and Navarre. Only one clause in fact smacked of centralization and this was the one which made French the judicial language in the principality. The right to worship according to the protestant faith was left untouched and

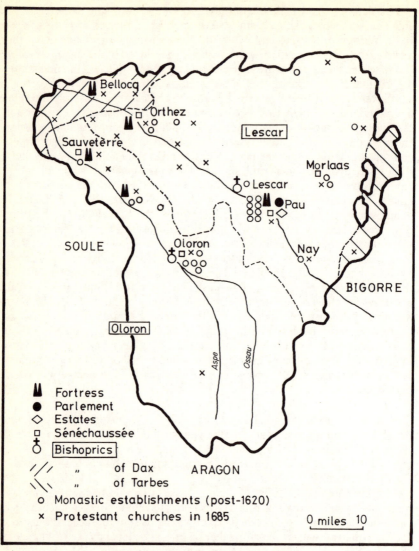

Belloc

Orthez

Lescar

Sauvetèrre

Morlaas

Lescar

Pau

Oloron

Nay

SOULE

BIGORRE

Oloron

Aspe

Ossau

ARAGON

⚔ Fortress
● Parlement
◇ Estates
▫ Sénéchaussée
☦ Bishoprics
／／／ „ of Dax
＼＼＼ „ of Tarbes
○ Monastic establishments (post-1620)
× Protestant churches in 1685

0 miles 10

Fig. 4.2 Seventeenth-century Béarn

would remain so until 1685. For its part, the Catholic Church did not become a vehicle for monarchical centralization either. The union introduced only a minimum of change in the life of the province and in 1789 the deputies of Béarn could still declare: 'The laws of the region, its liberties, privileges and rights have been preserved. . . . The general laws of France are entirely foreign to us; we live according to our own law, which can only be modified with our consent. We cannot be taxed either collectively or individually without our express consent. We have a national militia with which to protect ourselves'. What was the true position and what had happened to the liberties of Béarn after 1620?

The Estates General of Béarn, composed of the Grand Assembly (the *Grand Corps*, nobility and clergy together) and the Third Estate, retained their traditional format until the French Revolution. Representative of territory rather than of individuals, this assembly successfully resisted all attempts at reform proposed by the royal government. Through the existence of the *Abrégé*, a permanent council of the Estates when they were not in session, they preserved an unimpaired level of political activity. From the fifteenth century they had made themselves the guardians of the Béarn 'constitution'. They did their best to maintain this rôle which involved, primarily, the administering of the princely oath after each new accession. Louis XIII took his oath in Pau on 9 October 1620 and all the Bourbons after him took the oath in person and in the presence of representatives of the Estates.[5]

The 'pledge' or oath of Béarn was very distinct from that pronounced by the king of France at his consecration where the pledge to the Kingdom and the promise to the Church were entirely positive, devoid of any *non facere* clause, and there was no question of the sovereign agreeing to conform to the laws of the land. The French oaths, in any case, were oral pledges whereas those of the sovereign princes of Béarn were always drafted in writing and meticulously enregistered by the Estates. By his oath, the prince agreed to respect and to apply the custom of the land. He recognized the inalienable nature of his territory, accepted the limits which existed upon his right to declare war and make peace, and acknowledged that the Custom could not be changed without prior agreement from the Estates. The prince thereby confirmed the constitutional myth of the country which provided the preamble to the Custom and which proclaimed the superiority of law over princedom, the elective character of the early princes of Béarn and the theoretical right of insurrection.[6]

The ceremony of the oath, undertaken by all the kings of France, served to underline the reciprocal character of the engagement for both parties. The *sacramentum mutuum* was a veritable social contract, entered into by the king before he in turn received that of the deputies of the Estates. The Béarn nobility received the royal oath standing, swords at their sides. Only the Third Estate attended without swords and kneeling. The last oath received and exchanged was that of Louis XVI on 1 January 1776 at Versailles in the course of an exceptionally lavish ceremony. On the occasion of the *sacramentum mutuum* the Estates could present particular grievances (*doléances*), as distinct from the annual grievances, and they did so in both 1723 and 1776.

The Edict of Union in 1620 did not fundamentally challenge the characteristics of this engagement. Rather, it confirmed its essential purpose for the right of remonstrance if the Estates became subsumed into a genuine legislative authority. Every proposition from the Estates accepted by the king became a Statute and had the force of law equivalent to that of the Custom. The regulatory activity of the Estates of Béarn had been great in the period 1555–1620. The edict did not put a stop to it and it continued until 1675. From 1608 onwards, the Estates envisaged the preparation of a collection of these laws which would complete the Custom and bring it up to date. The union of 1620 appears to have stimulated their enthusiasm and a commission which met in 1628 led to the first collected edition of 1633. Two further expanded and corrected editions appeared in 1676 and 1716. At no point did the monarchy intervene to control or limit the initiative of the Estates. Yet it should be noticed how the example was imitated by the principal mountain valleys of Béarn, who compiled a version of their own individual statutes in 1645 whilst, for their part, the Estates of Navarre were never so active as during the reign of Louis XIV and continued issuing their own statutes until 1754. Soule also produced its first collection of regulations on 3 July 1695. The legislative activity of the Estates in the region covered by the *Parlement* of Navarre was at an unprecedented level in the years from 1620 to 1700, and there is little doubt that this was a local response to monarchical absolutism.[7] This legislation cannot be examined in detail here but some examples will illustrate the degree of autonomy which Béarn enjoyed under the union. In the economic sphere, the statutes preserved the monopolies and privileges traditionally enjoyed in the region. The ordinances of 1627 prolonged those of the great transhumance pastoral farmers of the uplands at the expense of the arable farmers on the plain and they would remain in place until the Revolution. With the tacit acceptance of the Estates, the rights of *compascuité* and free-range pasturage remained intact. As a result the royal edicts relating to enclosure and the abolition of free-range pasturage were never applied in Béarn. Some traditional pastoral agricultural practices, such as the right of *carnal*, a right to confiscate cattle in certain circumstances, remained in force until 1789, despite the contentions and violence which resulted from it. The confirmation of the privileges of the pastoral farmers became an insurmountable obstacle in the way of land reclamation schemes. These farmers found themselves supported in the Estates by the nobility which enhanced its monopoly over viticulture by official measures between 1648 and 1667. The nobles kept the sale of quality wines for themselves by keeping their monopoly over the good quality vineyards and by preventing smaller vine-growers in the river valleys from planting vines. The monarchy did nothing to stop this although, by the eighteenth century, it ran completely contrary to what the intendants were advocating.

In a similar fashion, the ordinances of the Estates perpetuated the exclusion of certain social and ethnic minorities from the province. A measure of 1633 reinforced the regulations of medieval customary legislation against the *cagot* (accused of being the descendants of lepers) although they were contrary to royal ordinances. By contrast, local legislation on the subject of mendicants and vagabonds was in advance of royal edicts. From the end of the sixteenth century, the Béarn regulations prefigured the policies of Colbert later in the seventeenth century. The legislation also attempted to put the finishing touches to a more strictly organized social inequality emulating Pyreneean tradition and founded upon an extended system of primogeniture for both noble and commoner property. Here, too, legislation enacted by the Estates anticipated that of the monarchy, laying down a strict hierarchy within some professional groups, such as the medical profession, and fixing wages as a way of controlling demands for increases. A large number of coercive measures attributed to monarchical centralization were, in reality, first instituted by the Estates themselves.

By leaving the Estates of Béarn unreformed, the monarchy thereby preserved intact one of the assembly's essential functions, that of determining noble status in the principality. Up to the French Revolution, nobility in this region remained a 'real' rather than 'personal' status; to be regarded as a noble it was necessary to be both a proprietor of lands declared noble and which carried membership to the Estates in the Great Assembly, as well as to renounce all artisan or commercial activity. There were times when the monarchy held that this arrangement tended to the proliferation of nobility, making the Estates ungovernable. In fact, the number of noble lands remained stable and the sale of such property was rare because noble families collaborated to ensure that it was kept intact. A complete political equality existed amongst these nobles which ensured the cohesion of the Great Assembly throughout this period. In 1770 the intendant was appalled by what he called the 'indecent arguments of an ignorant and prejudiced multitude' but the traditional structure of the Estates was never modified.

The Estates, guardians of the political and social institutions of the principality, served also as the protectors of the Béarnais language. The Edict of Union had imposed the French language only upon the acts of the judiciary; up to the Revolution, the debates of the Estates were recorded and their accounts drawn up in Béarnais. Of course, the official language gradually became a rather feeble kind of lingua franca but this was never the result of a requirement laid down by central authority. For their part, some notaries and many rural communities continued to record their deliberations in Béarnais up to the early eighteenth century. In 1789, the Béarnais still claimed that they were responsible for their own defence, which was not altogether without foundation since the regiment of Béarnais Bands, created after 1620, was never a unit of the ordinary militia and was kept exclusively for the defence of the frontiers of Béarn.

Between 1620 and 1789, it is undeniable that the Estates lost important aspects of their power. Although they maintained their right to present remonstrances to the king, their examination and acceptance was no longer an indispensable prerequisite to fixing the levy of tax. In principle, the Béarnais could only be taxed with their explicit consent, and there were still members of the nobility at the Estates in the eighteenth century who would argue that they would not consent to vote for any tax except in exchange for the right to elect their sovereign! In practice, the Estates were progressively forced to accept new permanent royal taxes which they had not the power to prevent. However, they retained the right to negotiate the amount of tax levied with the king's representatives and how it was levied upon taxpayers. These privileges ensured that Béarn was the most lightly taxed province of the kingdom after Corsica and the one where fiscal burdens were distributed with the least injustice. In 1788, the Estates were still declaring that taxes could be imposed only with their consent and that royal taxation remained 'provisional in its nature'; but the divisions between the Third Estate and the Great Assembly were damaging these claims and had made the monarchy the arbiter in taxation matters. In the end, although involved in the determination of how much tax was to be levied, the Estates had no rights to oversee the use which the royal government made of their levies since they had no powers of financial review.

The Estates of Béarn also lost the initiative in the areas of transport and forest administration. The latter is particularly instructive of both the powers of resistance at a local level on the one hand as well as the caution of central authority. The Forest Code of Colbert (1669) remained inapplicable for a long time in Béarn and the *Parlement* of Navarre and the Estates shared the responsibility of forest jurisdiction. This privilege was frequently threatened but it disappeared only in 1738 with the creation of a Mastership of Forest and River administration (*maîtrise des eaux et forêts*) subject to the Grand Master of Guyenne. However, this new institution was confirmed only in 1764 when the Estates had exhausted all the means at its disposal for opposition, not excluding an attempt to bribe the officials in Versailles.

In general, the monarchy displayed considerable flexibility in its attitude towards the Estates of Béarn and, although it reduced its power, it did so without fuss and almost always by exploiting either the incompetence or the internal dissensions of the provincial assembly. In any case, it would be wrong to imagine that the relationships between local and central authorities were always bound to conflict. Béarn never found itself engulfed by popular revolts, so frequent in neighbouring Aquitaine. In the seventeenth century, the Estates were concerned above all to institutionalize the social and economic privileges of the dominant groups in the principality, the large pastoral farmers and the nobility. The monarchy did not oppose this policy since it formed part of its own under another guise. In the eighteenth century there was even a renaissance of the Estates who willingly co-operated with the intendants and obtained significant results in areas as diverse as social medicine, education, agricultural techniques and commerce.

The monarchy was anxious to respect an institution which acted as a symbol of local liberties, and even worked to preserve the distinctive communal patterns of Béarn. The great mountain valleys preserved their traditional separate political organisms; their agents (*syndicats*) continued to look after the common pastures and negotiate with their Spanish counterparts over land usage in the high Pyrenees. 'Thoroughfare' treaties (*'lies et passeries'*) were drawn up or renewed up to the eighteenth century in order to settle the differences between transhumance farmers on both sides of the Pyrenees.[8] The federal organisms of the valleys remained in existence until the French Revolution and, with them, a society which attributed the reality of power to the 'notable families' of pastoral farmers at the expense of the broad mass of rural farmers. Proud of their independence, the people of the high Pyrenees were quick to remind the king that they were the most reliable guardians of the frontier. In 1688, the inhabitants of the Aspe valley resisted the introduction of the royal rights over property transfer by proving that they had once formed a republic and that their laws were older than those of the prince himself.[9] Versailles did not demur at this democratic interpretation of the valley's history.

In the end, the monarchy found itself in greatest difficulties with the institution which it had itself created in 1620. This was not because the *Parlement*'s creation had been, of itself, a radical departure. Since 1552, the composition and functions of the Sovereign Council of Béarn had been rather similar to that of a sovereign law-court. Besides, up to 1691, other independent institutions also existed, such as the Chamber of Accounts of Pau and Nérac, a Treasury (*Chambre du Trésor*), a Mint (*Cour des Monnaies*) and a Board for Forests and Rivers (*Table de marbre*). These were all transferred to the *Parlement* in 1691 and formed a separate Financial Chamber (*Chambre des Finances*) to sit alongside the *Grand Chambre* and the *Chambre Criminelle*.

Throughout the seventeenth century, the *Parlement* of Pau was submissive and self-effacing. This was a period during which its councillors acquired their social, cultural and economic pre-eminence amongst the Béarnais nobility. But after 1715, from the Regency onwards, the *Parlement* displayed its independence and took upon itself the rôle of defender of local liberties. Under the pretext that it was the descendant of the sovereign Councils of a kingdom, Navarre, and a principality, Béarn, it laid claim to daring political rights, particularly to share the king's legislative power and to question the government. Its remonstrances to the king became more numerous up to the fundamental crisis of 1765, during the course of which the councillors resigned and were replaced by judges nominated by the king. Reconstituted in 1775, the *Parlement* remained until the Revolution the champion of Béarn constitutionalism. Analysing the English constitution, an *avocat général* from Pau found himself writing: 'I have sketched without intending it the outlines of the constitution of Béarn; it satisfies the aspirations of a free man in his quest for a homeland'. It is easy today to criticize the *parlementaires* who, under the pretence of defending public liberties were in fact fighting to protect their individual privileges. The reality was certainly more complex and the noble councillors were not cynical when they saw analogies between the Béarn 'constitution' and English-style parliamentary government.

Over and above the opposition of the Estates or the *Parlement*, two points need emphasizing. On the one hand, there was a convergence of views between the intendants of the monarchy and those of the local deputies: whether over the poor, the mendicants, the social and professional order, the decisions of the Estates were often more advanced than those of the state itself. Centralization emerged more often than is generally realized from below and the provincial élites were never slow to sacrifice their political principles in return for allying themselves with the state and thereby protecting their social and economic interests. On the other hand, one cannot help but be surprised at the patience of the state and the relative lack of means at its disposal for the purposes of enlarging its hegemony. To secure compliance, the monarchy learnt how to live with interminable discussions about taxation, considerable delays in payment, and in the application of royal orders. The king never garrisoned military forces in Béarn and the *maréchaussée* could boast of scarcely more than 20 men for a population of approaching 200 000. The intendants made their appearance in 1631 but their presence was intermittent for some time thereafter. Between 1631 and 1739, the area covered by the intendancy was redrawn eight times, and of the 41 intendants serving during that time, not one took up residence in the province.

The implementation of the edict of 1620 was slow and, following the example of Louis XIII, it was never violent. The monarchy proceeded carefully by stages, above all associating the dominant groups in the province with its conquest. The evolution of the state thus became inseparable from that of society, and especially from the most co-operative, but also the most *frondeur* group in it, the office holders.

It was the French monarchy which completed the processes of annexation begun in 1620 when, doubtless against its better judgement, it called on the Béarnais to depute to the Estates General of France in 1789. The nobility of the *Parlement* and of the Estates as well as the clergy were against sending deputies. Anxious to preserve their individual privileges and their Custom, the Béarnais had never, until that moment, sent representatives to the Estates General of the kingdom. The reactions of the privileged orders was the same in 1789 as it had been in 1617 and 1620; they consistently believed 'that it would be a dangerous precedent to send deputies to the Estates General, because, if they were despatched this would have to indicate their quality as members of the French monarchy and that, to accede to this demand would be tantamount to accepting the Salic Law and all the other laws which together went to make up the French monarchy and that the Estates General had only been assembled to assign the immense royal debts upon the whole realm with equality. . .'.

It was not surprisingly this last point which was decisive in 1789. The nobility were preoccupied above all with the liberties and constitution of Béarn; the Third Estate was more concerned with the possibility of fiscal equality. Under the threat of a popular uprising, the Estates of Béarn agreed to send a deputation to the Estates General of France and, on 28 October 1789, the representatives of the six districts of Pau resolved to 'offer up as a tribute to their country an antique constitution which they held dear' for 'the moment had come when Béarn, united in affection and interest with France, should no longer uphold a separate constitution'. The people of Béarn entered at this moment, willingly and fully, into the larger nation of France.

NOTES FOR CHAPTER 4

* Professor of Modern History, l'Université de Pau et des pays de l'Adour. Translated by the editor.

1 See Abbé Puyol, *Louis XIII et le Béarn ou le rétablissement du catholicisme en Béarn et réunion du Béarn et de la Navarre à la France* (Paris, 1872).

2 See P. Tucoo-Chala and C. Desplat, *La Principauté de Béarn* (Pau, 1980) and C. Desplat, 'Les sièges de Navarrenx (1569–1620): le fait et les mots' in *Bull. Soc. Sciences Lettres et Arts de Bayonne*, cxl (1900), pp. 95–108.

3 '. . . franc taupin, prétendu gentilhomme aux épaules étroites, à l'échine longue faite en anguille, à l'écu noir . . .'.

4 France's Salic Law, which excluded the royal succession from passing through the female line and excluded queens from the throne, did not apply in Béarn where queens could rule.

5 C. Desplat, 'Les Etats de Béarn et la définition de la souveraineté béarnaise à l'époque moderne' in *Parliaments, Estates and Representation*, iii (1983), pp. 89–99.

6 See C. Desplat, 'Règlementation et société dans les Pays d'Etats des Pyrénées occidentales à l'époque moderne', *Société et monde ouvrier en Aquitaine* (Actes du XXXIIe Congrès Féd. Hist. du Sud-Ouest; Agen, 1982), pp. 185–202.

7 C. Desplat, 'Règlements et principes de la vie politique dans les Pays d'Etats des Pyrénées occidentales' in *Hommages à M. Bordes, Annales Faculté de Lettres de Nice*, xlv (1983), pp. 25–39.

8 See 'Lies et passeries dans les Pyrénées', *Actes 3e Journées de recherche de la Société des Sept Vallées* (Tarbes, 1986).

9 These feudal *droits de mutation*, chiefly *amortissement, nouveaux acquêts*, and *franc-fief* are explained in general terms in R. Doucet, *Les Institutions de la France au XVIe siècle* (2 vols., Paris, 1948) ii, pp. 483–7.

5

Louis XIV and Flanders

ALAIN LOTTIN*

The conquest of Flanders by Louis XIV was the culmination of a centuries-old conflict which began its decisive phase after 1635. With the capture of Arras in 1640, the victory at Lens in 1648 and that of the Dunes in 1658 there began a long piecemeal advance in which the first milestone in legal terms was the treaty of the Pyrenees in 1659. Artois, save for St-Omer and Aire-sur-la-Lys, was annexed, as well as some strongholds in coastal Flanders, such as Gravelines and Bourbourg, whose possession strengthened the position of Dunkirk which the king had purchased from the English in 1662.[1]

The second phase was completed in 1668 with the treaty of Aix-la-Chapelle. This brought to a close the lightning campaign of 1667–8 which saw the Sun King take possession of Lille, Douai, Tournai, Courtrai and Oudenaarde without a shot being fired. This conquest and the resulting changes of sovereignty were not welcomed amongst the local population. 'There was not much rejoicing in the towns belonging to the French' wrote Chavatte, the weaver from Lille, whose opinions well reflected those in the town at large.[2]

The final and critical phase culminated in 1678 with the treaty of Nijmegen. Louis XIV annexed the rest of Artois (St-Omer and Aire), a substantial part of Hainault and the Cambrésis including the towns of Valenciennes and Cambrai as well as part of the Flemish lowland with, notably, Cassel and Bailleul. To round it off (or, as Vauban advised him, to make his *pré plus carré*) he added Ypres to it, in return for Furnes and Oudenaarde, and the renowned military architect was called in for the express reason of constructing a sufficient number of powerful fortifications to give the military frontier a strong defensive capability.

The War of Spanish Succession threw these conquests into jeopardy and Louis XIV almost lost Flanders. Lille (1708), followed by Douai (1710) fell into the hands of Prince Eugene of Savoy and Marlborough. The victory of Villars at Denain in 1712 and the subsequent withdrawal of England from the war saved the day for the essential elements of the preceding acquisitions. At the treaty of Utrecht, Walloon Flanders and, with it, part of the Flemish coast, remained in French hands. This was not just the way things turned out but also what the local population wanted as the Anglo-Dutch occupation had left behind it too many

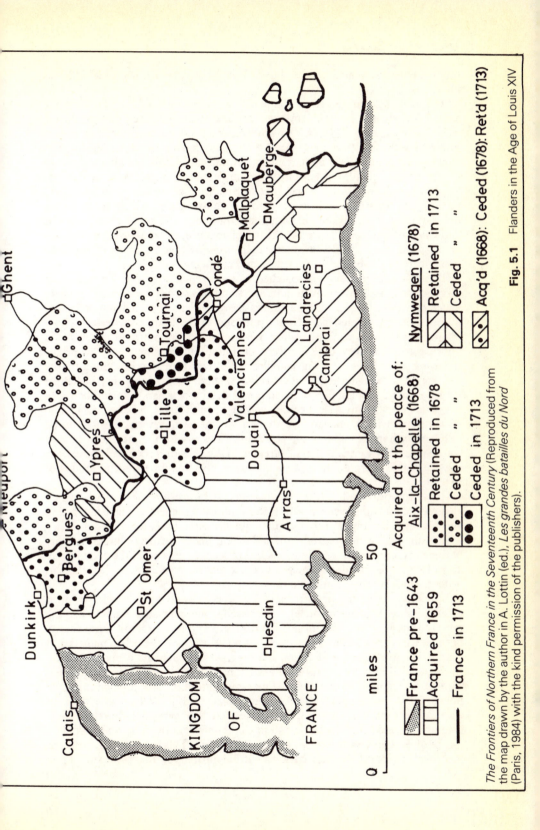

Ghent

Nieuport

Dunkirk

Calais

Bergues'

St Omer

Ypres

Lille

Tournai

Condé

Valenciennes

Douai

Arras

Hesdin

Cambrai

Landrecies

Maubeuge

Malplaquet

KINGDOM

OF

FRANCE

miles

0   50

Acquired at the peace of:

Aix-la-Chapelle (1668)
- Retained in 1678
- Ceded   "   "
- Ceded in 1713

Nymwegen (1678)
- Retained in 1713
- Ceded   "   "
- Acq'd (1668): Ceded (1678): Ret'd (1713)

- France pre–1643
- Acquired 1659
- France in 1713

Fig. 5.1 Flanders in the Age of Louis XIV

The Frontiers of Northern France in the Seventeenth Century (Reproduced from the map drawn by the author in A. Lottin (ed.), *Les grandes batailles du Nord* (Paris, 1984) with the kind permission of the publishers).

bitter memories, shattering the illusions of those who had seen the Allies as liberators.

The policies that Louis XIV and his 'servants' pursued to transform the annexed lands into French provinces, and the reactions which they produced, were evident as early as 1668. Two governmental systems corresponding to very different historical traditions found themselves having to work side by side. France with its absolute monarchy, its centralized régime, its officials and its intendants had to administer and integrate lands and populations used to the feeble and distant power of the king of Spain, represented by his governor-general in Brussels, and to methods of government which were highly decentralized.[3] Within the old communal traditions of Flanders, where towns and *bourgeoisies* were all-powerful, the urban notables, either enjoying noble titles or still commoners, held sway thanks to institutions which guaranteed them the lion's share of power both at provincial and municipal level.

The first administrators despatched by the French king were amazed, even disconcerted, to discover institutions and traditions so different from those with which they were familiar. 'These fellows are sovereigns of some kind' exclaimed the intendant Le Peletier de Souzy referring to the town magistrats. Those sworn in as mayors, burgesses, aldermen and councillors who collectively made up what were known as the *Laws* were, of course, chosen annually by the prince following procedures of varying complexity.[4] But those in office had the authority to organize a sophisticated rotation amongst these posts so that the substantial landed or merchant families retained power within their hands. In addition, in a world where mortality gave a certain substance to the *danse macabre*, the system remained sufficiently open to allow those newcomers whom fortune had favoured to entertain hopes of joining the governing élites. As for the provincial estates, whose rôle was essentially that of agreeing to the subsidies accorded annually to the ruler, they were dominated by the towns and thus by the same groups of notables.

Royal authority had, in the end, no interest in overturning a system which ensured that it had the co-operation and support of the élites. The French king and his representatives in the province quickly came to understand that. They limited themselves to controlling it and when, under financial duress, venality became evident among certain municipal officers at the end of the century, the king placed no opposition in the way of those towns who bought up the offices in order to preserve their constitutions.[5]

In reality, the urban magistrates of Flanders enjoyed considerable power in essential areas of government. They exercised sovereign justice and thus had the power to condemn to death those guilty of crimes within their remit. The security of the towns depended in large measure upon the *rewart*, the urban militias and traditional sworn bands of fencers, archers, crossbowmen and cannon-masters. In financial affairs, they controlled important resources and could spend them without a great deal of constraint. The regulation of industry, the craft guilds, public works and assistance to the poor equally fell upon their shoulders. In ecclesiastical matters, their authority extended over parochial churches, their institutional and religious fabric and to a certain extent over their personnel by means of the churchwardens whom they nominated. This state of affairs amazed the first priests of French background nominated to the province. They denounced in no uncertain terms a situation which seemed to them both incongruous and incompatible with the French monarchy: '*Messieurs* the Magistrates appear to believe themselves to be in something of the position that towns in a republic enjoy, where the Magistrate represents the town community which elects him. . . . These magistrates behave as though they were, after a fashion, sovereigns; but under a monarchy everyone is, in every sense, a vassal'.[6] Unruffled by this remark, the aldermen replied that they were but exercising the same powers as their colleagues and predecessors had done in Flanders and Brabant. This was, in effect, the nub of the problem. Towns and provinces in the conquered region wanted to continue to govern themselves as they had always done in the Burgundian, latterly the Spanish, Low Countries. But now they had stepped into another governmental régime and they would have to learn to adapt themselves to its rules.

In reality, 'central authority' had not been much in evidence under Spanish rule. Its principal representative, the provincial governor, was above all, preoccupied with military matters and had enough to do organizing the provisioning, garrisoning and disciplining of his troops. In all these matters, he had to deal as a matter of course with those who administered the country directly. As for the Chamber of Accounts in Lille, given responsibilities over finance, its members were drawn from the great local families or were closely bound up with them. In the towns, his provosts had only strictly limited police powers. The secular clergy, by definition more dependant upon civil authority since the king chose the bishops, cut a pale figure beside the regular clergy.

Things were very different under the French monarchy. The king of France made his presence felt in a much more overwhelming and personal way than the kings of Spain had done. Louis XIV came to Flanders not only in the course of military campaigns but also on official visits. He visited Lille, capital of the annexed region, six times. The organization of these trips and the receptions accorded him, like the respect for etiquette at Versailles, were methodically planned in order to impress and persuade the local population, and stimulate their attachment to and respect for the great king. These personal contacts were intensified by his methods of government. The king's representatives, his ministers, constantly referred to his orders and wishes; 'His Majesty' was ever-present in their correspondence and conversation in such a way that people were convinced that he knew about, and directed, everything; and in the case of Louis XIV they may have been very largely correct.

The central pivot of royal and ministerial action was the intendant of police, justice and finance, not only eyes and ears to the king but also the essential instrument of policy and imbued with considerable powers. The existence of the intendant was a great institutional innovation which allowed for a progressive change in governmental methods. To exercise this delicate task in this hard-won and difficult new province, Louvois, whose responsibility it became as secretary of state for war, chose someone from the Colbert clan, his 'cousin', Michel La Peletier de Souzy. Intelligent and subtle, hardworking despite a nonchalant manner, competent and efficient, he knew how to impose his will, and thereby the king's, throughout the first 15 years of deft negotiations. Never once, in any important respect, was he denied the support of the king and his powerful minister. When the members of the magistrature of Lille dared to despatch deputies to Versailles to complain about him and his 'infractions' upon their authority, Louvois assured the intendant that they would be received as they deserved to be and Le Peletier was delighted that this provincial delegation was going 'to learn the extent of the authority which the king has delegated to me'. At the first encounter, Colbert or Louvois reminded them that 'the king's service demands that we always give our intendants full consideration'.

But ostentatious support like this was always accompanied by private cautions which were sometimes in the nature of severe reprimands. 'The function of an intendant consists in informing the king of all that is done in his region and nothing else'; 'you are despatched only to carry out the orders His Majesty sends you'. Over-zealous or inappropriate actions are censured. 'To ensure that His Majesty is content with you does not require you to do more than he asks of you'. Intendants must be efficient but discreet, wield real power but not show it too much – in other words to be the king's servant and not a master, a political philosophy effectively encapsulated by Louvois; 'The more you enjoy the confidence of the king in the region to which you are assigned, the more everything takes place following your advice; and the greater, thus, should be your concern to make everyone think that you have had no part in it and that everything to the good occurs as a result of those who commanded it'.[7]

It was the task of this key individual, his collaborators and other royal representatives, to integrate Flanders progressively to the French administrative monarchy and kingdom. It required prudence, flexibility and intelligence, all of which involved, firstly, respecting the privileges of the province and the towns guaranteed by the treaties of 'capitulation' which the king had accepted and signed. Louis XIV had himself provided the example of his intention not to disturb urban privileges. Had he not been seen at Lille to swear to respect the privileges of the town before the Magistrature had sworn allegiance to the king, having been assured that this was the custom adhered to by the counts of Flanders? Subsequent orders transmitted through Louvois or Colbert were consistently along the same lines. To the intendant wanting to seize the opportunity provided by some new and inexperienced members of the sovereign council of Tournai to transform it into a commission with himself as its president, Louvois replied that there should be no question in anyone's mind of his harbouring intentions of 'harming the privileges of the region'. All must be so disposed so as not to confront any traditional privileges. When the magistrates, in accordance with custom, chose their permanent officials, and particularly their stipendiary councillors or syndics, he told the intendant to 'recommend nobody to them because this irritates the Flemings more than anything else in the world'. Colbert issued instructions for the greatest care to be taken in the regulation of markets, and Louvois, the greatest rigour in disciplining the soldiery. In general, the intendant had to be sure not to exceed his powers: 'Although the power to contradict the Magistrate has been included in our commission to you, it should only be exercised in extreme circumstances and in order to punish corruption'.

Yet this respect for privileges had its limits, as was brusquely recalled by Louvois when the magistrate insisted upon the right to judge a Lillois who had been found guilty of having lent assistance to deserters from the French army. He accepted it with ill grace but more or less gave orders as to the decision they should reach. 'It is vital to the *bourgeois* of Lille in general that they should carry out their duty as regards this *bourgeois* because, should they neglect it, it will surely be the last case they judge'. A still more abrupt formula went like this: 'The king, having confirmed their privileges, intends to keep his word to them absolutely until they give us cause to think otherwise'. This respect should be seen in the context of a long-term royal strategy revealed by the minister when he talked of 'the intention [of the king] being always to shape in every possible way and discreetly the customs of this region to those of his kingdom'.[8]

At the same time, the king strove to cut the ties of the province with the Spanish Netherlands and provide it with institutions typical of the French monarchy.

His priority was to ensure the security of the territories annexed by providing them with an 'iron curtain' or *ceinture de fer* of defence. Town fortifications were rebuilt, renewed and adapted to the new techniques of siege warfare. Vauban and his group of engineers studded the area with powerful citadels in a carefully conceived pattern, of which Lille and Douai were the centrepieces.[9]

These military constructions were primarily intended to deter any future invaders; but they also had a second function which was to prevent the success of any rebellion of the local inhabitants, as Louvois clearly stated: 'The King, believing that nothing was more important than to ensure that the *bourgeois* of the newly occupied towns were in no state to undertake anything . . . against his service, His Majesty has decided to set in hand immediately the works to close the bastion of St Sauveur close by the town and there to construct a rampart capable of carrying cannon which could assault the city if necessary.' And Vauban confirmed this when he wrote [this fort] can scarcely serve to contain the upheavals of this part of the city, heavily populated with the lower orders who have nothing to lose'.[10]

The same suspicions explain the decision taken after the conquest to suppress the sworn confraternal bands, worried by their para-military rôle, and only to re-establish them at a much later date. Similarly in 1672, after the declaration of war against the Dutch, the king ordered the transfer of all the gunpowder from the Lille cannon-masters into the citadel and had the aldermen who refused to surrender the keys to their magazines imprisoned. In 1673, the inhabitants were required to surrender all their firearms at the town hall and sworn oaths were ordered on a house-to-house basis.

The financial and judicial administration was reorganized. The king removed the annexed parts of Flanders from the appellate jurisdiction of the Council of Flanders at Ghent and replaced it with the creation at Tournai of a sovereign council which quickly became a *Parlement.* When Tournai was returned to the Dutch, the *Parlement* was installed at Douai (1714). At the same time, a *présidial* was created at Bailleul. In financial affairs, the old *Chambre des Comptes* at Lille, founded by Philip the Bold, hastily left for Brussels leaving behind it most of its archives. Louis XIV gave Denis Godefroy the task of classifying and cataloguing them. In 1691, he created at Lille a *Bureau de Finances* to exercise the functions of this Chamber of Accounts. In 1685, a *Hôtel des Monnaies* or mint was opened at Lille which rapidly grew in importance. Finally, in 1687, came the creation of the *Maîtrise des eaux et forêts* to administer rivers and forests.

Religious affairs and institutions were also the object of careful attention. These were sensitive matters, especially since the administration of a good deal of property was involved as well as the exercise of formidable power and also, above all, a surveillance of consciences and mentalities. The king and his ministers were particularly concerned with the mendicant orders, whose influence in the region was considerable. They had notably encouraged people to resist the king of France, who was suspected of sympathy towards heretics whom he tolerated in his kingdom. Louis XIV did not forget it; 'These are useless individuals and, for the most part, strongly attached to our enemies' wrote Louvois to the intendant. The king required the convents of the annexed territories to be detached from their provinces in the Spanish Low Countries. In 1671, the Récollets of Lille, in a conflict which engaged the sympathies of the whole population, finally had to submit. The general of the Capuchin order refused 'to divide the convents in the king's obedience from those under Spanish dominion'; but he nevertheless accepted a change of Superiors, replacing them with ones of French origin. The Jesuits had fewer problems because they had played a leading part in rallying the local inhabitants to the king through their public ceremonies and especially their famous processions. But the tone changed when the conflict with the pope grew more serious and Louis XIV became more menacing: 'Since the king is not satisfied with the conduct of *père* de Noyelle, General of the Jesuits, following his election', Louvois ordered the intendant to warn his family, who lived and had property in the region, 'that it was not out of the question that the King should punish them for the ill-conceived intentions of the said *père* de Noyelle'.

He was, above all, concerned with the secular clergy and the spiritual leaders of the dioceses. At Arras, he nominated a Gallican who served him loyally, Guy de Sève-Rochechouart. Louis XIV was fortunate in that he captured Tournai whilst the episcopal see was vacant. He recruited from Comminges in the distant Pyrenees a prelate, Gilbert de Choiseul du Plessis-Praslin, who, although suspected of some sympathies for Jansenism, was intensely Gallican and who had great intellectual and moral gifts. Upon his arrival, the new bishop impressed everyone with his pastoral zeal and the intendant, who admired the prelate's 'gifts of discernment which God has given him', emphasized the good impression which he made. 'It is regarded as some kind of marvel in this country to hear a bishop preach and it creates no less amazement than did the miracles of the Apostles'. At the same time, the new bishop was not liked because 'he was French'. Yet he became effectively the spearhead of Gallican and French politics. He controlled everything, nominating French priests to strategically vital posts, such as François Desqueux's appointment to the Oratory of St Etienne at Lille. One of his priorities was inevitably to create a seminary in which the future generations of his diocesan clergy would be trained; this was established in 1679 at Tournai. And when the great quarrel between France and the papacy broke out, the king left nothing to chance in his choice of representatives from the province at the Assembly. 'As it is vital that the prelates who are charged with this delegation have both zeal for the good of the Church and also for the service of His Majesty, he has commanded me . . . that you are to go immediately and see Monseigneur the archbishop of Cambrai and explain to him personally that it would please His Majesty if he would arrange that himself and Monseigneur de Tournai should be entrusted with the deputation from this province'. Gilbert de Choiseul became the prelate who drew up the first draft of the Declaration of 1682. The royal control and intervention upon both religious institutions and ideas was thus considerable. This was often evident at the University of Douai which the intendant visited upon the king's instructions to demand its submission to the Declaration of 1682, to suspend the payment of the wages of those who opposed it and to require that, in future, no professors should be appointed 'who did not agree to teach the doctrine contained in the Declaration of the clergy'.[11]

But in a province with old and intensive manufacturing traditions and where the textile industry, in particular, was of considerable importance not only in the towns but also in the outworking villages and the countryside, the economic and commercial patterns were more difficult to modify. For centuries, the territories annexed by Louis XIV had formed part of the economic zone of the old Netherlands along with Ghent, Antwerp, Brussels and Amsterdam. Colbert recognized that there were 'great links, commercial ties, family and kin relationships amongst these urban communities'. The conquest, however, set up a clean break between French Flanders and its former partners without, however, entirely pulling down the borders with France. The conquered lands had, in reality, the status of 'designated foreign province' (province réputée étrangère). Imports and exports were thus paid at both frontiers. 'Wishing to give favourable consideration to his numerous subjects in the town of Lille', the king agreed not to apply the duties on certain goods entering France, particularly manufactured cloth, at the higher rates laid down in 1667 but at the lower tariffs of 1664. The same applied to imports from the French tax-farm area of northern France known as the *cinq grosses fermes*.[12]

The most serious problem was provoked, however, by the establishment of a frontier, and therefore customs duties, along the new frontiers with the Spanish Netherlands. This took place in a climate of hostility and rivalry which alarmed the local population. When Colbert promulgated the Council edict of 21 September 1668 'to the effect that the traffic and merchandise entering and leaving from countries owing obedience to the Catholic King ... would pay duties at the rate of 30 per cent' until the governor-general in Brussels revoked those which he had imposed, the result was almost popular insurrection. In private, Louvois did not hesitate to express his disapproval for this measure, proposed by his great rival, for 'it would entirely ruin trade', whilst adding prudently that as 'he was not encharged with these kinds of matters' the intendant should interpret his comment as his personal 'rationale'. In any case, this drastic measure was quickly suspended 'for the goods and materials necessary for manufacture' as the situation was an explosive one. However, the customs posts were installed and it was not long before the tariffs were set at those generally applying in 1671. But the local population never accepted this state of affairs and, in 1698, the intendant Dugné de Bagnols wrote that the merchants considered that these customs duties were in danger of 'ruining them' and that they 'would do anything not to have to pay them'.[13]

Just as disturbing were the changes in trade patterns imposed by French authority. Colbert saw this as an essential element not only of his commercial politics but also of the fundamental integration of the annexed territories with France. Writing to Le Peletier de Souzy, he said: 'You must consider the point of making them use the routes via France for the despatch and traffic of all their goods to Spain, Italy and Germany, as one of the most important matters which could fall to your responsibility'. He undoubtedly envisaged this as a mechanism for expanding France's foreign trade; 'This will enable our merchants to profit from other countries'. But he also thought it would have a beneficial psychological effect; 'By these means, merchants will all be persuaded to detach themselves from their Flemish and Dutch counterparts and, at the same time, become more linked to the French by commercial ties and links'. To encourage this to happen, he used both the carrot and the stick. He suppressed the taxes or lightened the duties at the French frontier whilst multiplying the difficulties and inconvenience on the Dutch border. But commercial ties with Rouen, the other side of Picardy, held little attraction for the merchants who preferred the shorter and infinitely more convenient links with Ghent, Ostende or Antwerp. Because of the numerous wars, this policy was, however, fairly successful. But in his Memorandum of 1698 the intendant remained realistic; 'The Flemings despise the French; to such a degree that they would not hesitate to load their cargo on any other ship rather than a French one plying the same route'.[14]

At all events, it is indisputable that the populations of the annexed regions, merchants, artisans and craftsmen, attributed economic changes, the economic crises and the misery which resulted from them to the customs tariffs and wars of Louis XIV. They discreetly or overtly wanted to return to the Spanish Netherlands. Thus, when the Lille cloth-weaver, Chavatte, learnt that the prince of Orange had to retreat towards Maastricht in 1677, he wrote; 'This brought sadness to Lille'.

More generally, it is clear that, at the end of the seventeenth century, the populations of the conquered Netherlands were unreconciled in either heart or mind to the France of Louis XIV. In 1690, a Lille attorney declared 'that he would still prefer to be Spanish and see the last Frenchman dead', upon which the intendant commented that this was a common expression amongst the native population. At the same time, an important body of notables in Douai condemned French policy in all its aspects, and particularly the reduction of communal liberties. Charles Caudron, one of their number who had responsibility for looking after orphans, spoke of the 'tyranny' of the French, their 'shabby treatment' and 'ill-will and pretence' towards them.[15]

Paradoxically, it was the Anglo-Dutch occupation of 1708–13 which served as a revelation and hardened convictions in favour of France. The allies, welcomed as liberators by part of the population, quickly earned universal detestation by behaving as though they were conquerors and exploiters. The councillor of the *Parlement* of Douai, Le Febvre d'Orval, in refuge in Béthune, wrote: 'These poor people are more French than ever'. The victory at Denain (1712) made the maintenance of French sovereignty possible and it was assured in the Peace of Utrecht. This time, Louis XIV had annexed no territories at all; the inhabitants of Artois and the Flemings in the conquered territories were henceforth French not only in law but in heart and spirit. And this attachment was profound and irreversible. The Austrians and the English were to discover this to their cost in 1792–4. At this decisive point in its history, there was no defection in the north and it became, rather, the rampart for the Revolution and the young French Republic.

NOTES FOR CHAPTER 5

* Professor of Modern History and President, l'Université de Lille III.

1 On the war and process of conquest, see A. Lottin (ed.), *Les grandes batailles du Nord* (Paris, 1984).

2 A. Lottin, *Chavatte, ouvrier lillois. Un contemporain de Louis XIV* (Paris, 1979).

3 There is no shortage of excellent studies of the French administrative monarchy. G. Pagès, *La monarchie d'Ancien Régime en France* (Paris, 1932) provides a brief and clear analysis. The most recent substantial treatment is to be found in R. Mousnier, *The Institutions of France under the Absolute Monarchy* (2 vols., Chicago UP, 1979–84).

4 On these different urban constitutions see the recent *Histoire des villes du Nord/Pas de Calais* published successively by the Presses Universitaires de Lille for the towns of St-Omer, Cambrai, Valenciennes, Villeneuve d'Ascq and Boulogne-sur-Mer and then by Editions des Beffrois (Westhoek), Dunkirk, for the towns of Roubaix, Mauberge, Béthune, Douai, Arras, Tourcoing and Calais.

5 For these problems, see A. Croquez, *La Flandre wallonne et les pays d'intendance de Lille sous Louis XIV* (Paris, 1920).

6 See A. Lottin, 'Messieurs du Magistrat de Lille. Pouvoir et société dans une grande ville manufacturière' in *Pouvoir, Ville et Société en Europe, 1650–1750*. Actes du Colloque internationale du CNRS, 1981 (Strasbourg, 1983). A. Lottin, 'Un mémoire des curés de Lille contre le Magistrat à la fin du XVIIe siècle', *Revue du Nord* liii (1971), pp. 21–32.

7 A. Lottin, 'La fonction d'intendant vue par Louvois', *Mélanges historiques et littéraires sur le XVIIe siècle offerts à G. Mongrédien* (Paris, 1974), pp. 63–74.

8 These quotations are taken from the registers of correspondence between the ministers Louvois and Colbert and the intendant Le Peletier de Souzy, preserved in the château of Beloeil, which have been consulted on microfilm and which are cited with the kind permission of the prince de Ligne.

9 See Map 5.2.

10 Lottin, *Chavatte, ouvrier lillois*, p. 47ff.

11 M. Rouche (ed.), *Histoire de Douai* (Dunkirk, 1985), pp. 129–30 (chapter by A. Lottin on the sixteenth and seventeenth centuries).

12 Lottin, *Chavatte, ouvrier lillois*, p. 47ff.

13 *L'intendance de Flandre Wallonne en 1698*. Edition critique du mémoire pour l'instruction du duc de Bourgogne par Louis Trenard (Paris, 1977).

14 *Ibid.*

15 *Histoire de Douai*, p. 138, see note 4.

6

The Decline of the Irish Kingdom

CIARAN BRADY*

The kingdom of Ireland, established by statute in the Irish parliament of 1541, was at the outset, and remained, a constitutional fiction. An aspiration rather than an achievement, it was a perfect illustration of the gap between the intentions of state-makers and political realities. The Kingship Act's assertion that Henry VIII was the monarch of all the inhabitants of Ireland, extending to each the order and protection of his royal justice and receiving, in return, allegiance and obedience from each one, was, in the context of mid-sixteenth century Ireland, manifestly untrue.[1] For political life in Ireland at the time was at once fragmented and unstable. Divided into a congeries of about 60 lordships of varying size, in which some great lords attempted to exert suzerainty over lesser fry, while others sought to maintain their independence from outside pressure and others again struggled to prevent internal rivalries from producing yet further fragmentation, Ireland's dominant political mode was that of chronic, if generally moderate, war-making and ceaseless intrigue, faction formation and betrayal.

It has become customary to divide the communities of Ireland into three relatively distinct groupings.[2] In the small region of the Pale [*see Map 6.1*], the basic, although somewhat decayed, institutions of English social and economic organization were still to be found. There, too, the conventional instruments of law – the four central courts, assize circuits and shire government – functioned in a normal though often discontinuous manner. But outside this narrow area, distinctive elements of English political culture decayed rapidly. In the great feudal lordships of Kildare, Ormond and Desmond, the institutions of English local government existed in only a shadowy form. Palatine jurisdictions in Tipperary, Kerry and (until 1531) in Kildare allowed the great earls to dispense whatever form of justice they pleased, while their acceptance of Gaelic tenants, their attachment to Gaelic allies and their inter-familial links with leading Gaelic dynasties allowed them to exploit the arbitrary modes of Gaelic politics to their own benefit. In Connacht and in most of the midlands their surrender to Gaelic ways had become almost total.

By the early sixteenth century, then, the largest (though not necessarily the most powerful) grouping in Irish politics was constituted by the Gaelic lordships. Following the collapse of the Anglo-Norman earldom in the later fourteenth

Fig. 6.1 Sixteenth-century Ireland

century, Ulster had again become predominantly Gaelic, with the great dynasties of O'Neill and O'Donnell rivalling each other for hegemony over the lesser Gaelic lordships in the province and over the surviving Anglo-Irish elements in the north-east. In the midlands the Gaelic families of O'Connor and O'More had also recovered strength, and regularly threatened the security of the Pale, while in south Leinster the lesser septs of the O'Brynes, O'Tooles and the Kavanaghs posed an intermittent danger both in the Pale and also in the Anglo-Irish settlement in Wexford. In Munster and Connacht the Gaelic lordships lived in an uneasy relationship with their Anglo-Irish neighbours. Some, like MacCarthy More and O'Flaherty, paid general allegiance to the lords of Desmond and Clanrickard respectively, although they renounced or re-negotiated it whenever the opportunity arose, whilst others, like the O'Briens in Thomond, retained a proud but uncertain autonomy.

The idea of Ireland's 'English Constitution'

In the face of this divided and highly unstable political scenario, the belief that Ireland could be reshaped within a single constitutional framework requiring obedience to a single absentee sovereign appears to have been not only over-optimistic but wholly impracticable. For this reason few historians have been willing to regard the Kingship Act as anything more than an aberration, a curious and insignificant digression from that central process of confrontation and dispossession enframed within the traditional historical canon as 'the Tudor conquest'. Of late, however, this brisk dismissal has itself been seriously questioned. Brendan Bradshaw has shown that the alteration of King Henry's title from 'lord' of Ireland to 'king' of Ireland was not merely a change in the royal style, but a declaration of a profound change in the way in which the Tudor monarch regarded his Irish inheritance. The Kingship Act constituted a formal renunciation of the traditional aim of subordinating Ireland to English rule by means of military conquest. Instead it affirmed a commitment to constructing a model constitution in Ireland through the gradual introduction of the same legal, social and political institutions that had shaped England into a stable and orderly polity.[3]

In accounting for the appearance of this radical change in Tudor political thinking toward Ireland, Bradshaw has drawn attention to more general intellectual forces acting upon English political thought as a whole. The new view of Ireland was but another aspect of that renewed confidence in the efficacy of constitutional and administrative reform which Sir Geoffrey Elton has posited at the heart of English government in the 1530s. This emphasis on the intellectual origins of Irish reform has been invaluable, but it should not deflect attention from the importance of somewhat more practical sources for the emergence of the new political outlook which had their roots in the recent history of the Irish colony itself.

In surveying the condition of early sixteenth-century Ireland, locally based political commentators provided an analysis that was at once bleak and yet surprisingly promising.[4] They bewailed the contraction of the Pale, the degeneration of the Anglo-Irish and the recovery of the Gaelic lords. They acknowledged the failure of English government in Ireland in the past and warned that, were it not immediately revived, it would disappear altogether. Yet on the basis of these gloomy observations they advanced some rather more positive observations. Firstly, they affirmed that, despite its subsequent fate, the initial conquest of Ireland in the twelfth century had been an undoubted success, demonstrating the superiority of English government over whatever Gaelic institutions had existed at the time, and confirming thereby the right of the conquerors to establish their laws and institutions in the land.[5] The momentum of that conquest had thereafter been lost and the Anglo-Norman colony had entered into a long period of decline. But in recent centuries, they asserted, this decline had not been the result of some unexpected Gaelic resurgency; rather it had been due to the failure of the conqueror's descendants to build upon their forefathers' achievements. Having established their military and political superiority, these later generations had not sought to construct the model English society which the conquest had made possible. They had been satisfied merely to consolidate their power by the continued application of the same practices of aggression and intimidation by which the colony had been established in the first place.

Such a rudimentary mode of political control was inherently unstable, and, as leading Anglo-Irish dynasties failed or took to feuding among themselves, Gaelic lords in every province recovered partial or (as in Ulster) full independence. As the balance of power see-sawed uncertainly throughout the island, Gaelic-Irish and Anglo-Irish lords began to fashion alliances and rivalries with one another in accordance with the demands of local conditions and a new and complex political configuration began to emerge in Ireland towards the close of the Middle Ages. The operations of this new system were highly unpredictable: old alliances and rivalries could be changed overnight as a consequence of dynastic upheaval or through the appearance of new opportunities. But two fundamental principles, one particular and the other general, remained firm throughout. The first was an acknowledgement of a clear hierarchy in the system in which the Kildare Geraldines and their less powerful rivals, the Butlers of Ormond, exercised a national influence, forming and sustaining alliances that transcended and con-founded the old ethnic distinctions of the conquest. The second was a general agreement that, whatever his ethnic background and his place in the grand national networks of alliance, each ruling lord would maintain or increase his status within the system through the application of the same extra-legal practices of intimidation, protection and extortion which the commentators referred to generically as 'coyne and livery'.[6]

A composite term, derived from *coinnmhead*, the Gaelic term for a lord's right to lodging with his vassals, and from the English term for the free maintenance of his horses, 'coyne and livery' symbolized both the manner and the degree to which the different communities of Ireland had become united and oppressed under a common political system.[7] Its emergence, all the commentators were agreed, had been nefarious. It had enervated the drive of the conquest and spelled ruin to all hopes of establishing a model civil society in Ireland. Yet this emphasis upon the evils of 'coyne and livery' allowed, ironically, for the formulation of a solution of the Irish problem that was not only economical and conservative, but intellectually compelling as well.

Since this powerful inter-ethnic system had arisen in the wake of a successful military conquest, any proposal to re-enact the conquest was patently futile.

Rather the system itself would have to be confronted, carefully dismantled, and replaced by the English political culture which ought to have been planted in the wake of the conquest in the first place. Such an undertaking may have appeared daunting, but its feasibility was underwritten by two apparently undeniable facts of recent historical experience. The first was the manifest success of English constitutional and social institutions in preserving and restoring order in England itself. Despite the calamities of the Wars of the Roses, the fabric of the constitution had remained sound, exerting through its traditions, procedures and institutions a continuously conservative force strong enough to withstand the depredations of the most ambitious magnate. Its essential power having thus been tested under the most critical conditions in England there seemed little reason to doubt that it would bring about the same effect when prudently and patiently applied in Ireland.[8]

The second undoubted historical lesson more specifically concerned Ireland. Despite all its evil effects, 'coyne and livery' had none the less succeeded in producing significant developments in Ireland's political structures. Through its influence, as has been indicated, an integrated national system of alliances had been constructed, one that linked the war-lords of Gaelic Ulster and the merchants and lawyers of Dublin in common allegiance to some great patron. But it had also maintained a clear social and political hierarchy in every region and in the country at large which, however regrettable its methods, had maintained an elementary order in society which all commentators regarded as absolutely essential. In dismantling 'coyne and livery', then, it was both unnecessary and undesirable that the social hierarchy which had been shaped under the system should itself be destroyed. Rather, Ireland's political élite was to be persuaded merely to alter the means by which they maintained order in society. They should be encouraged to abandon their arbitrary, violent and undependable ways in favour of the manifestly superior processes of English law. The 'god-fathers' of Ireland's protection and intimidation rackets were not to be flushed out; they were simply to be induced to go legitimate.[9]

Because it was gradualist, because it was relatively cheap, but above all because it was grounded upon conventional political thinking and a sound analysis of Ireland's recent history, the conviction that Ireland could be reduced to order, not by force but by piecemeal constitutional reconstruction, became the central tenet of English strategic thinking until the end of the sixteenth century. The crown's commitment to this programme was officially declared in the Kingship Act. But it was to be practically affirmed by a long series of diplomatic, political and administrative initiatives which began before, and were to continue long after, the passage of the statute in 1541.

The Tudor enterprise in reform through diplomacy began with Thomas Cromwell's ill-starred effort to persuade the earls of Kildare and Ormond to agree to a gradual abandonment of 'coyne and livery'. The Butlers were amenable, but the Geraldines brusquely rejected Cromwell's overtures, preferring (fatally as it turned out) to mount a traditional feudal challenge against the king's upstart minister. Even after the débâcle of the Kildare rebellion (1534–6), however, the government remained anxious to reconcile the Geraldines. In the 1530s and 1540s English governors in Ireland carefully cultivated James Fitzgerald of Desmond, effectively backing his claims to the disputed succession to the earldom and appointing him to the Irish council in the senior honorary position of Lord Treasurer. In addition, Gerald, the heir to the Kildare earldom, was himself restored to all his lands and titles in 1554, allowed to return to Ireland, and given a seat on the council.[10]

Meanwhile, during the years of the Kildare eclipse, government patronage was directed primarily toward the house of Ormond. The earl and his heir, Lord James Butler, both became influential counsellors to the government. Both benefited greatly in the lavish distribution of monastic lands which occurred in the 1530s and 1540s, advancing their own projects in Leinster and even securing the dismissal in 1540 of a viceroy, Lord Leonard Grey, when he attempted to cross them.[11] At the same time the Dublin government pursued an independent and equally intense campaign of conciliation amongst the Gaelic lords, great and small. Sir Anthony St Leger (viceroy, with brief intermissions, between 1540 and 1556) concluded a large series of initial agreements with the principal Gaelic lords in every province. His campaign, moreover, was by no means an isolated endeavour. For, although it has often been forgotten, his efforts were renewed and developed by almost all of his Elizabethan successors in office between the later 1550s and the late 1580s, who attempted to conclude mutually binding arrangements with almost every independent Gaelic lordship in the island.[12]

From the beginning, of course, it had been realized that such diplomatic agreements would be of little significance unless they were accompanied by an extensive programme of political and administrative reconstruction. Such an operation, it was understood, would, of necessity, be gradual and would require careful reform on a number of levels. The reform of the principal institutions of English governance, parliament, the four courts and the central administrative offices which survived in the Pale in a gravely decayed condition, was considered to be a priority. The viceroys and their superiors in London from the 1530s onwards made repeated efforts to improve the efficiency of royal administration through the establishment of commissions of inquiry and reform and through the gradual replacement of older servitors with more dependable appointees. Parliament too was to become a more representative and more effective constitutional instrument. Each of the major viceroys of the sixteenth century followed the aspirations of St Leger and hoped to launch their governments on the basis of an elaborate statutory programme which would grant authority to their actions within the constitutional framework of the Irish kingdom. It is significant that the Kingship Act itself was passed by a parliament in Dublin at which, for the first time, representatives of the major Gaelic lordships were present as observers.[13]

Outside the central administration, Tudor governors sought progressively to extend the ambit of English law through the revival and extension of assize circuits, through the despatch of special commissions of peace into more lawless areas and through the regular tours of the viceregal court throughout the whole island. The need to establish more permanent institutions for the enforcement of law in the darker corners of the country was also recognized from the outset, though it was not until the later 1560s that provincial councils, modelled on those for Wales and the north of England, were at length established in Munster and Connacht.[14]

Yet it should not be assumed that the drive to establish an English constitution in Ireland was entirely tolerant and conciliatory. Implicit in the Kingship Act itself was the assumption that those who denied its statutory authority were traitors to the new Irish king and would be treated as such. Thus the dispossession and destruction of rebellious subjects was regarded from the outset as a legitimate right of the Irish government, though one which was to be employed with discretion. Indeed, the first attempt to establish a plantation in Ireland amongst the O'Mores and O'Connors in the midlands was begun under St Leger, the viceroy who had long sought to reach a peaceful accommodation with them.[15] Confiscation and plantation were perceived, then, to have an important exemplary value, demonstrating the seriousness of the government's commitment to the idea of the Irish kingdom and its willingness to apply sanctions against those who would reject it. But plantation was also considered to be exemplary in a more positive sense. The establishment of small English colonies in the underdeveloped and underpopulated lands of Gaelic Ireland was seen as a means of demonstrating to the Gaelic lords just how profitable the adoption of English social and economic customs could be. Such an argument, as advanced by English and Anglo-Irish colonial exponents, was somewhat disingenuous; but that it was not entirely without conviction may be seen from the positive response which several Gaelic lords, O'Sullivan Beare and O'Neill of Glandeboy, for example, displayed towards particular enterprises.[16]

The government's determination to carry out reform, if necessary by means of coercion, was revealed, not in its somewhat half-hearted interest in colonization, but in its more persistent concern to establish military garrisons in the country. In the 1540s and 1550s attempts to erect garrisons were confined to what were considered to be key strategic sites, in the midlands, on the borders of the Pale and along the southern coastline which was vulnerable to foreign invasion. Under Elizabeth, however, the need for a greater, if more dispersed, military presence became apparent. Though initially intended to function as a largely civil institution, the provincial councils established in Munster and Connacht soon took on the appearance of small mobile military garrisons. In Leinster and parts of Ulster the constables of forts were renamed 'seneschalls' and given wide discretionary powers to maintain order in the territories surrounding them. But the clearest indication of the Elizabethan conviction that political and constitutional reform required coercion as well as diplomacy was to be found in the policy of 'composition' devised by the viceroy Sir Henry Sidney and his private secretary Edmund Tremayne in the 1570s, and applied by Lord Deputy Sir John Perrot in the mid 1580s.[17]

The ultimate objective of the strategy of the 'composition' was conventional. It aimed gradually to transform the Irish lordships into English shires. Such a goal, Tremayne and Sidney argued, could be attained only when political life within each lordship had first been stabilized through the commutation of all arbitrary and 'bastard-feudal' dues claimed by the lords over their vassals into a fixed sum acceptable to both sides and guaranteed by the government. In principle, commutation of this kind appeared to be in everyone's interest. The freeholders and tenant-farmers of a lordship would not be totally released from all exactions but they would enjoy significant relief from the depredations of the lords' private armies. Correspondingly, the lords would be required to make some compromise with their vassals but they would be compensated for any loss by the assurance that their income would from henceforth be certain and that they would no longer be compelled to support highly wasteful bands of retainers in order to collect it. Finally, the government itself would reap the benefit of having a small but effective security force in every territory which would politically and financially be supported by both partners in the 'composition'.

The long-term benefits of 'composition' were clear. The critical question remained how to persuade the local community that the government was capable of establishing the scheme in the first place. For this reason the scheme's devisers recognized that an element of coercion would be essential to its success, at least in its earliest stages. 'Composition' was to be introduced in each province by means of a large campaign army (Tremayne recommended about 5 000 men) which would persuade the lords that the government was capable of imitating and surpassing them in their practices of extortion and intimidation. Yet, having once convinced the lords of its ability to destroy 'coyne and livery' by dominating it, the government would then proceed to establish a new standardization of the old system's relationships and the great army would be dispersed into small bands sufficient for the collection of the agreed composition rents and their own maintenance charges. As a means of establishing political reform, therefore, 'composition' was neither naively conciliatory nor brutally exploitative. It was simply a realistic and well-considered attempt to lay the foundations of the new society in the most effective manner possible.

The foregoing review of the theory and practice of constitution-making in the sixteenth century ignores, however, one central problem. For if, as has been indicated, the strategy of legal reform was based on a realistic analysis of Irish political circumstances, and if the strategy itself was developed in a patient, flexible yet hard-headed manner, the question arises as to why it turned out to be such an unmitigated failure.

The Tudor failure in Ireland

Fail the Tudor strategy most certainly did. Within a decade of the Kingship Act there began a series of confrontations between the government and the native communities which was to last until the latter were finally defeated in a major nationwide war at the close of the Tudor period. By the late 1540s a rebellion had broken out in the midlands which, though it resulted in the dispossession of the natives and the establishment of the first effective English plantation in Ireland (in Laois and Offaly in 1556), also provoked a protracted and extremely costly guerrilla war which plagued the government until the end of the century. Also in the late 1540s, the decision of the O'Neill chieftain who had been made earl of Tyrone by the crown in 1543 to alter the terms of his agreement by choosing his younger son, Shane, as his successor gave rise to a major rebellion in Ulster which was to preoccupy every English governor until Shane was eventually assassinated in 1567. In the later 1550s, the house of Desmond, which had been carefully rehabilitated by St Leger, began a series of increasingly sharp disputes with the house of Ormond and with the Dublin government. These broke into full-scale war in Munster in 1568–73 and finally resulted in the rebellion and extinction of the dynasty in the period from 1579 to 1583 and the establishment of the second major Tudor plantation in Munster in 1586. The early 1580s also witnessed the uncovering of a conspiracy in the Pale under the leadership of the

Viscount Baltinglass in which the restored earl of Kildare was shown to be seriously implicated. Finally, after years of uneasy relations with the Dublin government, the great lords of Gaelic Ulster joined in an unprecedented union to present the most serious challenge ever faced by the Tudors in Ireland, the nine years war of 1594–1603.[18]

These events have been easily and almost inevitably reorganized in historical retrospect as the principal stages of that familiar juggernaut, 'the Tudor conquest'. Yet in the light of recent research and revision, they present the historian with a major interpretative problem. Not only did they form no part of any predetermined plan of conquest, but they also appear to have occurred in direct contradiction to the avowed aims and practical efforts of English reform in Ireland. Far from providing the benchmarks of the Tudor success in Ireland, these wars and rebellions constitute instead the clearest demonstration of the extent of the Tudors' failure. And the question for the modern historian is, of course, why?

This central paradox of Tudor rule in Ireland does not lend itself to easy resolution. But a variety of factors suggest, through their interconnection, one possible account as to how it took shape. One obvious, though ultimately inadequate, explanation is the sheer ambitiousness of the reform enterprise itself. The lordships of Gaelic Ireland were arguably too primitive, economically, socially and politically, to be amenable to the fundamental cultural transformation being forced so rapidly upon them.

The problems raised for each lord by the prospect of reform were indeed major, but they were not insuperable. Traditional descriptions of the condition of Gaelic lordships, being based largely on the extremely hostile commentaries of late Elizabethan soldiers and planters, have greatly exaggerated their primitive character.[19] More objective research has revealed a society that was far more sedentary and stable, in which a mixed, though predominantly pastoral, economy prevailed in accordance with climatic conditions and in which succession to property through partible inheritance took place under carefully controlled conditions. Scholars have also noted the emergence of a strong freeholder interest in several lordships who, though unwilling to compete for political dominance in their own right, were jealous of their autonomy and capable of forcing their nominal chieftains to respect it. Even as the great lords pursued their traditional politics, exploiting their weaker subjects and neighbours in whatever way they might, they were compelled to acknowledge the existence of an increasingly influential group which imposed a limit on their ambitions and their abilities to realize them.[20] Seen in this context, surrender and re-grant and, more specifically, 'composition', required no radical departure from the mores of Gaelic politics but simply a development of tendencies already at work. Offering guarantees of future stability both to existing ruling families who stood to gain financially and politically from the establishment of primogeniture and to the freeholders anxious to consolidate their position, the new policy appeared to establish the basis for a powerful consensus within each lordship in favour of political reform and the new Irish kingdom.

The coalition of support shaped by this 'new deal' was immediately confronted, however, by an alternative coalition of resistance. For a lord's younger sons, for his nephews, uncles and cousins, the acceptance of primogeniture implied a surrender of their succession rights which some (though by no means all) were unwilling to make. A more serious source of opposition was to be found within the ranks of the lords' private armies now threatened with redundancy by the lords' and the freeholders' agreement to settle their disputes through the arbitration of the English government. For these professional swordsmen, faced with the prospect of extinction or reversion to the plough, constitutional reform was wholly unacceptable. Thus they formed the basis of the movement against reform which existed to a greater or lesser degree in every lordship.[21]

This alliance of displaced relations and disappointed soldiers could present a serious difficulty to any lord. But it was rarely sufficiently powerful to compel lords already convinced of the long-term benefits of reform to forfeit the initiative. Instead such potential dangers generally induced caution, persuading the chiefs to advance the case of reform slowly, to tolerate open opposition to change, and most commonly to contain such internal tensions by encouraging their own sons to assume positions of leadership within both groups. The inherent delicacy of the lords' position thus determined that reform would be a lengthy and uncertain process, but it by no means ensured its failure. The essential prerequisite was that the lords should retain confidence in the government's willingness to support their general efforts and to tolerate their occasional lapses.

It was in relation to this latter condition, however, that two independent factors began to impede the course of Tudor reform. The first and more restricted of these was the sudden intrusion of the Scots of the Western Isles into several parts of Gaelic Ulster from the middle of the sixteenth century. The result of increasing pressure by the Edinburgh government on the clansmen of the north, this Scottish migration took two forms. In the Glens and the Route of Antrim and in the decayed neighbouring lordship of Glandeboy, large numbers of the MacDonnells began permanently to settle, thereby simply displacing the Anglo-Irish and Gaelic-Irish natives and defying the region's overlords to repel them. At the same time, equally substantial numbers of seasonal migrants presented themselves to Gaelic lords throughout Ulster and to their rivals as hired swords of potential utility in provincial politics or merely to be bought off. As either seasonal or permanent intruders, the Scots constituted a highly destabilizing force in Ulster's politics, deflecting the lords from their business with the reforming Dublin government, impressing upon them the continuing need to defend their status in the traditional Gaelic manner, and so deepening their dilemma in balancing the promised benefits of law against the immediate value of force.[22]

The Scottish problem, though acute, was intermittent and regionally limited. But a far more general disruptive force had come into play even before the Tudor reform plan had been officially inaugurated in 1541. The defeat of the Kildare rebellion, though swift and effective, set in motion a series of reverberations that spread throughout every province in the island. For though the rebellion ruined (temporarily) the house of Kildare itself, it did little structural damage to the Geraldine alliance as a whole. But now leaderless and vulnerable to attack from the government and, more seriously, from their triumphant Butler rivals, the members of this nationwide affinity became politically highly unstable, seeking at once to make a favourable peace with the crown while intriguing secretly for a Geraldine resurgence. This increased Geraldine volatility in the wake of the rebellion was paralleled, however, by the equally disturbed condition of the Butlers and their adherents who were now presented with an unexpected opportunity to establish their predominance within the factional system and to settle old scores. Like the Geraldines, therefore, their attitude to the English government was inherently ambiguous, being conditioned by the wholly independent consideration as to whether any particular reform initiative tended to their own benefit or served to rescue the hated Geraldines. In thus disrupting the national structure of alliances, the Kildare rebellion ensured that the Tudors' carefully conceived and well-intentioned plan of reform would be perceived and interpreted through a complex filter of factional considerations which the reformers could do little either to influence or to dispel.

The reforming governors of Tudor Ireland, of course, made strenuous efforts to contain the disruptive effects of faction. Lord Leonard Grey and St Leger attempted to shape a loyal following from within the Geraldines through the extension of government patronage. Neither was particularly successful (Grey indeed failed disastrously) and it was the sheer difficulty of controlling this group that lay behind the decision to grant a full restoration to the Kildare heir in 1554. The re-establishment of the house of Kildare did much to stabilize the Geraldine alliance, allowing for a return to conventional politics and rendering treasonable intrigues unnecessary. Yet, in so doing, it tended in the short term to intensify the reformers' problem by concentrating the Kildare leadership's energies on gaining influence over the English viceroy, the central political figure they had once rejected, but had now agreed to obey. This readjustment in Geraldine strategies was inevitably followed by the Butlers. As the Geraldines moved to influence the viceroy by promises of support or threats of obstruction, the Butlers also assumed an attitude toward the Dublin governor in inverse relation to that of their rivals. This concentration of factional pressure upon the office was in itself unacceptable to reform-minded governors. But in their efforts to escape from the worst effects of factional influence, they proceeded to introduce an apparently sensible, but ultimately fateful, alteration in their style of administration which more than any factor so far considered, led to the disruption, deflection and final exhaustion of the Tudor reform enterprise.[23]

The ultimate failure of both Grey and St Leger to manipulate the politics of faction in their own interests provided a highly instructive lesson to their Elizabethan successors in the office of viceroy. Both men had for some years withstood the criticism and obstruction of the Butlers in their cultivation of the Geraldines. Both, too, had even survived the propensity of the Geraldines to renege on their promises. Yet for both, Butler subversion and Geraldine treachery proved fatal when they formed part of political intrigues against the viceroy at the court of Westminster itself. Grey fell suddenly, a victim of the coup that brought down Thomas Cromwell. St Leger, after years of evasion, was dismissed and disgraced in a Marian reaction against old Edwardian hands. The restoration of Kildare, however, and the concentration of intrigue around the appointment and career of the English viceroy which it entailed, ensured that the double exposure of the governor both to obstruction in Ireland and to slander at Court, elements hitherto occasional, would now become a permanent fact of political life. At once the prey of jealous court intriguers and of a reconciled Irish nobility determined to assert its influence through the subtle stratagems of court politics rather than by the crude methods of rebellion, the viceroys became the prisoners of faction, the unwilling friends and unintentional enemies of thousands of Irish subjects even before they took office.

It was to escape this terrible dependence upon private interests that the English governors who succeeded St Leger introduced one important administrative innovation. Before accepting office in Ireland they chose to present their plans for the advance of reform there in the guise of clearly outlined, precisely timed and tightly costed programmes. By seeking in this way the prior approval in London for a set of priorities, a list of objectives whose attainment would guarantee the final success of reform, and for a budget and a timetable necessary to attain them, the new governors thus pre-empted serious criticisms of their actions for as long as their time and their money held out. This tactical attempt to overcome the difficulties in being Irish viceroy implied no departure from the conventional aims of Tudor reform in Ireland. For underlying the viceroys' belief that the problems of Irish government could be isolated and resolved in order of importance was the continuing confidence that, once these salient obstacles had been removed, the successful transformation of Irish political culture was inevitable.[24]

The governors' assessment of the nature of these central problems varied considerably, and developed markedly over time. The earl of Sussex, viceroy in the late 1550s and early 1560s, believed that all that was necessary to clear the path of reform was a determined resolution of those issues on which St Leger had revealed his own fundamental weakness. Thus the re-establishment of the midlands plantation, the expulsion of the Scots from the north-east, and above all the enforcement of the original surrender and re-grant agreement among the O'Neills of Tyrone formed the central elements of his programme. Over time the character of these priorities became more sophisticated. Sussex came to recognize that mere determination was insufficient, and that the introduction of permanent regional councils was an immediate requirement. His successor in office, Sir Henry Sidney, built his own programme on Sussex's recommendations of central and regional administrative reform, but in time he too came to see the inadequacy of provincial councils as originally conceived and proposed, as we have seen, as the policy of 'composition' which was in turn to become the centrepiece of Sir John Perrot's reform programme in the mid 1580s.

Despite such changes in their programmes' content, however, the reforming Elizabethan viceroyalties all shared several features in common. Each believed that the reform of Ireland could be organized and conducted in separate stages, that sheer executive action could solve Ireland's political problems, and that such action could be successfully discharged at a predictable cost and within a given period of time. Where earlier reformers had assumed that Ireland's political transformation would take place gradually through a process of ingestion and acclimatization within which the collaboration of the indigenous powers would be central, the Elizabethans were convinced that the operation could be accomplished briskly, through the application of an administrative programme alone, and with the minimum of dependence upon local vested interest.

The programmatic strategies of the Elizabethan viceroys also shared some rather more negative features. In discounting the importance of maintaining local connections, each underestimated the degree of difficulty which their untested programmes faced, misjudging in consequence the costs they involved and the time required for their completion. Each programme, therefore, soon fell behind schedule, failed to meet its targets and raised in its increasingly desperate efforts to do so a whole variety of unanticipated difficulties. Between the late 1550s and the late 1580s the careers of the great reforming viceroys collectively displayed the same dismal pattern of overambition and miscalculation ending in their successive failure, recall and disgrace.

The immediate consequences of these successive failures varied in relation to the content of the programme itself. Sussex's inability to expel the Scots and to quash the midlands rebellion did little to enhance the reputation of the Dublin government as a power to be reckoned with in the country. More seriously, his refusal to compromise with Shane O'Neill and his failure to dislodge him transformed a specific succession dispute into a crucial test case concerning the viability of surrender and re-grant in general. Sidney's repeatedly unsuccessful attempts to establish conventional provincial councils in the west seriously discredited these institutions in the eyes of local lords and convinced the English administrators themselves that only more forceful methods would bring order to these provinces. Finally, Sir John Perrot's sudden and abortive effort to impose 'composition' upon the intricate political and social relations of Gaelic Ulster divided the province into bitterly opposing camps, placing those lords who had shown themselves to be amenable to reform under unprecedented pressure within their own lordships. But the end result of these varied failures was always the same, namely disillusion, fear and rebellion.

The Irish response: rebellion, subversion, alienation

Seen in this context, the increasing incidence of rebellion in the later sixteenth century becomes more explicable. Confronted by a government fixed in its commitments of time, money and targets, and unwilling to be deflected by considerations of local or factional sensitivity, those who had most to fear from reform and those who had least to gain by it found little difficulty in forging an alliance of resistance to all change. The initiation of this reactionary momentum both within and between lordships greatly intensified the pressure on all reform sympathizers; and the dilemma of these compromising and politically compromised figures was worsened by the governors' unwillingness to respond sensitively to particular needs and their sheer inability to bring their own programmes to fruition. The conditions for a domino syndrome were thus established in any region where reform was introduced in the framework of a viceregal programme, as the most hostile gradually forced the more amenable to realign themselves or face isolation and ruin. This pattern of rapidly accelerating disorder can be seen in each of the major rebellions of the later sixteenth century, and indeed it became their defining characteristic. It accounts for the remarkable success of Shane O'Neill in maintaining control over the province of Ulster for so long in his war with Sussex, and for the collapse of the earldom of Desmond following the introduction of 'composition' in Munster. Above all, it explains the long-delayed but decisive rôle reversal of Hugh O'Neill, earl of Tyrone, from principal agent of English reform in Ulster to that of rebel commander-in-chief in the 'nine years war'.[25]

Once made, moreover, the decision was generally irreversible. Despite a number of efforts to reconcile him, the forces upon which Shane O'Neill had depended for his power in Ulster locked him into an ever-expanding war against the crown in which either total victory or total defeat could be the only result. The Desmond Geraldines also tried to make their peace with the government on a number of occasions but in the later 1570s the temporizing earl found the pressures driving him toward total rebellion to be irresistible. Finally Tyrone, having negotiated a remarkably generous peace with the crown in 1603, decided within four years that a continuing compromise with the Dublin government was impossible and fled into exile to prepare for a renewal of outright war.[26]

This growing sense of inevitable and irrevocable conflict with the English government produced, and was in turn sustained by, a radically determinist interpretation of recent events that was supplied by religious teaching. Though they had remained largely untouched by any practical efforts on the part of the government to initiate reform in ecclesiastical matters, the clerical dynasties and religious orders of many Gaelic and Anglo-Irish lordships were opposed from the beginning to any innovations which threatened their property, their social status and (most importantly) their claims to a monopoly of spiritual authority. Initially the influence of this hostile group was, like the other interests, muted. But as the difficulties of reform mounted, so the priests' radical insistence that any concession to reform was ruinous began to acquire greater currency. Thus notwithstanding the remarkably tolerant attitude of the viceroys toward all forms of religious non-conformity, the arguments of this beleaguered special interest group began to be shared by those who had become disillusioned with reform for very different reasons. For these secular interests the adoption of a religious justification for their resistance to English reform entailed several practical advantages. It increased the likelihood of support from Rome and, more significantly, from Spain. Most importantly of all, it formed the centrepiece of an ideological defence of the old ways which provided a far more powerful rallying point in each lordship than the material concerns of disappointed individuals or sectional interests. Gradually, therefore, as the failure and abandonment of successive reform programmes left more and more natives estranged from the Dublin administration, the disparate discontents of widely varied interests became fused in a 'crusade' or holy war.[27]

Rebellion, war and fixed ideological confrontation thus became the most distinctive results of the failure of English reform programmes in Ireland. But this failure also led to a further series of consequences which, though less dramatic, were to prove equally fatal to the prospects for constitutional reconstruction in Ireland. Not all of those who had become estranged from the Dublin administration looked upon rebellion as either a feasible or a desirable option. For some, most notably the apparently loyal community of the English Pale itself, resistance could take on more subtle and covert forms. Unimpeachable advocates of English rule in Ireland who had long supported the crown's efforts at reform, the Palesmen became progressively more disillusioned with their own administration in Dublin as they were compelled to bear the ever-increasing costs of one reform programme after another. In particular they became steadily more aggrieved at the cost of supporting the royal army through the supply of food, horses and carts, and, above all, through enforced billeting. The governors themselves were genuinely concerned to minimize the burden and made several efforts, none of them successful, to find alternative and more efficient means of supply. Yet ultimately the grievances of the loyal Palesmen took second place to the priorities which they imposed upon themselves when they assumed office and as the cost of these characteristically underestimated programmes grew, so they turned unwillingly but inevitably to the country to make good the short-fall. The helplessly oppressive conduct of the reform governors determined the strategy of their loyalist victims. Unable to gain relief from the representative of the sovereign in Dublin, the Palesmen turned directly to the monarch for the protection of their rights as freeborn Englishmen, and were almost invariably sympathetically received.[28]

The Palesmen's disillusion with the Dublin government as the centre of a new Irish kingdom was considerably deepened by the one systematic effort which the viceroys made to solve the problem of supply. Both Sidney and Perrot attempted to find a permanent source of income for the army by proposing a commutation of all victualing and billeting charges into a fixed annual tax along the lines which they were currently negotiating with the Gaelic and Anglo-Irish lords. The scheme was administratively sensible and, in view of the real extortions of the soldiers, financially generous. But this particular illustration of the reform governors' intention of treating all the inhabitants of Ireland in the same even-handed manner was entirely unacceptable to the Palesmen. The proposal entailed a violation of that constitutional right which they, in common with other English subjects, regarded as fundamental, namely, the right of parliamentary consent to taxation.

The Palesmen's direct appeal to Elizabeth I led in both cases to the withdrawal of the scheme and the recall of the viceroy. But their success in this constitutional conflict not only validated the tactics of resistance and subversion which they had developed in recent decades, but also served to confirm their doubts as to the practicality of an Irish kingdom guaranteeing to all the island's inhabitants the same rights and liberties as those enjoyed by Englishmen. By the end of the sixteenth century, then, the Palesmen had determined to dissociate themselves in full from the project of Irish constitutional reform. Instead, looking directly to London as the focus of their allegaince and the source of their redress, they displayed an equal disregard both for the rebel Irish lords and for the newly arrived English administrators and settlers whom they believed had done so much to provoke those rebellions. And as a means of affirming this dual separation, that is both from the Irish and from the English *arrivistes*, they began to refer to themselves in a highly exclusive way. They called themselves 'the Old English'.

The Palesmen's withdrawal from the Irish kingdom, like that of the rebel Gaelic Irish and Anglo-Irish, gradually found ideological expression in religious terms. Though it had been largely sympathetic to the alterations of the Henrician reformation, the Pale had, like many parts of England, remained cool toward the doctrinal reformation until the 1570s. But whereas Englishmen thereafter conformed in large numbers, the Palesmen moved in the opposite direction. While they had, in the past, been suspected of church-papistry, they now revealed themselves to be thoroughgoing recusants, defying both threats and inducements to attend the services of the Established Church as well as refusing outright the oath of allegiance required to hold office in the Dublin administration. Those native-born lawyers, churchmen and administrators who did conform found themselves to be part of a tiny minority, increasingly isolated and without influence in their own community. At the same time, recent English arrivals who had hitherto integrated with ease into the Pale community by means of intermarriage found themselves frozen out and debarred from local alliance on the grounds of their religion.[29]

Religion thus provided the Palesmen, as it had provided the rebels, with an ideological defence of resistance. But, unlike the rebels who had embraced the Counter-Reformation as a justification for total war, Catholicism served the Palesmen as a powerful means of ensuring both their internal unity and their separation from not only the recently arrived English Protestants, but also from the rebel Irish. So whereas militant and highly politicized monks became the chaplains of the rebels' 'holy war', respected notables and lawyers from the Pale travelled to Court to defend their countrymen's religious nonconformity in the most conciliatory and loyalist terms while the new personal disciplines of an ostensibly non-political catholic reformation were quietly introduced into the households of the Pale by the secular clergy and by the Jesuits.[30]

By the first decade of the seventeenth century, therefore, the principal achievement of more than 70 years' effort at constitution-making had been to drive the native communities of Ireland not closer together but further apart, with both sides agreeing upon little other than the unreality of the common constitutional framework which had been imposed upon them. Yet this process of division in the midst of reform had operated not only on the subjects of the reform enterprise but also upon its agents themselves.

For the servitors of the crown, the English administrators, soldiers and settlers in Ireland, the effect of repeated failures in reform was equally decisive. At the most obvious level, the introduction of English planters into territories confiscated after rebellion ensured that the new arrivals would be greeted with hostility and fear by those natives who remained. The exemplary intent of the colonies was therefore severely handicapped in these areas from the outset. But the settlers' difficulties were further exacerbated by the inability of the government to provide the necessary support for their secure establishment in unknown territories. In the midlands, Munster and a number of lesser areas in Ulster this chronic neglect of colonies produced a complex reaction among the planters themselves. Furthering their sense of isolation, it gave rise to a series of bloody confrontations with the natives in which massacres perpetrated by both sides were a frequent occurrence. Among some planters, however, this ready adaptation to their environment took more positive forms. Settlers like Francis Cosby and Edward More in the midlands, William Piers in Ulster and, later, Valentine Browne in Munster, came to integrate themselves into the deeply divided patterns of local politics, making alliances and attracting enmities among the ranks of natives and planters in the traditional manner. As relations with their neighbours and their fellow-settlers evolved in an ambiguous way, so the planters' attitude toward their own government acquired a somewhat uncertain character. When faced with the threat of rebellion, their concern for the defence of English government, law and order was unlimited. But their loyalism was soon qualified when government policy came into conflict with their own particular interests. Thus where the crown's concern to enforce the law threatened their patronage of local septs, the planters frequently resorted to obstruction and downright deception to protect their clients. More commonly, however, when the official policy of tolerant, piecemeal reform conflicted with their primary aim of enforcing their will in the country, the same manipulative methods were employed to discredit the natives and frustrate the aims of the state.[31]

By the close of the sixteenth century, however, such a distinction between the government and the settler interest had become quite artificial. Many of the planters of the midlands and in Munster held civil or military office within the Irish administration. For these men, the aspiration of establishing a model kingdom in Ireland in which all would be equal subjects under the same law held few lasting attractions once they had been given the opportunity to establish themselves as major speculators in attainted Irish lands in their own right. Ironically, therefore, the longer the English government in Ireland persisted in its attempts to carry through reform in Ireland, the more it became dependent upon the services of men who had nothing to gain by the policy's success and much to look forward to from its failure.

It was not simply planters who acquired a particular interest in subverting crown policy. By the closing years of the century, there had emerged around Dublin Castle a significant official and semi-official cadre whose original ambitions and expectations had been disappointed or frustrated by the failure of one of the several viceregal programmes to which they had attached themselves. Soldiers without commission, administrators without further prospects, clerics without parishioners and merchants with failed investments, all looked to the government as a means of compensating for their losses. For many, an investment in plantation was too long-term, too costly or too risky. But they could exploit their influence with the administration for more modest or more immediate speculations. One opportunity which beckoned was the acquisition of large numbers of reversions on crown leases which, even when the leases were not due to fall in, had acquired a speculative value in their own right. Dealing in reversions, however, was secondary to a far more aggressive mode of property speculation. The recovery of allegedly concealed crown titles in both Gaelic and Anglo-Irish territories, and the recovery of leases on which ancient conditions had apparently been violated was, as Terence Ranger has shown, the principal means by which a minor official like Richard Boyle rose to become earl of Cork and one of the richest men in early seventeenth-century Ireland. But Boyle was only a spectacular example chosen from a much larger administrative group which had decided to regard the use of English law in Ireland not as a means of reform, but simply as an aid toward personal advancement.[32]

By the end of the century, even the chief governors themselves had come to share in this change of attitude. Sir William Fitzwilliam, Perrot's successor, not only renounced 'composition' as a means of reform, but engaged in a series of private adventures within the Ulster lordships of Tyrconnell, Breifne and Monaghan which proved to be the final trigger of rebellion in the province. Lord Mountjoy, the only governor who (following the surrender of Tyrone) had the opportunity to renew the policy of reform, chose instead to abandon Ireland, retaining office purely as an absentee. Yet, even in his absence, he managed to acquire a substantial (though covert) interest in crown leases in Munster and in the Pale through the offices of an agent, John Wakeman. His successor in office, Sir Arthur Chichester, was already a substantial land-holder in north-east Ulster before the flight of Tyrone and his followers in 1607 provided the grounds for even more lavish plantation ventures for the governor and his colleagues in the rest of the province.[33]

Like all of the other withdrawals from the idea of a united Irish kingdom, this desertion of the administrators acquired, in time, an ideological defence of its own. In the later sixteenth century, as confidence in the reform policy faltered amidst persistent administrative failure, an increasingly sceptical attitude toward the potency and value of the common law began to become apparent among English servitors in Ireland. The need to supplement the law's intrinsic attractions by some coercive sanction had been appreciated by reformers from the outset. In the strategy of 'composition' the use of force came to be regarded as an essential preliminary to further reform. Arising out of the premises of 'composition' and its subsequent failure in practice, there developed the notion, common amongst military commanders and their spokesmen, that coercion itself was the best – and indeed the only – way of maintaining English control over Ireland.

Such an argument was easily formulated and gave much satisfaction to those who did so. Yet it raised fundamental problems concerning the entire English presence in Ireland. For any demand for wholesale force implicitly conceded both the failure of English law to establish its superiority in Ireland and the consequent invalidity of the Tudors' claim to be monarchs of the whole island. It was for this reason that many of those who advocated the use of force did so in a qualified manner, defending its use in particular places or at specific times as a necessary or preliminary derogation from the general programme of legal reform. The risks inherent in a more radical argument were made plain by the suppression of Edmund Spenser's *View of the present state of Ireland* (1596) which advocated a campaign of ruthless suppression to destroy all the elements of Ireland's existing political culture. It was not, however, the violence of his proposals that shocked Spenser's censors, since appeals for the use of extreme force in Ireland were no longer uncommon. Rather it was the means by which he justified them. Spenser insisted that reform had failed in the past and was inapplicable to the present, not through negligence or some other contingent factor, but because the entire programme was itself fundamentally misconceived. Reform by law was not merely the victim of all the tumults and disorders of the later sixteenth century, it had in many cases been their cause. Spenser's case was supported by much recent practical experience, but its theoretical implications, challenging at once orthodox belief in the efficacy of reform and an even deeper conviction of the universal value of English law, were quite unacceptable. So Spenser was silenced.[34]

It was not, therefore, until after the end of Tyrone's war and the completion of a ruthless campaign, similar in its character (though not in its intentions) to that which Spenser had envisaged, that a more theoretically orthodox defence of an aggressive political strategy began to be formulated. Writing in the calm of 1612, Sir John Davies, the new English attorney general and speculator in attainted lands in his own right, asserted in his *Discovery of the true causes why Ireland was never subdued* what all the Elizabethans short of Spenser had been loathe to argue. Since the conquest of Ireland, he contended, had not been completed, all

previous assumptions concerning what needed to be done in that part of Ireland
which had not accepted this fate were necessarily false. But since the conquest
had indeed been brought to a conclusion in his own day, the process of legal
reconstruction could now commence in Ireland and the Irish kingdom made into
a reality. Davies's insistence on the completion of the conquest, and upon the
readiness of Ireland to receive English law, gave his treatise a reassuringly
conservative tone. On a superficial reading it might appear like a rehearsal of the
Tudor reform case. Yet his concern with the appearance of orthodoxy masked an
important departure from Tudor assumptions. Because the conquest had only
recently been completed Davies therefore regarded all the political and social
structures of the 'pre-conquest' period which the Tudors had accepted and
sought to work through as wholly invalid and, indeed, as impediments to
constitutional reform. The function of law in post-conquest Ireland was not to
transform the existing political structure, but to dismantle it and the mechanisms
by which it had been preserved. Law, then, was seen not as an alternative to the
forceful establishment of English rule in Ireland, but as an integral part of that
process – the continuation of conquest by other means. For this reason, the use of
particular English laws and procedures was to be assessed not in terms of their
own intrinsic values, but only in relation to their ability to bring about the perfect
consolidation of English power in Ireland. Thus the exploitation of statute,
customary law and due process in cases that exposed the vulnerability of the
natives and strengthened the hands of the newly arrived settlers was not merely
pragmatic and materially advantageous: it was the only valid means of ensuring
that a new English kingdom in Ireland would finally be brought into being.[35]

In the early years of the seventeenth century, the kingdom of Ireland survived in
the manner in which it had been founded in 1541, only as an idea representing
aspirations rather than realities. For the rebel exiles and their sympathizers in
Ireland it survived in its most shadowy form as a symbol of a political and cultural
unity fused in common resistance to English reform and to be revived in 'holy
war'. For those calling themselves 'the Old English' it served as a convenient
means of attaching themselves more closely to their absentee monarch and to this
court in London where they believed their best security lay. And for the new
English planters and administrators it provided the necessary framework for their
campaign of piecemeal expropriation. For each group it helped to maintain a
common sense of identity and a common political strategy. But the visions of the
future which it represented to each were, in total negation of the hopes of its
creators, fundamentally different and utterly irreconcilable.

NOTES FOR CHAPTER 6

* Lecturer in Modern History, Trinity College, Dublin.

1 The Kingship Act (33 Henry VIII Session 1 ch. 1) was passed by the Irish
Parliament in 1541. On the immediate circumstances of its drafting and passage see
Robert Dunlop, 'Some aspects of Henry VIII's Irish policy' in T. F. Tout and J. Tait (eds.),
Owen College Historical Essay (Manchester, 1907) pp. 279–306: but the deeper aims and
implications of the statute are most fully analysed in Brendan Bradshaw, *The Irish
Constitutional Revolution of the Sixteenth Century* (Cambridge UP, 1979).

2 For a good general survey see D. B. Quinn and K. W. Nicholls, 'Ireland in 1534' in T. W. Moody *et al.* (eds.) *A New History of Ireland. Early Modern Ireland, 1534–1691* (Oxford, 1976) pp. 1–38; see also N. P. Canny, *The Elizabethan Conquest of Ireland: A Pattern Established, 1565–76* (Hassocks, 1976), ch. 1.

3 Bradshaw, *Constitutional Revolution*.

4 Two important contemporary tracts are the 'Report on the state of Ireland, 1515', *State Papers Henry VIII* ii, pp. 1–15 and Patrick Finglas, 'A breviate of the getting of Ireland and of the decay of the same, 1533' printed in Walter Harris, *Hibernica*, i (1747) pp. 39–52.

5 In addition to sources cited in note 4, see Sir William Darcy's 'Articles on Ireland', Calendar of Carew MSS. 1515–74 pp. 6–8 and an unsigned tract, *c.*1528, B[ritish] L[ibrary], Lansdowne MS. 159 no. 1.

6 Sustained contemporary descriptions of the working of coyne and livery are provided in, *State Papers Henry VIII* ii, pp. 477–80 and for a modern analysis of the functions of coyne and livery which largely confirms the views of early Tudor writers see Art Cosgrove (ed.), *A new History of Ireland: Medieval Ireland 1169–1534*, chs. 18, 20–2.

7 *Ibid.*, pp. 541–2; for a fuller discussion of the variety of exactions imposed by the great lords see C. A. Empey and Katherine Simms, 'The ordinances of the White earl and the problem of coign in the later Middle Ages', *Royal Irish Academy, Proceedings*, lxv (1975) section C pp. 178–87.

8 See, esp. the 'Report on the state of Ireland, 1515', cited above. On the conservative bases of institutional reform thought in Henrician England, see A. B. Ferguson, *Clio Unbound: Perceptions of the Social and Cultural Past in Renaissance England* (North Carolina UP, 1979), chs. 7, 10; also D. W. Hanson, *From Kingdom to Commonwealth: The Development of Civic Consciousness in English Political Thought* (Harvard UP, 1970), ch. 6.

9 In addition to the sources cited above, see Bishop Edward Staples's treatise on reform, *State Papers Henry VIII* (1537) ii pp. 480–6; for a full commentary see Bradshaw, *Constitutional Revolution*, chs. 2 and 7.

10 Brendan Bradshaw, 'Cromwellian reform and the origins of the Kildare rebellion' *Transactions of the Royal Historical Society* 5th series, xxvii (1977), pp. 60–93; Lawrence Corristine, *The Revolt of Silken Thomas* (Dublin, 1978); on the recovery of the Geraldines, see Bradshaw, *Constitutional Revolution*, pp. 241–3, 272–6.

11 *Dictionary of National Biography*, (art. Lord Leonard Grey).

12 Bradshaw, *Constitutional Revolution* ch. 7; for the continuation of the reform strategy, see W. F. T. Butler, *Gleanings from Irish History* (London, 1925), ch. 3 and Ciaran Brady, 'Ulster and the failure of Tudor reform' in Brady *et al.*, *Ulster: An Illustrated History* (1989).

13 On the character of Tudor administration in Ireland, see Steven Ellis, *Tudor Ireland* (London, 1985), ch. 6 and Ciaran Brady, 'Court, castle, and country: the framework of government in Tudor Ireland' in C. Brady and R. Gillespie (eds.), *Natives and Newcomers: Essays on the Making of Irish Colonial Society* (Dublin, 1986), pp. 22–49.

14 Canny, *Elizabethan Conquest*, ch. 5.

15 D. G. White, *The Tudor Plantations in Ireland to 1571* (Unpublished PhD thesis, University of Dublin 1967), p. 247.

16 D. B. Quinn, 'Sir Thomas Smith and the beginnings of English colonial theory', *Transactions of the American Philosophical Society*, xcviii (1945), pp. 4543–60; Hiram Morgan, 'The colonial venture of Sir Thomas Smith in Ulster 1571–5', *Historical Journal*, xxviii (1985) pp. 261–78.

17 See Tremayne's proposals, in P[ublic] R[ecord] O[ffice]. SP 63/32/64–6; *BL* add MS. 48015 ff 357–60; for the practice of composition, see Bernadette Cunningham, 'The composition of Connacht in the Lordships of Clanricard and Thomond', *Irish Historical*

Studies, xxiv (1984), pp. 1–14 and Ciaran Brady, 'Faction and the origins of the Desmond rebellion of 1597', *ibid.*, xxii (1981), pp. 289–312.

18 For a general survey of Elizabethan military history in Ireland, see Cyril Falls, *Elizabeth's Irish Wars* (London, 1950).

19 For a representative selection with good critical commentary, see D. B. Quinn, *The Elizabethans and the Irish* (Yale UP, 1966).

20 The work of K. W. Nicholls has been of central importance to this revision; see his *Gaelic and Gaelicised Ireland in the Later Middle Ages* (Dublin, 1972); also his *Land Law and Society in Sixteenth Century Ireland* (O'Donnell lecture, Dublin, 1976) and 'Gaelic society and economy in the high Middle Ages' in Art Cosgrave (ed.), *A New History of Ireland; Medieval Ireland* (Oxford UP, 1987), pp. 397–438. See also Mary O'Dowd, 'Gaelic economy and society' in Brady and Gillespie (eds.), *Natives and Newcomers*, pp. 120–47.

21 For case-studies see Brady, 'Faction and the origins of the Desmond rebellion' and 'The O'Reilly's of east-Breifne and the problem of surrender and regrant'. *Briefne*, vi (1985) pp. 233–62.

22 George Hill, *The MacDonnells of Antrim* (Belfast, 1973); James McDonald, *Clan Donald* (Loamherd, 1978); G. A. Hayes McCoy, *Scots Mercenary Forces in Ireland 1565–1603* (Dublin and London, 1937); Donal Dorrian, 'The cock-pit of Ireland: north-east Ulster in the later sixteenth century' (Unpublished BA thesis, Trinity College, Dublin, 1984).

23 Brady, 'Court, castle and country', pp. 41–9.

24 *Ibid.*, for a further discussion see Ciaran Brady, *The government of Ireland c.1540–1583* (Unpublished PhD thesis, University of Dublin, 1980), chs. 3–5.

25 Brady, 'Faction and the origins of the Desmond rebellion'; Hiram Morgan, *The Origins of the Nine Years War in Ulster* (Unpublished PhD thesis, University of Cambridge, 1987).

26 Nicholas Canny, 'The flight of the earls 1607', *Irish Historical Studies*, xxvii (1971), pp. 380–99.

27 Colm Lennon, 'The counter-reformation' in Brady and Gillespie (eds.), *Natives and Newcomers*, esp. pp. 85–7. For an earlier study which prints many relevant documents see M. V. Ronan, *The Reformation in Ireland 1558–1580* (Dublin, 1930); see also R. Dudley Edwards, *Church and State in Tudor Ireland* (Dublin, 1935).

28 N. P. Canny, *The Formation of the Old English Elite* (O'Donnell lecture, Dublin, 1975); Ciaran Brady, 'Conservative subversives: the community of the Pale and the Dublin administration, 1556–86', in P. J. Corish (ed.), *Radicals, Rebels and Establishments* (Belfast, 1985), pp. 11–32; Aidan Clarke, 'Colonial Identity in Early Seventeenth Century Ireland' in T. W. Moody (ed.), *Nationality and the Pursuit of National Independence* (Belfast, 1978).

29 See especially Colm Lennon, *The Lords of Dublin in the Age of Reformation* (Dublin, 1989) esp. chs. 5–6.

30 Helga Hammerstein, 'Aspects of the conventional education of Irish students in the reign of Elizabeth I' and John Bossy, 'The counter-reformation and the people of Catholic Ireland, 1596–1641' in T. D. Williams (ed.), *Historical Studies VII* (Dublin, 1971), pp. 137–53; 155–69; P. J. Corish, *A History of Irish Catholicism* (Dublin, 1986), chs. 5–6.

31 For general surveys of the new English settlers and administrators see Nicholas Canny, 'Dominant minorities: English settlers in Ireland, and Virginia 1550–1650' in A. C. Hepburn, (ed.), *Minorities in History* (London, 1978), pp. 51–69 and 'The permissive frontiers: social control in English settlements in Ireland and Virginia, 1550–1650' in K. P. Andrews *et al.* (eds.), *The Westward Enterprise* (Liverpool, 1978), pp. 17–44. For the conduct of settlers in the midlands and in Munster, see Vincent Carey, 'The Laois-Offaly plantation' (Unpublished MA thesis, St Patrick's College, Maynooth, 1985) and Michael MacCarthy Morrough, *The Munster plantation, 1580–1641*. The older articles by Robert Dunlop on both settlements in *The English Historical Review* iii (1898),

pp. 250–69; vi (1891), pp. 61–96 retain their value. Cf. Anthony Sheehan, 'Official reaction to native land claims in the plantation of Munster', *Irish Historical Studies*, xxxvii (1982–3), pp. 297–318.

32 For the trade in reversions see C. Brady, 'Distribution of monastic lands in Co. Dublin, 1540–1640', an unpublished paper presented to the *Conference of Irish Social and Economic Historians*, September 1986. For escheatments and concealed lands, see Terence Ranger, 'Richard Boyle and the making of an Irish fortune', *Irish Historical Studies*, iv (1957), pp. 257–97, and Nicholas Canny, *The Upstart Earl: A Study of the Social and Mental World of Richard Boyle, First Earl of Cork 1566–1643* (Cambridge UP, 1982).

33 On Fitzwilliam, see Hiram Morgan, 'Origins of the Nine Years War', ch. 2; on Mountjoy, F. M. Jones, *Mountjoy: The Last Elizabethan Deputy* (Dublin, 1968); on Chichester, John McCovett, 'The government of Sir Anthony Chichester' (Unpublished PhD Thesis, The Queen's University, Belfast).

34 For a debate concerning the significance of Spenser's *View* see Nicholas Canny, 'Edmund Spenser and the development of an Anglo-Irish identity', *The Yearbook of English Studies*, xiii (1983) pp. 1–19. Ciaran Brady, 'Spenser's Irish crisis; humanism and experience in the 1590s', *Past and Present* (1986) pp. 14–49. Brendan Bradshaw, 'Robe and sword in the conquest of Ireland' in Claire Cross *et al.* (eds.), *Law and Government under the Tudors* pp. 139–62; on the general intellectual background, see Ciaran Brady, 'The road to the *View*; on the decline of reform thought in Tudor Ireland' in Patricia Caughlan (ed.), *Spenser and Ireland* (Cork, 1990) pp. 25–45.

35 There is a useful edition of the *Discovery* in M. Morley (ed.), *Ireland under Elizabeth and James I* (1890); for commentary, see Hans Pawlisch, *Sir John Davies and the conquest of Ireland* (Cambridge, 1983) and Fimnuala Bymre, 'Sir John Davies; an intellectual in Ireland' (Unpublished MA thesis, University College, Galway, 1985).

7

The Hanoverians and Scotland

DANIEL SZECHI*

It is a historical commonplace to stress the peculiarity of events in a given context. Circumstances, it is often argued, so dominate cases that comparisons are rarely fruitful. An analysis of Anglo-Scottish relations between 1702 and 1782, taken from the European perspective, explodes any such assertion in this case. While it is true that Anglo-Scottish union and Scotland's integration into the new English-dominated polity depart considerably from what has been assumed to be the general European pattern, this makes comparisons between Britain and the continental experience all the more valuable. Whereas in the continental European context we can see examples of strategic planning, systematic administrative overhaul and calculated repression, Scotland's case illustrates how integration worked when none of these elements was in evidence. The most striking feature of England's covert annexation of Scotland was its almost complete lack of co-ordination and planning. Beyond organizing the passage of the Act of Union through the Scottish Parliament, the English ministers showed remarkably little interest in promoting Scotland's involvement in the new British polity. As long as the Union was allowed to stand, British ministers were content to let Scotland go its own way so long as it did not create problems for them at Westminster. Scotland's absorption by 'Britain' provides, then, a case-study in what occurred when a people were subjected piecemeal, spasmodically and reflexively by a state with little substantive material interest in the acquisition.

Preconditions for integration

By the time of the Union of England and Scotland in 1707 England was one of the most unified countries in Europe. National identity was the key to this phenomenon, and beside it the power of the English state to enforce conformity (which, contrary to orthodox opinion was substantial) pales into relative insignificance. The common assumption has always been that because England enjoyed a common legal code, a virtual absence of internal tariffs and a common representative assembly at Westminster, a common national identity naturally developed, epitomized by that glorious eighteenth-century archetype: John Bull. Yet we know from the experience of our own times that common laws and common markets do not a nation make. Englishmen were English because they thought they were, not because the state told them so.

'England' as a concept, like most European *ancien-régime* states, encompassed a wide diversity of ethnic, linguistic and cultural groups. The Cornish language, with all its associated traditions, assumptions and mores, only disappeared about 1780, and as late as 1549 ill-feeling about the issuing of a new prayer-book in English rather than Cornish was strong enough to foster the Western Rising of that year. Well into the eighteenth century the Cornish gentry retained a keen interest in the Parliament of the Stanneries, a local assembly technically to do with the regulation of tin-mining, but actually the repository of a good deal of local patriotism and the focus of much local political endeavour. The Welsh-speaking 'Englishmen' of Glamorgan retained a proud sense of their separate, Welsh traditions despite their integration into the English national economy and proximity to English culture and society. Welsh bards and Welsh poetic traditions were patronized by the Glamorgan gentry and eagerly attended to by the common people at least as late as the mid-eighteenth century.[1] Channel Islands French and Manx were still living languages throughout the eighteenth century, and, like Cornish, they came with a baggage-train of cultural traditions and strong local patriotic feeling. Moreover it is impossible to take into account in any brief survey such as this the power and vitality of local dialects and regional feeling in areas such as Yorkshire, the Welsh Marches, and the Scots borders.

The survival of such linguistic and cultural diversity in England into the eighteenth century is a striking illustration of the power of the English national myth. For, despite the latent fissiparousness outlined above, almost all these groups thought of themselves primarily as English, with all the connotations of patriotism, pride and superiority over foreigners that came with it. To a significant extent, and without minimizing the exceptions already noted, a common language and its associated vernacular literary culture did foster a general sense of 'Englishness', but more important by far were two powerful institutions: the monarchy and the church.

To be an Englishman was to share John Bull's twin loyalties to the sovereign and unflinching (indeed unthinking) devotion to Protestantism. Patriotic pride in England was expressed through the acceptance of powerful historical myths and a participation in ritual celebrations stemming from them. The monarchy was seen in the light of its glorious tradition of drubbing foreigners and resisting internal and external enemies. These conceptions were popularly based on great events like the defeat of the Spanish Armada, the thwarting of the great popish conspiracy by the discovery of the Gunpowder Plot, the restoration of the monarchy in 1660 and William of Orange's saving England from the popish menace in 1688.[2] The church had a special place within the concept of 'Englishness' because it embodied English superiority on a spiritual, in contrast to the monarchy's temporal, basis. The Church of England was seen as the one pure, primitive, Christian (i.e. protestant) church in Europe, and one with a noble record of martyrdom for true Christian principles, particularly during the reign of Queen Mary I.[3] It may easily be appreciated how events like the Gunpowder Plot, Restoration, etc, were seen as vindicating both the monarchy and the church. Together, the monarchy and church created an amalgam of traditions in which they were seen as one body, the equal and coterminous guardian of Englishness.

The finest hour of both institutions was embodied, for most Englishmen, in one event: the execution of Charles I/murder of St Charles the martyr.[4] Inevitably (as in the case of most national myths) certain groups were excluded from, and stigmatized in, the celebration of these events: primarily the Roman Catholics, and, to a lesser extent, the protestant Nonconformists. In some ways their position in English society was on a par with that of Scotland in British society after the Union. They were numerically, geographically and socially marginal, and consequently generated little or no modification of the national myth.

By 1707, so far as the English were concerned, England had been unified and Englishmen had proved their superiority over foreigners time out of mind. In fact an articulate national identity, as opposed to the semi-tribal monarchism strongly associated with acute xenophobia for which the English were renowned in the fifteenth century, emerged only in the 1590s.[5] England's victory over Spain during Queen Elizabeth's wars coincided with the *de facto* conversion (at least in their own eyes) of most Englishmen to Protestantism, and created a popular tradition of protestant, English glory that was celebrated every year on the anniversary of Elizabeth's accession. It was in part due to this that English national feeling was still so aggressive. It was a relatively recent phenomenon, whose full implications for the English mentality were still evolving – an important factor in any analysis of relations between England and Scotland.

Moreover, for all the cohesion the English drew from their national myth, it produced, and was more than a little dependent on, its own collective 'neuroses'. In the main, the myth depicted England as permanently under threat, either from popish conspiracy or foreign catholic invasion. In order to be safe from such threats, so the argument ran, England had to guard itself against attack from within the British Isles and the need for vigilance was never more acute than 'at the present time'. This 'national interest' justification of English imperialism within the British Isles led to attempts throughout the seventeenth century to manipulate Scottish and Irish politics to suit England's perceived interests. Such interference inevitably generated a nationalistic 'backlash' in Scotland and Ireland which intermittently expressed itself in armed uprisings against those local élites who were perceived as the agents of English hegemony.[6] The 1638 Scottish rebellion against Charles I and the Irish rising of 1641 were still potent memories, even as late as 1707. Their immediacy was reinforced in English eyes by Scottish and Irish resistance to the Revolution of 1688. England was felt to have been under dire threat from the popish menace between 1685 and 1688, in the shape of the catholic James II. The country had been saved by William of Orange, but a great deal of blood and treasure had been expended to overcome resistance in Scotland and Ireland. In addition, the Revolution precipitated England into over 20 years of warfare between 1689 and 1713 to defend the protestant Revolution Settlement. The question of how England could best control Scotland and Ireland so as to preserve the hegemony 'vital' to its security in such a crisis was a matter for violent political debate between the burgeoning English Whig and Tory parties. The assumption that it was necessary was common ground.

In Ireland's case English responses in the light of these fears were straightforward: the Irish were incorrigible popish rebels who needed to be thoroughly intimidated and repressed. Scotland, however, was a more difficult problem. It was an overwhelmingly protestant country. In addition, both Scotland and England had been ruled by the same dynasty for over a century and, technically, both countries were equal partners in the Union of Crowns inaugurated in 1603. English fears of Scotland's potential disruptiveness largely stemmed from its supposed responsibility for England's slide into civil war and interregnum in the mid-seventeenth century, and it was on this basis that most Englishmen rationalized the need for English oversight of Scottish affairs. This perception, and the apprehensions from which it grew, gained increasing urgency as Queen Anne, the last legitimate protestant Stuart, became older and frailer. If there were to be a disputed succession between the English Parliament's nominated protestant heir, Georg Ludwig, Elector of Hanover, and James Stuart (the 'Old Pretender', the legitimate, but catholic, son of James II) many, if not most, English politicians were uncertain as to which way Scotland would jump.

Economically there was little impelling England towards union with Scotland. England's population was at least four times that of Scotland, and England was the regional superpower in economic terms. Both Scotland and Ireland had already been reduced to being the raw-material suppliers who serviced the English economy. Scotland's population was 80–90 per cent rural while England's demographic centre of gravity was slowly but steadily shifting from a rural to an urban one. Even Scotland's flourishing west-coast ports ultimately relied on the English economy, dependent on systematic smuggling operations in the English West Indian and North American colonies.

Scotland's economic weakness was made more apparent by the trends in contemporary warfare. England's economic superiority was directly translatable into military force. By the early eighteenth century armies and navies had become professional, highly trained bodies armed with the high-technology weapons of the age. They accordingly represented a huge investment for any state, and a constant, often crippling, drain on revenue. The Scottish state effectively bankrupted itself mobilizing what were, by English standards, tiny forces during the Highland war of 1689–91.[7] In addition, improvements in the conduct of war meant that even Scotland's last, oldest military resource, its rugged terrain, no longer had the stopping-power it had once enjoyed. Without outside support, Scotland could no longer take England on in any sustained conflict.

This was a sad prospect for Scottish patriots like Lord Belhaven and Andrew Fletcher of Saltoun. England was Scotland's 'auld enemy' and hostility between the two kingdoms played a vital part in forging a Scottish national identity in conscious opposition to that of the English. From the fourteenth to the sixteenth century England's interminable and futile efforts to subjugate Scotland had effectively brought a dynamic, independent Scottish polity into being. Even their common alignment with the protestant cause in Europe in the late sixteenth century had only muted, rather than removed, this traditional hostility.[8].

For a century before the Act of Union, it had been increasingly apparent that the Union of Crowns was a thinly disguised form of English domination and the incorporating Union under discussion in 1706–7 offered little more than a regularization of Scotland's subordination. It was also evident to many that Scotland alone could no longer resist English military force with any hope of success. That distasteful truth coloured, and significantly weakened, Scottish opposition to the Union, but perversely it probably heightened English apprehension over Scotland's possible future conduct on the death of Queen Anne. If Scotland could not resist English power without outside help, might not the Scots seek it among England's enemies, and particularly from Scotland's 'auld alliance' with France?

Scotland had been quietly but effectively orientated in various ways towards the Union of 1707 for almost a century. The anglicization of the monarchy occurred within less than one generation of the Stuarts succeeding to the English throne (Charles I was born in Scotland but was thoroughly anglocentric in his attitudes and actions), and the greater nobility was not far behind. During the course of the seventeenth century the soft and fashionable pleasures London could offer (and, as importantly, the hope of preferment at court) drew more and more of the penurious Scots nobility southwards. For most of the seventeenth century the rhythms of Scottish politics reflected the strongly hierarchical order of Scottish society, with the nobility at the top playing the decisive and mobilizing rôle. Hence the increasing absenteeism of the Scottish peerage made a considerable, negative impact on the vitality of Scottish politics. Naturally enough, with the notable exception of the period of the Covenanting Revolution in Scotland (1637–52), Scottish politics also became more orientated towards English rather than native sensibilities. Any Scottish politician worth his salt was playing to an English audience and an English monarch in London, which inevitably detached him from Scottish affairs.[9] By the end of the seventeenth century the chronic lack of relevant leadership offered by the Scots nobility began to foster a rise in the social authority of the landed gentry and the urban bourgeoisie. More decisive in terms of paving the way for the eventual absorption of Scotland into an anglocentric British polity was the anglicization of the Scottish nobility. In practical terms its most significant (and apposite) impact came during the passage of the Act of Union in 1706–7. Throughout the process the Marlborough-Godolphin ministry in London directed and financed an impressive phalanx of Scottish noblemen and their followers in bulldozing the measure through, so that when it came to the final vote on the ratification of the Treaty of Union on 16 January 1707, the government mustered more than a 2:1 superiority in peers.[10]

Scottish misgivings about the possible future absorption of the Scottish polity by the English dated from before the time of James I's accession to the English throne. In part the abortive 1603–7 negotiations for a constitutional union between the two kingdoms that accompanied his arrival in London, just like those of 1668–70, 1689–90, and 1702–4, arose from a desire to negotiate a union before the insidious process of anglicization achieved a *fait accompli* to Scotland's disadvantage. There were also some Scottish nobles, lairds and merchants who prospered as a result of Scotland's steady reorientation of its exports from the Netherlands to England during the course of the seventeenth century. Many of these individuals came to favour political integration to match Scotland's new economic direction. By 1707 there was, then, a substantial minority of the Scottish ruling élite who wanted a constitutional union with England. However, such a radical constitutional change required a majority in the English Parliament too and until English apprehensions about Scotland's potential as a future source of trouble overcame the MPs' innate Scotophobia this would simply never materialize.

Once the Union had become reality, its origins in these English 'neuroses' about Scotland made it a constitutional shibboleth. As it so admirably served English political and strategic interests there was virtually no pressure to get rid of it from the English side. And since the English had an overwhelming majority in the new British Parliament that meant it was never going to be dissolved by peaceful means. The initial breakthrough in English prejudices was the crucial one, and that can only be accounted for by the unusual political circumstances operating on both sides of the border during the period from 1705 to 1707.

For most of the seventeenth century (excluding the period from 1637 to 1652) the Scottish Parliament was a legislative body which was tightly controlled by the monarch and which compliantly supplied both money and statutes when they were demanded of it. This changed completely with the Revolution of 1688. The Scottish Parliament, temporarily under the dominance of a radical minority, abolished the Lords of the Articles, a watchdog committee controlled by the crown to which all proposed legislation had to be submitted in advance. Direct monarchical (and, by 1689, English-orientated) control of the Scottish Parliament was thus destroyed. The position was made more complicated by William III's insistence on employing and rewarding all those he regarded as supporters of the Revolution whatever their factional allegiance. His government in Scotland therefore was not able to make good use either of the carrot of royal patronage or the stick of threatening its suspension in its attempts to construct a parliamentary majority out of the rival magnate factions. Consequently the traditional 'treasure-hunt' among the great magnates grew completely out of control.[11] By 1700 the Scottish state had been virtually bankrupt for nine years as a result of the administrative and fiscal disruption engendered by this faction-fighting. By way of a culmination, the first stirrings of 'party' alignments appeared in the 1690s among the barons and burgh members of the Scottish Parliament (the equivalents of the knights of the shires and borough MPs in the English Parliament). These were initially on a national or 'Country' party basis and arose partly out of disgust at the blatant cynicism of the magnates' in-fighting over patronage, and partly as a result of outrage at what was felt to be national humiliation stemming from the English connection, most notably the massacre of the Macdonalds at Glencoe in 1692 and the Darien fiasco.[12]

By 1704 clear-cut magnate factions were on the wane, while party feeling was burgeoning. In the early years of Queen Anne's reign the amorphous 'Country' grouping effectively separated out into three distinct parties. A rump of the 'Country' party remained, but two new alignments grew to far greater prominence: the *Squadrone Volante* and the Cavaliers. The *Squadrone* were basically anti-court Scottish Whigs, but with a significantly deeper ideological base than the self-interested 'Whiggism' of the duke of Queensberry's faction which dominated Scotland's administration by this time. The Cavaliers were in general the Scottish counterparts of the English Tory party, but in one crucial respect their political ideology openly diverged from that of the English Tories: they were Jacobites to a man. Moreover, a loose Cavalier-'Country' party alliance appeared increasingly to gain the upper hand in the Scottish Parliament.[13]

This development coincided with one of the brief interludes of Whig ascendancy at Westminster during the reign of Queen Anne. Though the Whigs did not have a Parliamentary majority between 1705 and 1707, they became increasingly influential as the Marlborough-Godolphin ministry's unflinching policy of war to the death with France began to alienate the ministry's original, Tory constituency in Parliament. The English Whigs, led by the 'Junto' of Lord Halifax, Lord Wharton, Lord Somers, the earl of Sunderland and the earl of Orford, dominated the Union negotiations from the start, and were primarily responsible for the character of the final agreement. As a result, it was a document that was very satisfactory from a Whig point of view on both sides of the border. The cardinal point for both the English and Scottish Whigs was that, as a result of the Union, Scotland was denied the possibility of a separate, Scottish (and probably Jacobite) successor on the death of Queen Anne. The much vaunted trade provisions of the Act of Union, along with the protection afforded the Kirk in the new British polity and the preservation of a separate Scottish legal system, were all window-dressing. These minor concessions (from an English Whig viewpoint) were needed by Queensberry's faction and the *Squadrone* to conciliate powerful interest groups like the clergy and the lawyers, and to sweeten the unpalatable fact that the Union was to be an 'incorporating' rather than 'federal' act which would leave Scotland permanently at the mercy of an in-built English majority. Without both the basic ideological identity of interest of both Scottish and English Whigs and their common determination to ensure a protestant, Hanoverian succession, the Union would never have come to pass. As it was, the passage of the Union bill against furious Opposition resistance still required the investment of at least £20 000 (about £200 000 in 1987 values) by the government in London to fortify the Scottish political managers and their friends.[14]

In the final analysis the English apprehensions and suspicions which fuelled the drive towards Union in 1705–7 arose from the inescapable geographical fact that Scotland was the only country with a land frontier common to that of England. A hostile régime in Scotland could admit an enemy of England onto the British mainland. This possibility was one which any English administration was bound to try to remove. Before the mid sixteenth century the nature of the Scottish polity and the intrinsic limitations of contemporary warfare denied England any long-term success in its alternate wooing and bludgeoning of its neighbour. After 1603, however, the more gentle seduction of the monarchy and, increasingly, of the aristocracy by English ways delivered what English force had consistently failed to. Scottish government steadily came under the effective control of the monarch's English ministers. Ironically, the first stirrings of Scottish resistance to this subordination, from the late 1690s onwards, and hence the possibility that the dormant northern threat might be reactivated, created the need for closer control from England out of which the Union emerged.

The experience of acquisition

Scotland ceased to exist as a separate political entity through mutually agreed fusion with its English neighbour. Technically, both kingdoms' representative assemblies voted themselves into oblivion and a new, British state had succeeded them. In reality, the English polity remained completely intact and a truncated Scottish representation was grafted on to it. For the new order to have any legitimacy for the acquired people, the Scots, the façade of a true, lasting bond had to be created. This occurred in due course but it owed little to government efforts. In the short term, London-based governments took a 'hands-off' approach intended to achieve the entirely practical objectives of keeping Scotland quiet and running it cheaply. This had two important repercussions from a Scottish point of view. One was that it led Westminster, by and large, to rule Scotland through loyal, but Scottish, agents who mediated, and to some extent softened, the impact of its demands. The other was that those same loyal Scottish agents, who, naturally, did not wish to think of themselves as unpatriotic, fostered a myth of 'Britishness' in which the Union, and thence support for it, became a moral act. The rhetoric and propaganda generated by official attempts to rebut Opposition charges of treachery in 1705–7 was the basis for this, and matured over the next century into a noble vision of (Scottish) Britishness and Scotland's significance for the new polity. It also consolidated the political divisions the Union created in Scottish society.

The Union was achieved through expert political management in Scotland under orders from London. Daniel Defoe and others busy propagandizing in favour of the measure were financed and encouraged by the government in Scotland and England, but the principal target for their efforts was always the Scottish Parliament rather than the Scottish people. Consequently, though a majority of their representatives were brought over to the idea, the Scottish people were not. Key interest groups such as the Kirk, the lawyers, the peerage and central government officials, the paucity of whose numbers was inversely related to their influence in Scottish society, probably contained a majority in favour of the Union. The population at large, however, showed its sympathies by rioting and demonstrating against the Union in Glasgow, Edinburgh, Dumfries and many other towns.[15] The lower orders in these places were doubtless encouraged to act as they did by hostile sections of the political nation but it is illuminating to note that there was not a single popular demonstration in favour of the Union in response to them.

Higher up the social scale, among the 'heritors' (landowners) and burgesses who made up the bulk of the ruling élite and the political nation, the pattern was the same. One third of Scotland's Parliamentary constituencies sent addresses to the Scottish Parliament against the Union in spite of all that the government could do to discourage and obstruct them. Conversely, despite its best efforts the government failed to generate a single address in favour of the Union. The best evidence for the unpopularity of the Union can be seen from the way the government avoided any form of plebiscite on the measure. Throughout the passage of the Union Bill the government studiously ignored the Opposition's reasonable demand that the voters should be allowed to express an opinion on the demise of their own polity. And in the final days of the Scottish Parliament the government used its synthetic majority there to have the 45 MPs supposed to represent Scotland in the new British Parliament until the next general election co-opted from among its supporters.[16]

The deep divisions in Scottish society created by such shameless political jobbery were traumatic and they determined the pattern of Scottish politics for the next 50 years. Until at least the 1750s Scotland's rulers were a beleaguered native oligarchy, dependent in the final analysis on English armed force to keep them in power. There can be few better illustrations of this than the relative musters for government and rebels in 1715. The rebels only ever loosely controlled less than half of the Scottish population at any time, but they managed to mobilize a *minimum* of 20 000 men – even though the government had all the textbook advantages such as weapons, fortresses and control of communications. By contrast, the government managed to recruit at most 1 500. Taking Scotland as a whole, between 5 and 10 per cent of the adult male population took up arms for a catholic (and anti-Union) Stuart against a protestant (but pro-Union) Hanoverian. A similar-sized uprising in Scotland in 1987 would field in the region of 250 000 men, which gives some idea of its seriousness.

The net effect of government control of Scotland resting on the support of a minority (albeit a growing one) was that for the next half century Scotland became a client society administered on semi-colonial lines by a select inner group within the traditional ruling class. The government at Westminster ruled Scotland through a narrow oligarchy of 'reliable' families with connections. These in turn controlled Scottish society through patronage in the form of government jobs, favourable legal decisions, and so on. This effectively demoralized Scottish politics. Given the way Scotland was being run, politicians operating within legitimate politics (as opposed to Jacobite conspiracy) were obliged to play to English ministers' prejudices because it was in London that all the crucial decisions were taken. In Scotland their activities had to be restricted to building up cadres of client officials with which to battle against similar opposing groups over who should control the access to favours and rewards. Faction became the keystone of Scottish politics and sterile, parasitic exploitation of its government's meagre resources the sole objective of Scottish politicians.[17]

This degeneration in the tone of Scottish politics was assisted by the way certain Scottish institutions such as the Assembly of the Kirk and the Convention of Royal Burghs were preserved by the terms of the Union. Without a native legislature to lobby, influence and co-operate with, these institutions were effectively emasculated. The new British Parliament, dominated by English MPs and peers, was indifferent or even hostile to the purely Scottish concerns these institutions dealt in. Consequently, they were left curiously stunted. Still retaining some local authority and economic power, their power and prestige was left unrelated to any larger political reality. Inevitably they became introverted and unresponsive to the needs of the society they had been created to serve. More damagingly, these institutions represented local resources of patronage, and were therefore seized upon by the Scottish Whig oligarchy as spoils to fight over in their interminable factional struggles. Within five years of the Union even the General Assembly of the Kirk, which for most of the previous century had been a ferocious watchdog of the moral order in church and state, was reduced to a rubber-stamp which endorsed government policies. Its exploitation as a source of rewards for faithful servants of the new order soon followed.[18]

Because it was a key instrument of government control, the Scottish legal system was a partial exception to this general decline in Scotland's institutions. Nonetheless it too was warped by alien influences. Whenever the government at Westminster found Scottish legal traditions a hindrance it simply swept them away. For example, Scotland still preserved general rules of evidence in treason cases, requiring two witnesses for conviction. Under this rule, four over-zealous Jacobite Stirlingshire gentlemen, arrested after having turned out prematurely to assist the abortive French invasion attempt of 1708, were acquitted. Annoyed by the decision, the ministry used its English Whig majority to pass a law aligning Scottish legal practice with that current in England (where only one witness was needed). This was despite a near unanimous protest in Scotland at the breach being created in Scotland's legal tradition, and the combined opposition of Scottish representatives of all political persuasions at Westminster.

A more disruptive change was the introduction (under the terms of the Union) of a higher Court of Appeal than the Lords of Session: the English House of Lords. In 1711 the Episcopalian Scottish Tories (Jacobites almost to a man) used this new avenue to outflank the Presbyterian Whig establishment in Scotland. The Tories appealed to the Lords to reverse the conviction of an Episcopalian clergyman, James Greenshields, under laws upholding the Kirk's position as the established Church of Scotland. Capitalizing on the Tory majority in the Parliament of 1710, the Scottish Tory MPs and peers incited strong emotions among their English counterparts over the 'persecution' by sour and fanatical Presbyterians of a clergyman using the English liturgy. In due course, they succeeded in having the conviction quashed. In the process the Kirk's position as the established Church of Scotland (guaranteed by the Union) was casually breached, and events set in train that were to lead to a major Cameronian schism in 1712 which was not to be healed until 1718.[19] Only the advent of the Hanoverian Whig régime in England after 1714 put an end to the potential wastage of the Scottish judiciary's authority. Because the now Whig-dominated House of Lords could usually be relied on to back up the Whig establishment in Scotland it became a dormant rather than an active problem.

Whiggish domination of Scotland's administration after the Union flowed naturally from the divisions it created. Only men committed to the Union could be trusted to man the government in 1706–7, and the coalescence of hostility to it in Scottish Toryism after 1708 initiated a process whereby Whiggery and Unionism became coterminous. Hence there were few changes in personnel accompanying the passage of the Union even during the Tory ascendancy of Queen Anne's last years. The Harley ministry and its Whig successors wanted Scotland run reliably and cheaply and, by those lights, the existing officials or their ilk were quite adequate. During the Tory ministry of 1710–14 and the Whig faction fighting before and after it, a few high placemen and sinecurists, Scottish Secretaries, Commissioners of Chamberlainry, Keepers of the Signet and so on, were dismissed in favour of the successful party or faction. Yet the minions and underlings who did the real work remained a constant in terms of both personnel and political sympathy. The only area of Scottish administration extensively reformed as a result of the Union was that of the customs and excise. An influx of English personnel and expertise took place there so as to keep English and Scottish collection and enforcement of customs and excise tariffs uniform. It was bitterly resented by Scotsmen of all political hues at the time, but this was necessarily a transient phenomenon incapable of stirring up sustained opposition.

The patterns of everyday life in Scotland were, on the surface, little affected by the existence of the Union. The next two generations of the peerage, lairds and gentry contained large elements that were politically frustrated, or even disaffected, but for most of the population the pace and tenor of life went an unchanged. Indeed, in this respect, the Union was designed to be placatory. Over the next century Scottish society was changed out of all recognition, largely through the social impact of the Union. But in the short term all that was visible was a slight acceleration of existing trends. Scotland was already on the way to being deserted by its peerage and greater gentry before 1707; by 1832 the social vacuum created by their absence had been filled by men and families of less exalted social station: the urban middle classes.[20] Economically based social relations eventually overpowered the old hierarchical bonds of Scottish society too, but in the immediate aftermath of the Union there were very few signs that such a change was underway.

Likewise, in the short term, Scotland's international importance was little affected by the Union. By 1700, few major European powers had any interest at all in Scotland's fate, and those that did were too preoccupied to show much concern. Sweden had some trading links with Scotland and had acted as a major source of mercenary employment for Scottish soldiers for over a century. In 1707, however, Charles XII and his ministers were too busy fighting the Great Northern War to worry about the demise of a satellite kingdom in the British Isles. The Dutch Republic was formerly Scotland's major trading partner; Denmark had some old dynastic ties. Both were allies of England's in the English dominated Grand Alliance against Louis XIV's France, and neither cared to irritate their powerful ally by protesting about the Union. Only France, Scotland's ancient ally, showed any interest at all in Scotland's pending disappearance. An expedition nominally led by the 'Old Pretender' and intended to link up with a planned Scottish uprising was launched in 1708. The French officers involved were unenthusiastic about the project, conducted it incompetently and precipitated its demise in dismal failure. It was hardly surprising that they were so half-hearted: the expedition was plainly a desperate gamble on Louis XIV's part. By 1708 the armies of the Grand Alliance under the Duke of Marlborough and Prince Eugene had inflicted a series of catastrophic defeats on the French and were close to breaking through the northern defences into France proper. Louis XIV's aim in sending an expedition to Scotland was transparently that of distracting his adversaries.[21] A century of Scotland's foreign relations being subsumed in those of England had wrought its inevitable result: none of the major European powers cared if Scotland vanished or not – their relations with England were far more important to them.

Ironically though, the long-term discontent engendered in Scotland by the Union initiated a recrudescence of international interest in the kingdom. Patriotic anti-Unionism in Scotland had nowhere else to go but Jacobitism after 1707, as the great anti-Union Whig patriot Fletcher of Saltoun indicated by his retirement from all active politics thereafter. Jacobitism alone offered unconditional dissolution of the Union as part of its political platform, thereby gaining an enduring body of support in Scotland that was to prove its mainstay in the British Isles. Because the Jacobites were perceived as strong in Scotland, powers that were inclined to destabilize (or distract) the new British polity became interested in Scotland. The French expedition of 1708 was the first actualization of an analysis that cast Scotland as Britain's Achilles heel, but the same reasoning influenced a succession of Britain's enemies over the next 50 years. Sweden in 1717, Spain in 1719, France in 1745–6 and Prussia in 1752–3, all flirted with the Jacobite government in exile with a view to stirring up an insurrection in Britain, and Scotland was always a key element in their plans.[22]

Acquisition and integration

The new British Parliament, like its English and Scottish predecessors, claimed absolute sovereignty over its territories and peoples, so there was no question of Scotland being allowed any constitutional autonomy after the Union. By the same token nothing left in Scotland was sacrosanct, whether mentioned in the articles of Union or not. After the Union any law passed by the anglocentric British Parliament automatically applied to Scotland unless it was specifically exempted (a very rare event). Existing Scottish laws were altered whenever it facilitated government action in Scotland, while at the same time attempts to protect Scotland's economic interests at Westminster met with hostility.

The 1709 Treason Act was passed to facilitate government prosecution of treason suspects in Scotland despite the outrage it provoked among Scotland's representatives in Parliament, and various disarming Acts were passed after the 1715 rebellion despite warnings that it would mainly be the Government's supporters that were affected (as indeed proved to be the case).[23] One of the first examples of legislation that causally harmed Scotland's economic interests occurred in 1711, when the Scottish linen industry had revenue duties imposed on it. This occurred despite Scottish protests that this was its staple industry, equivalent to England's revenue-exempt woollen cloth industry. In the same vein, the Scottish linen industry was denied similar protective legislation against the Irish linen industry to that enjoyed by the English woollen industry against all comers.[24] Conversely, where no constraints on governmental freedom of action were felt to be involved or sustained consideration of Scottish interests required, remarkable anomalies were preserved. Heritable jurisdictions continued to operate in Scotland until 1747, when they were belatedly abolished in the wake of the '45, and the death penalty for witchcraft was not removed until 1735, nearly 50 years after its effective abolition in England (the last witchcraft execution in Scotland was in 1727).

Such lack of concern for Scottish affairs is not surprising in an English-dominated representative assembly. Nonetheless many Scotsmen were taken aback by Westminster's partiality. They were shocked that the terms of the Union, particularly those relating to the status of the Kirk, were not considered an immutable part of the constitution. The Kirk's naivety on this score was revealed in 1711–12 through a series of measures which were passed despite the terms of the union, which limited its authority in Scotland and imposed an extremely distastefully worded oath of loyalty on all Scottish clergymen. In time the Kirk accepted the breaking of its legal religious monopoly, but only after a lengthy period of schism and theological disputes.

The Kirk's acceptance of its diminished status stemmed, in part, from a more general awareness of the precariousness of its hold on Scottish society. In 1707 the Kirk chose to accept the risk of association with 'white popery' (Anglicanism) rather than risk the return of a catholic dynasty with its attendant risk of 'black popery' (Roman Catholicism). The Kirk's acceptance of the Union however, went against the clearly expressed sentiments of most of its adherents. It therefore became reliant on the secular magistracy to bolster its position, and that magistracy was firmly tied to the post-Union Scottish Whig establishment. In return for the régime's support, the Kirk zealously upheld the Union in its teaching, thereby also highlighting its reliability compared to its openly seditious Episcopalian rival.[25] The net effect of this intertwining of Kirk and state was to give the Whig establishment a wider body of support than it would otherwise have enjoyed. A consequence of such sectarian backing, however, was that it tended to limit the new order's support for a particular confessional alignment, with all the geographical and social consequences attendant on that. Where Episcopalianism was strong, the hold of the new régime was weak. The Highlands and most of northern Scotland, particularly the regions north of the Tay (comprising something between a half and a third of the population), were implicitly alienated by the continued alliance of Kirk and State after 1707. It was to take considerable military effort and the passage of a good deal of time to reconcile these regions to the government.

Another group for whom the English bias of the British legislature would prove to be a rude shock was the Scottish nobility. In order to help ease the passage of the Union Bill through the Scottish Parliament a good number of them were promised British peerages once the kingdoms were united. As well as those to whom specific promises were made, many others were also encouraged to cherish hopes that promotion out of the second-class status laid down for the Scottish peerage by the terms of the Union would be quick and easy. The English peerage however refused to be (as these aristocrats would have seen it) 'swamped' by beggarly Scottish noblemen. In a rare display of cross-party unity, the English aristocracy decisively threw out the duke of Hamilton's patent to sit as the duke of Brandon in December 1711.[26] Despite repeated challenges the English peerage held to this precedent until 1782, to the impotent fury of a host of disappointed Scottish peers. In addition, not only the Scottish peerage's increasing absenteeism, stemming from their growing anglicization, but also the abolition of their hereditary jurisdictions in 1747 steadily reduced the social authority of the Scottish peerage over the same period. For most of the eighteenth century they were a declining caste.[27]

Nevertheless during their increasingly infrequent visits home the Scottish peerage still wielded considerable social power, which, added to their increasingly anglocentric outlook, meant they acted as a force for integration. The Scottish peerage's growing anglocentricity sprang from their disproportionate involvement in the armed services, diplomatic corps and colonial administration, all of which expanded hugely during the course of the eighteenth century as Britain acquired a world-wide empire. Intermarriage with their English counterparts, common residence in London and at fashionable resorts, and a growing tendency to have their children educated in England naturally followed.[28] Though the Scottish peerage's influence on those in power was small, they nonetheless did well out of the Union. Those who could not stomach what was happening, or even those who, on occasion, did not consider themselves to be doing sufficiently well (like the earl of Mar in 1715 and the earl of Kilmarnock in 1745), eliminated themselves by rebellion and forefeiture. By the early 1800s, the English, Scottish and British peerages formed a single cohesive social group.[29] In the process, the Scottish peerage shrank in size and ceased to be representative of anything Scottish. Yet, like the Kirk, they carried a constituency with them. It may have been a diminishing asset, but during the crucial opening years of Anglo-Scottish Union it too broadened the basis of the régime.

Economic integration with England was one of the carrots used to entice the Scottish Parliament to accept the Union. Like many other inducements, it proved a severe disappointment. England's economy appeared to be flourishing around 1707 from a Scottish perspective. In accordance with contemporary mercantilist theories, it was assumed that association with it would expand Scotland's markets and lead to some of that prosperity rubbing off. In fact, the results were distinctly mixed for at least 50 years after the Union. Glasgow did strikingly well out of free, legal access to England's empire, passing easily from wholesale smuggling to a burgeoning transatlantic trade. Against this, however, must be set the decline of Scotland's east-coast ports, their trade strangled by legislation designed to protect nascent English industries against European competition. Overall (excluding Glasgow), Scotland, with a semi-stagnant economy, remained a poor supplier of raw materials and primary products for the English market until the late eighteenth century. Then, economic circumstances in and around Glasgow fostered an industrial boom akin to that occurring around Liverpool and Manchester. The Industrial Revolution eventually created the prosperity which pro-Unionist Scotsmen yearned for in 1707 but, until then, Scotland's economic integration with the English economy merely maintained its poverty.

Apart from suppressing the occasional Jacobite pamphlet, the new British state also showed little interest in changing Scottish culture so as to facilitate the integration of Scottish society into the English-dominated whole. This was not a deliberate policy of *laissez-faire*; it was owing to the fact that such ideas simply did not figure in English politics. If they thought about it at all, which is doubtful, English ministers probably assumed that the attractions of English life would seduce Scotland's élite, that the Kirk would give collaboration the necessary respectability, and that the rest of the population would be won over by the approval of their social superiors. The one exception to this general indifference was the Highlands. There, successive Scottish governments since at least the early seventeenth century had, in alliance with the Kirk, been trying to 'civilize' the Gaelic-speaking clans by exposing their leaders to lowland culture and converting their followers to a recognizable form of Christianity.[30] The Scottish Society for the Propagation of Christian Knowledge's efforts to undermine Gaelic culture and disseminate Lowland (after 1707, English) values through its schools continued under the new régime and appear to have been taking effect by the early eighteenth century. The impact of such efforts was considerably boosted by government measures to pacify the Highlands in the wake of the Jacobite rebellion of 1745. The abolition of hereditary jurisdictions removed the key institution underpinning the chieftains' control of their clansmen. It enforced the exposure of the Highlands to the delights of the outside world, through exile and imprisonment, and fostered the same anglicization of clan élites as that taking place among the Scottish peerage. By the end of the eighteenth century the clan chiefs had, by and large, shifted their attitudes from paternalistic overlordship to straightforward landownership, as may be seen from the accelerating rate of Highland clearances at the close of the eighteenth century.

The kind of upheavals Scottish society was undergoing in the mid eighteenth century would not usually be expected to engender an artistic and philosophical renaissance. However, in Scotland, they did. From the 1740s until the end of the century there was a flowering of intellectual, literary and artistic activity now known as the Scottish Enlightenment. It was fundamentally a provincial culture that blossomed in these years; all of its leading figures (apart from Robert Burns who affected a sentimental nationalism) accepted the political *status quo*. Many, like David Hume the philosopher and Adam Smith the economist, overtly supported the Union and were proud of their newly discovered Britishness.[31]

In part, this phenomenon was symptomatic of the increased self-confidence and social leadership of Scotland's urban bourgeoisie and improving Lowland landowners. The subjects that Enlightenment intellectuals were interested in were those that interested the urban bourgeoisie too, such as political economy, scientific improvement and the philosophical basis of rational self-interest. Likewise the literary and artistic flowering exemplified by Robert Burns and Robert Adam came mainly in forms agreeable to the bourgeois patrons who were increasingly usurping the rôle of the nobility in that sphere: vernacular poetry and grand civic architecture. The bourgeois input into the Scottish Enlightenment profoundly influenced its impact, and, with hindsight, we can see that it shaped the outlook of the Scottish middle class in the next century. Yet its effects should not be exaggerated. The teachings of the Kirk remained the guiding light for the overwhelming majority of ordinary Scotsmen. Noble influence and patronage, though declining in relative importance, still set the tone of much of the Enlightenment. No bourgeois patron was likely to evince much interest in the brilliant outpouring of Gaelic poetry taking place at the same time as these more 'progressive' developments.[32] The civic pride that lay at the root of the enduring elements of the Scottish Enlightenment in many ways expressed the final stage of the provincialization of Scotland. If it had a common theme, that theme was the celebration of Scottish Britishness, a regional rather than national pride.

Conclusion

To state that each acquisition of a neighbouring polity considered in this volume is a special case would be a truism. Nonetheless that must be the starting point of any analysis of the strengths and weaknesses of the early modern state highlighted by the Union of England and Scotland. The decisive move in the kind of legitimated annexation which took place in Scotland between 1707 and 1782 has to be the winning over of the social élite in the acquired territory. Of necessity, such seduction is inseparable from local circumstances. By any criterion the fact that, by 1700, the majority of the Scottish people spoke a form of English intelligible to their southern neighbours was of crucial importance. No linguistic distinction has figured in this account of Anglo-Scottish relations because it simply was not an issue. Elsewhere in Europe language problems have dogged the absorption of smaller polities by larger ones down to the present day. In the same vein, Scotland and England enjoyed more than a geographical affinity in two vital areas: religion and politics. The Church of England and the Kirk in Scotland had major, acrimonious differences, but they were both militantly protestant and both profoundly afraid of the popish Antichrist. Out of this common 'neurosis' came the ideological affinity of the English and Scottish Whigs. The Covenanting Revolution of the mid seventeenth century created a lasting split in Scottish society along fundamental ideological lines. In the process, it also expanded the basis for co-operation between kindred English and

Scottish religious/political alignments. In the end, it was the common interests and shared analysis of the likely course of future events between the English and Scottish post-Revolutionary political establishments that brought about the Union.

So much for the peculiarities of the Union of England and Scotland. What strengths of the early modern state does it reveal? One element of the power exercised by the British state stands out as decisive in bringing about and maintaining the Union: its control of surpassing physical force. The rebellions of 1715 and 1745 certainly posed problems for the British state, but there was no question in either the establishment's *or the rebels'* minds but that, if the rebels did not win quickly, they were not going to win at all. What each side recognized was that if the state was allowed time to mobilize its resources its challengers must be defeated. In this context, it is instructive to note the Jacobites' desperate attempts to establish their own countervailing administrative and fiscal structures both in 1715 and 1745, in a vain attempt to draw on the economic and demographic resources otherwise monopolized by the government.

On a more technical level, that of actually waging war, the state had the advantage over its opponents. The courage of the Highland clansmen was second to none. It enabled them to win startling successes at the battles of Prestonpans and Falkirk. But their victories were ultimately empty and their defeats were final. Enthusiasm was simply no match for professionalism. By the early eighteenth century, professional soldiers who would fight on remorselessly through encounter after encounter, rally after each defeat, and ruthlessly follow up after each victory, were the way wars were won. When it came down to fixed, positional warfare (the essence of being able to hold territory and resources) the rebels were hopelessly outclassed. It took cannon, organized supply lines, trained men, and the expertise of specialist professional officers to conduct a siege or fight a formal battle. The rebels had virtually none of these prerequisites in 1715 and suffered from a massive inferiority in them in 1745. By the early eighteenth century the state could almost always defeat its opponents in an armed confrontation.

Military force however, was prohibitively costly. No régime could afford the expense of relying solely on its armed forces to control and administer its population. The major weakness of the early modern state followed from this: in the end the state needed to have the co-operation of local élites. European society was still overwhelmingly hierarchical, with bonds of paternalism and deference running vertically up and down the social order, so that, if the state wished to control an area without directly using its armed forces, it had to have the co-operation of at least some of the area's 'nobility'. There was of course a price to pay for such collaboration. In return for their falling in with its desires, the state had to allow its local élites a substantial degree of autonomy. In practical terms it also meant that the collaborating elements had to be allowed to distribute the state's patronage and interpret its requirements in accord with local circumstances as they saw them. *De facto* the burgeoning ability of the early modern state to coerce its subjects was thereby limited to more socially acceptable proportions. In the round, power was held in check by exigency.

NOTES FOR CHAPTER 7

 * Professor of History, Aubern University, Alabama, USA.

 1 P. Jenkins, *The Making of a Ruling Class. The Glamorgan Gentry 1640–1790* (Oxford UP, 1983), pp. 5–6, 205–6, 213–15.

 2 N. Rogers, 'Popular protest in early Hanoverian London', *Past and Present*, 79 (1978), pp. 70–100.

 3 P. Collinson, 'A chosen people? The English church and the Reformation', *History Today* xxxvi (1986), pp. 9–14.

 4 J. P. Kenyon, *Revolution Principles. The Politics of Party 1689–1720* (Cambridge UP, 1977), pp. 64–82.

 5 R. A. Griffiths, *The Reign of King Henry VI* (London, 1981), pp. 169–71.

 6 For examples of which see: D. Stevenson, *The Scottish Revolution 1637–44* (Newton Abbott, 1973); T. W. Moody, F. X. Martin and F. J. Byrne (eds.), *A New History of Ireland*, (Oxford UP, 1976), pp. 289, 299–302.

 7 P. Hopkins, *Glencoe and the End of the Highland War* (Edinburgh, 1986), pp. 180, 191, 209, 267, 359.

 8 J. Wormald, 'Gunpowder, treason, and Scots', *Journal of British Studies*, xxiv (1985), pp. 141–68.

 9 J. Buckroyd, *Church and State in Scotland 1660–1681* (Edinburgh, 1980), pp. 27, 33–4, 93; P. W. J. Riley, *King William and the Scottish Politicians* (Edinburgh, 1979), pp. 53–5.

 10 P. W. J. Riley, *The Union of England and Scotland* (Manchester UP, 1978), pp. 330–4.

 11 Riley, *Scottish Politicians*, pp. 11–116.

 12 *Op. cit.*, pp. 131–8; Hopkins, *Glencoe*, p. 495. The Darien affair of 1698–1700 was a disastrous attempt by the Scottish Royal African Company to establish a Scottish colony on the isthmus of Darien in South America. It was a national project which seized the imagination of the political nation, who consequently invested heavily both emotionally and financially in it. William III and the English Parliament did not directly undermine the venture, but they withheld vital naval support and financial backing so that in due course the Spanish (with whom William was determined to stay on good terms because of the likelihood of war in Europe over the Spanish succession) forced the colony to surrender. As a result, the outraged Scottish public blamed William and the English for the loss of the colony and all the advantages they believed Scotland stood to gain by it.

 13 Ferguson, *Scotland's Relations with England: A Survey to 1707* (Edinburgh, 1977), pp. 197–213.

 14 *Op. cit.*, pp. 235, 246–52.

 15 *Op. cit.*, pp. 255–6, 267–8.

 16 *Op. cit.*, pp. 257, 265, 266.

 17 B. Lenman, 'A client society: Scotland between the '15 and the '45', in J. Black (ed.), *Britain in the Age of Walpole* (London, 1984), pp. 81–93.

 18 J. S. Shaw, *The Management of Scottish Society 1707–64* (Edinburgh, 1983) pp. 95–113.

 19 D. Szechi, 'The politics of "persecution": Scots Episcopalian toleration and the Harley ministry', in W. J. Sheils (ed.), *Toleration and Persecution. Studies in Church History*, xxi (1984), pp. 275–89. The Cameronians were originally the followers of Richard Cameron; fanatical Presbyterian separatists active in southwest Scotland between 1680 and 1687, who violently resisted Government attempts to impose an episcopalian church settlement. After the Revolution they rejoined the (now Presbyterian) Kirk, wherein they constituted the most inflexible and intolerant group on all issues relating to Presbyterian dogma. The imposition of the 1712 Toleration Act's 'Erastian' oath of loyalty on all Scottish clergymen accordingly triggered a secession by the heirs of this extremist group,

who withdrew from the regular Kirk to establish field conventicles in a schism which lingered on until 1718.

20 Shaw, *Scottish Society*, pp. 14–15.

21 D. Chandler, *Marlborough as Military Commander*, 2nd edn (London, 1979), pp. 123–50, 166–83, 205–7.

22 J. J. Murray, *George I, the Baltic and the Whig Split of 1717* (London, 1969), pp. 285–315; B. Lenman, *The Jacobite Risings in Britain 1689–1746* (London, 1980) pp. 189–94; F. J. McLynn, *France and the Jacobite Rising of 1745* (Edinburgh UP, 1981), pp. 80–1, 87, 175–204; Sir Charles Petrie, 'The Elibank Plot, 1752–3', *Transactions of the Royal Historical Society*, xiv (1931) 175–96.

23 R. C. Jarvis, *Collected Papers on the Jacobite Risings* (2 vols, Manchester UP, 1972), ii, p. 37.

24 D. Szechi, *Jacobitism and Tory Politics, 1710–14* (Edinburgh, 1984), pp. 85, 158–9.

25 B. Lenman, 'The Scottish episcopal clergy and the ideology of Jacobitism', in Cruickshanks, *Ideology and Conspiracy*, pp. 36–48.

26 G. Holmes, 'The Hamilton affair of 1711–12: a crisis in Anglo-Scottish relations', in C. Jones and D. L. Jones, (eds.), *Peers, Politics and Power: the House of Lords 1603–1911* (London, 1986), pp. 151–76.

27 Shaw, *Management of Scottish Society*, pp. 1–17; J. Cannon, *Aristocratic Century: the Peerage of Eighteenth Century England* (Cambridge UP, 1987), p. 31.

28 Shaw, *Management of Scottish Society*, pp. 8–10, 196–8; M. W. McCahill, 'The Scottish peerage and the House of Lords in the late eighteenth century', in Jones and Jones, *Peers, Politics and Power*, pp. 285, 288; Cannon, *Aristocratic Century*, pp. 87–8 incl. footnote 47.

29 McCahill, 'Scottish peerage', pp. 306–7.

30 D. Stevenson, *Alasdair MacColla and the Highland Problem in the 17th Century* (Edinburgh, 1980), pp. 16–17, 28–30, 274–7, 281, 297–9; G. P. Insh, *The Scottish Jacobite Movement* (London, 1952), pp. 158–64.

31 T. C. Smout, *A History of the Scottish People 1560–1830* (London, 1985), pp. 461, 477–8.

32 *Op. cit.*, pp. 452, 453–9, 460–4, 465, 468–9, 471–8, 482–3.

8

The Habsburg Monarchy and Bohemia, 1526–1848

R. J. W. EVANS*

The case-studies in this volume mostly involve a process of clear political incorporation: the absorption of a lesser entity, a 'province', into a larger, reasonably well-established and coherent corpus, or body politic.[1] Whatever the ramifications, there is a definite relationship of centre and periphery, conqueror and conquered, or patron and client. Austria's acquisition of Bohemia was markedly different. Although the long-term fruits of the process yield many points of comparison and cast light on the general issues raised elsewhere in the book, no one could have predicted which party would predominate over the other in 1526, when sovereignty over the lands of St Wenceslas passed by election to Ferdinand I of Habsburg.[2]

The beginnings of Habsburg rule in Bohemia

The kingdom of Bohemia formed one of the prime political and economic constituents of late medieval Europe. With its core territory of Bohemia proper, looking nationally and administratively to the capital city of Prague as its focus, and the associated lands of Moravia, Silesia and Lusatia, it possessed a population of some three million (more than lived in contemporary England) and extensive resources. These included the rich farmlands of the Elbe valley and the southern Moravian plain, Silesia's textiles and flourishing merchant communities, and, above all, the famous silver mines at such places as Iglau (Jihlava), Kuttenberg (Kutná Hora), and the new boom-township of Joachimsthal, which gave its name to the [Joachims]thaler or 'dollar'. Moreover, Bohemia was often felt to be the central region of the continent in a way which transcended her purely geographical location. A widely circulated sixteenth-century print depicts Europe as a queen with head in Iberia, arms in Italy and Jutland, and dress billowing out eastwards: if Spain represents her crown, Sicily and Denmark her orb and sceptre, Bohemia, symbolized by many-towered Prague, is her heart.

By contrast, the Habsburg patrimony in central Europe before 1526 consisted of a congeries of provinces, stretching irregularly from the Rhine to the Danube, none of them especially distinctive or influential. Several contained towns favoured as residences of the ruling family: Innsbruck, Linz, Vienna, Wiener

Neustadt and Graz. Young Ferdinand, who had just inherited these territories after considerable haggling with his elder brother, Charles V, was only in the initial stages of developing Vienna as his headquarters. That decision would soon be confirmed by the city's proximity to his new realms of Bohemia and Hungary, where Ferdinand was likewise elected in 1526. But even his simultaneous acquisition of part of Hungary left Bohemia distinctly wealthier than the rest of Ferdinand's lands; and neither those lands nor their young ruler were yet sustained by any other purpose, myth, or principle of government than the dynastic ambition of the house of Habsburg.

The events of 1526 did not anyway seem to call for novel prescriptions from the Habsburgs. Rather they looked like merely a fresh twist to Bohemia's two long-standing international relationships, with both of which the Austrian dynasty had also been concerned for generations. The first was the country's position inside the Holy Roman Empire, to which Bohemia still belonged, even though her native Přemyslid kings had long ago assured her complete autonomy. Membership of the Reich cut two ways constitutionally: Bohemia's residual vassalage, particularly in respect of a small but important piece of her western territory around Eger (Cheb), could be set against the king of Bohemia's status as senior imperial elector. Practically speaking, the implications of the settlement of a large number of Germans in Bohemia, forming a substantial proportion of burghers everywhere as well as a majority of the population in Silesia and Lusatia (which had only been joined with Bohemia and Moravia during the fourteenth century) were of far greater importance.

The extinction of the Přemyslids in 1306 inaugurated a period in which a second kind of international association achieved prominence: the union of crowns between Bohemia and neighbouring lands. Such unions had been successfully pursued, above all, by two dynasties. Beginning inside the Empire, the Luxemburg dynasty combined sovereignty over Germany with the kingship of Bohemia under the resplendent Emperor Charles IV (Emperor, 1346–78), and his feeble eldest son Wenceslas (Emperor, 1378–1400), and extended it to Hungary as well under the younger son Sigismund (Emperor, 1410–37), though only for a single year did the last manage to operate as effective ruler of all three realms. Outside the Empire the house of Jagiellon, whose roots lay in Poland (or, more accurately, in Lithuania, joined in a condominium with Poland from 1387), spread to secure the thrones of Hungary, then of Bohemia, combining the latter two after 1490 in the persons of Vladislav II and Louis II. The resultant links with Poland, where the main line of Jagiellons reigned until 1572, remained distant (although the descendants of the earlier Polish house of Piast continued to rule over parts of Silesia). The closer bond with Hungary evidently foreshadowed later developments.

As emperors for a time in the later thirteenth century, and uninterruptedly since 1437, the Habsburgs were an international dynasty in their own right, well used to operating in this milieu, and to including Bohemia in their calculations. Rudolf I (Emperor, 1273–91), the first Habsburg of European standing, built up the power of the family on his crushing defeat of the most prominent Přemyslid king of Bohemia, Otakar II, at the battle on the Marchfeld in 1278. He then promptly arranged a double wedding between his children and those of his Bohemian rival. When the male line of Přemyslids failed in 1306, Rudolf's grandson of the same name married the widow of Otakar's son and made good his claim as king of Bohemia: but for his sudden death the following year, the Habsburgs might then have established themselves permanently in Prague. They came equally close to this objective in the mid fifteenth century. Charles IV of Luxemburg married two of his daughters to the next generation of Habsburgs; his son Sigismund did the same, so that, in the absence of a male Luxemburg heir, Albert of Habsburg (Albert II; Emperor, 1438–9) ascended the throne of Bohemia in 1437 – as he would those of Germany and Hungary in 1438. Again the new ruler expired soon afterwards. So did his only son, Ladislav Posthumus, nominal king of Bohemia and Hungary between 1453 and 1457. Meanwhile, however, Albert's daughter married Casimir of Poland, father of Vladislav II, whose successful claim to Bohemia in 1471 thus rested on his Habsburg blood. In his turn Vladislav was responsible for the double matrimonial alliance with Emperor Maximilian I which, first mooted in 1491, finally took effect in 1521, when Archduke Ferdinand became brother-in-law to the ill-fated King Louis.

Such dense genealogical information is bewildering; but it is necessary in order to indicate the extent of Habsburg involvement in Bohemia before Louis perished at the hands of the Ottomans on the battlefield of Mohács. Ferdinand's formal bid for the vacant throne rested on grants by rulers of the kingdom stretching back to the early fourteenth century, as well as on the rights of his wife, Anna, which had been expressly confirmed by the diet, or estates, of Bohemia in 1510. The estates of the realm could retort that they had not officially approved Anna's marriage to Ferdinand although such approval had been stipulated by them as essential in 1510. But opposition to the Habsburg claim contained a large element of shadow-boxing. The only realistic rival candidates in 1526, the Polish king and the dukes of Bavaria, were half-hearted, readily warned off by imperial diplomacy and bought off by hand-outs to their supporters from the Habsburgs' south German bankers, re-enacting on a smaller scale the election of Charles V as Holy Roman Emperor seven years before. Ferdinand's offer to pay off the crown's debts to its chief citizens struck a similar chord. Besides, the need for firm kingship was reinforced by the recurrent threat of peasant disturbance and by the Turkish advance into Hungary, although Bohemia's lords had recently done much to permit the latter by their failure to rally in time to their late king's Mohács campaign.[3]

If the Bohemian political establishment faced a 'Hobson's choice', then the king whom it duly elected in October 1526 could hardly escape his manifest destiny. In a way, the precedents were attractive: the chance to revive the empire of Charles IV or Sigismund, or of his short-lived Habsburg ancestor, Albert. But the new ruler also inherited a major liability. As he crossed the border into Bohemia through the mid-winter snows, Ferdinand must have reflected uneasily that he was entering the very homeland of heresy – heresy which he was already engaged under oath to sustain. Bohemia's great expansion under Charles IV had itself nurtured the twin cankers of ecclesiastical abuse and German domination which had given rise to the Hussite revolt. Under the limp hand of Wenceslas it had fermented, especially at the newly founded Caroline University in Prague, around its professor, Jan Hus. Under Sigismund, it exploded into a virulent struggle for a purified national church controlled by laymen, and for its symbol of the chalice, or communion in both kinds (hence the designation 'Utraquism').

Against the odds, the heretic nation had triumphed, and with it Czech culture and a predominantly Czech aristocracy. But Bohemia paid a terrible price in terms of social, ethnic and regional tensions, and was left debilitated and internationally isolated. Like seventeenth-century England or nineteenth-century France, Bohemia became notorious as the most disordered polity and ungovernable people of the day: the sick heart of the continent, with unsteady beat.[4]

An uncertain overlordship (1526–1618)

Ferdinand I's qualities as ruler – his enterprise and ambition, firmness and method – are generally acknowledged. Historians have also tended to stress the significance of the fact that he came to Bohemia as a stranger. That argument is less persuasive. Certainly the Hussite legacy attached its own dimension of foreignness to those who were not 'Utraquist' and spoke no Czech. It was also important that Ferdinand was often absent from Bohemia in his Austrian (and Hungarian) lands. On the other hand, many native Bohemians were catholic and used German, like Ferdinand himself, who at least made sure that his sons should learn Czech. As to absentee government, the recent example of the Jagiellons showed that this regularly signified weak, rather than strong government. What mattered most was that the new Habsburg monarch aimed specifically to emulate the energetic *domestic* rulers of Bohemia's past – Charles IV, or the Hussite king, George of Poděbrady (or *mutatis mutandis* Matthias Corvinus of Hungary). Reform and reorganization were to run parallel in Bohemia and in the Austrian (and Hungarian) territories, where Ferdinand, born and bred in Spain, was similarly regarded for a long time as a stranger.[5]

The Habsburgs' policy during this first period of their governance of Bohemia thus aimed at a limited dominion in the country rather than full control over it. Faced by the distended expectations of many leaders in the Bohemian estates, whose financial and military support Ferdinand urgently needed, the king's task was to transform those whom he had already mobilized to support him in 1526 into a genuine court party. To further this objective, he employed various forms of patronage and inducement, above all the appointments to high office. Apart from certain court positions more ceremonial than substantial, these included specifically the posts of Grand Burgrave of Prague, Bohemia's senior royal lieutenant, and of Chancellor, the keeper of the seals and head of the day-to-day administration. Ferdinand had indeed promised to consult the estates before nominating individuals to such offices (all of them reserved for the nobility), but he found ways of limiting the force of that requirement, the more so in the case of the royal Chamber (*Kammer*), newly reconstituted in 1527 to manage crown finances. No less crucial to the objectives of Habsburg government were three kinds of major dissension which disconcerted the efforts of its opponents.

Immediately upon his accession Ferdinand had the opportunity to exploit inter-provincial rivalries. 'Inter-provincial', though, is hardly the *mot juste* for the severe historical tensions between, on one hand, the kingdom of Bohemia, and, on the other, the margravate of Moravia, together with that motley assemblage of semi-autonomous duchies loosely bound together under the description of Silesia, and the twin northerly margravates of Lower and Upper Lusatia. Bohemia sought to call the constitutional tune, but these other, so-called 'incorporated' regions, larger collectively in both area and population, objected strongly when the Bohemian estates pointedly failed to involve them in the electoral process. They forthwith declared their acceptance of Ferdinand and his descendants as hereditary rulers. The lands of St Wenceslas possessed remarkably little institutional cohesion. 'General', or common, diets were vigorously resisted outside Bohemia proper, as was the writ of the Chancellor, the only overall officer of state. Indeed the other provinces acknowledged the authority of their own Land Captain or *Landeshauptmann*, not that of the Grand Burgrave. Socially, the sole (albeit important) bond consisted in an equal and uniform noble status, such that individual nobles could move around freely and hold office anywhere, provided that they owned land in the province concerned. Intellectually, the dominant Bohemian culture, shaped by the Czech language in its Hussite manifestations, extended through much of Moravia, but hardly at all to Silesia or Lusatia. More alarming was the wide divergence in their external concerns, with Moravia always more inclined to look south and east (Matthias Corvinus of Hungary had ruled Moravia as margrave in the later fifteenth century), whilst Silesia and Lusatia (though they too belonged among Matthias's conquests) were preoccupied by relations with the Holy Roman Empire as well as (at times) with Poland.[6]

This clash between Bohemia's claim to hegemony and the separatist response of the incorporated lands proved, time and again, to be at least as effective as enemies from without in frustrating the best efforts of its patriots. It allowed the king to employ two alternating strategies. He could either use Bohemia to press for tighter control throughout the territories (as with the chamber administration of 1527), or else favour the other provinces as a lever against Bohemia (as over regulation of the succession). But within each body of provincial estates he enjoyed hardly less scope, since the divisions everywhere between privileged corporations of lords, knights and burghers of the royal towns became ever more pronounced in the course of the sixteenth century. In part such divisions were the fruit of Hussite disorders, especially the feuding of over-mighty barons among themselves and with the rest of society (and Ferdinand made valuable capital out of his dismissal in 1530 of the unpopular Grand Burgrave, Zdeněk Lev of Rožmitál).[7] Increasingly, however, these tensions resulted from new rivalries, particularly over shares in buoyant sectors of the economy like brewing, fish-farming, and the wool trade. Meetings of the Bohemian and other diets were a focus for resistance to the demands of the crown, but they proved to be an equal focus for the disunity of the opposition.

The third and most fundamental area of conflict surrounded religion. Fifteenth-century struggles had left large pockets of catholic survival, an ill-defined and turbid Utraquist mainstream dominated by lay, not to say worldly, influences, alongside communities of radical sectaries repeatedly outlawed, though in practice usually tolerated. Instead of simplifying this picture, the Protestant Reformation – which of course acknowledged a debt to the Hussite impulse – only complicated it. It introduced further confessional subdivisions and meshed in intricate ways with the existing lines of political fracture.[8] Most German-speakers soon gravitated towards Lutheran beliefs propagated from the Empire. Many Utraquists did the same, though more guardedly. Meanwhile, the chief sect, the Unity of Bohemian Brethren, became increasingly Calvinist, while others espoused Anabaptist and similar tenets. Ferdinand could not stem this tide: the continuing catholic loyalties of his house left him dangerously isolated. Yet his position offered certain advantages. He stood as a rallying-point for the orthodox remnant, which included some powerful noble families. This orthodoxy would prove an attraction to conservative Utraquists, who feared the collapse of all ecclesiastical authority. Most importantly, he offered an obstacle to effective organization by protestant groups. Operating with considerable pragmatism, he awaited the chance to exploit the unbridled dissensions of his subjects.

That chance came in 1546–7 with the outbreak of the Schmalkaldic War in Germany and Ferdinand's call for the country to assist his brother, Charles V. However fortuitous the circumstances it was entirely predictable not only that more extreme Protestants in Bohemia would take the side of their co-religionists in the Empire, but that the bulk of the estates should hesitate to follow them. By the time a majority had decided to resist the king, the issue was settled in Germany without them, and Ferdinand could retaliate. He instituted tougher measures to discipline the towns, which were the ringleaders of the opposition, and to crush the sects. He established a new court of appeal for all the Bohemian lands. Over the next years he introduced the Jesuit order and revived the archbishopric of Prague, defunct since Hussite times. Yet these policies were not pressed very far or consistently; they still fell far short of lasting confrontation. In Moravia and Silesia, which had remained broadly loyal, liberties were infringed even less.[9]

The events of 1546–7 possess a further significance for our purposes. It was the first occasion when the wider context of Habsburg politics could be turned to advantage in Bohemia. Previously that context – the costly and disruptive Turkish wars, the obligatory catholic stance (preventing the launch of some kind of national church), the abortive experiment of general diets – had been, on balance, a drawback. Now close co-operation bore fruit, a process confirmed in 1556 (formally in 1558) when Ferdinand succeeded to his brother Charles V's title. At the same time, his 'Austrian' institutions, the Court Chamber (*Hofkammer*), Aulic Council (*Hofrat*) and newly established War Council, became fully-fledged imperial ones. Henceforth Ferdinand enjoyed greater authority to introduce uniform models of government, especially to tighten the financial grip on Bohemia, which yielded over half his revenue, and to employ foreign experts in the Chamber there. Again, however, we must beware of exaggeration. Bohemia's administration was still quite distinct and, despite the occasional royal protégé, Florian Griespeck for example, who made his career there, the prerequisite of naturalization by the estates (*inkolát*) remained difficult to evade. Moreover – a great contrast with the future, as we shall see – practically no Bohemians found advancement in the other direction, across the Austrian border.

By the time of his death in 1564, Ferdinand I's everyday involvement in Bohemia had anyway greatly diminished. From 1548, he installed his second son Ferdinand as a regent governor (*Statthalter*). When the latter's elder brother Maximilian (Maximilian II as Emperor) succeeded, he restored direct rule and spent long periods in Prague. But Maximilian was less resolute and more tolerant than his father. His 12-year reign forms essentially an interlude, during which the estates recovered their nerve and developed a modicum of solidarity. After much hard bargaining in 1575, they extracted from the king a verbal promise of security for protestant worship, which they had subsumed under the awkward umbrella of a single *Confessio Bohemica*.[10] But their opposition was muted, not least because service at the court of the cultivated, opulent, and generous Maximilian afforded many attractions.

With the advent of Rudolf II, this aspect of Habsburg-Bohemian relations was vastly enhanced. From 1583 Rudolf, alone among the sovereigns of his dynasty, made Prague his permanent residence. In so doing he reanimated Charles IV's conception of Bohemia as the focus for the government of the whole Holy Roman Empire, and simultaneously fulfilled one of the main demands of the local estates. Some administrative overlap between the ruler's domestic and his broader activities was bound to result, but it seems to have stayed irregular and limited, given Rudolf's touchy personality and fitful, sometimes wayward, conduct of business. Nor did the king, ensconced in his castle on the Hradschin, often intervene directly in Bohemian politics before the end of the century. The dominant aristocratic clans of Rožmberk, Pernštýn, Hradec, and the like, continued to hold sway over public office, and an uneasy religious truce lived on. Meanwhile the cultural magnetism of the Rudolfine entourage helped to accomplish what the artistic and literary patronage of earlier Habsburgs had already furthered; the reintegration of Bohemia's nobility and burghers into the world of the European Renaissance and international humanism, from which the aftermath of the Hussite wars had long largely excluded them.[11]

After 1600, however, a wider crisis of Habsburg affairs entailed correspondingly grave consequences for the Bohemian lands. In Germany, there was religious polarization and constitutional breakdown. In Hungary, unreal plans for the assertion of royal power coincided with another devastating war against the Turks. These problems, along with the *Bruderzwist* or fraternal feud between Rudolf and his next of kin, disturbed the political balance inside Bohemia. So also did the inception of a semi-official campaign of domestic counter-reformation to which the ailing king lent partial support. Protestant majorities among the various estates were pitched first into opposition. Then, as the bitter struggle between Rudolf and his brother Matthias split the Habsburg camp, they climbed into the saddle. They insisted on written guarantees of religious equality and of full participation in government, those for Bohemia proper being enshrined in the famous 'Letter of Majesty' conceded by the embattled Rudolf in 1609.[12]

What made possible the dramatic discomfiture of the dynasty in the early years of the seventeenth century was the remarkable success of a movement of confederacy among the territories of the Austrian Habsburgs. Once the Bohemian lands had become involved in the broader destiny of Rudolf's empire, it made obvious sense to seek support beyond their borders, and to ally with malcontents in Hungary and Austria too. The outcome was an ambitious and unique experiment in self-government by the estates on an international scale which both offered a genuine alternative to Habsburg rule and incorporated some markedly progressive constitutional features. Yet the experiment was fraught with problems from the start. Firstly, the two most important oppositional groups did not see eye to eye. A nadir in relations between Bohemian and Moravian Protestants was reached in 1608. They almost came to blows over Prague's unwillingness to rally to the side of Matthias, and Moravia would return the disfavour in 1618. Besides, it remained extremely difficult for the estates, which (in a real sense and in contrast to the ruler) *embodied* the separateness of different parts of the crown, to concert their activities in time of need. Lastly, there were pointed disagreements, even among the newly appointed official 'defenders' of the protestant cause, about how far disloyalty to the dynasty could or should go.[13]

The Habsburgs did nothing to accommodate these doubts, and matters came to a head rapidly after Rudolf's death in 1612. Matthias, anxious to exorcise his brother's spirit and chasten a rebellious capital, withdrew his court back to Vienna. Then openly partisan actions by the catholic lieutenants, entrusted with royal government in his absence, provoked the defenestration of two of them from the windows of the Hradschin on 23 May 1618, a messy and inefficient procedure full of Hussite symbolism. This response by Bohemia's protestant estates was nevertheless a reluctant one, lacking in real Hussite resonance: not a year earlier, they had accepted without serious protest the notorious counter-reformer, Ferdinand of Styria, as heir to his cousin Matthias. They did not initially seek to break the ties with the Habsburgs completely, even with an army in the field to lend force to their demands. Nor could their behaviour be construed as a Czech patriotic outburst – after all, the victims, Jaroslav Martinic and Vilém Slavata, were more authentically 'old-Bohemian' than several of their accusers. The rebels were now the first to invoke the *casus foederis* with their confederates abroad and look to help from Germany as well. The events of 1546–7 were about to be replayed in reverse.

Happily the events of the Bohemian Revolt, prelude to the Thirty Years War, are reasonably well known, for there would not be space to summarize their intricacies here.[14] The crucial constitutional dates which concern us here all lie during 1619 and they need to be grasped in their sequence. The death of Matthias on 20 March foreclosed the last chance of compromise. The confederal programme was eventually agreed with Moravia and Silesia on 31 July. Ferdinand was deposed on 19 August, and the elective principle was unilaterally reasserted in favour of Frederick of the Palatinate a week later (just two days before Ferdinand was chosen as emperor). The incompetence of the new monarch, the resulting religious and political frictions, and the failure of Protestant alliances then combined with the effectiveness of a Habsburg fifth column and the very un-Hussite passivity of the population at large to encompass the defeat of the insurrection. We are left to ponder the dramatic irony of Bohemia's international relationships in these years. The rebels denied her link with the Holy Roman Empire in order to facilitate Ferdinand's deposition and Frederick's kingship. Yet they hoped to rely on that same link for support, although most of Germany's backing actually went, along with the imperial crown, to the Habsburgs. The rebels revived the medieval arrangement of a loose union of thrones; but now as a union for dethronement instead.

Bohemian 'provincialization', 1620–1740

The defeat of the forces of revolt on the afternoon of 8 November 1620 upon a featureless tableland called the White Mountain outside the gates of Prague turned into a catastrophe with the precipitate flight of its leaders. It abruptly heralded the next phase in Habsburg relations with Bohemia, a phase which lasted exactly 120 years. Now, for the first time, royal powers could be unequivocally asserted over the estates, and the restored Ferdinand II lost no time in doing so, even while the seismic waves of European disturbance were spreading out from the Bohemian epicentre. For a few years after his comprehensive success the king could wield the authority of a conqueror; and his decisions therefore afford an important insight into the priorities of the dynasty in the crown of St Wenceslas. Totally persuaded that such a military coup must betoken the hand of God, Ferdinand and his advisers sought above all to make Bohemia safe for Catholicism.[15]

Religious enactments came first and last in those years. Hardly had the dust settled than the most pernicious heretics were forced to leave the country. It is instructive that these included not only Calvinist preachers, many of whom had indeed agitated strongly in the heat of confrontation, but also the harmless communities of Moravian Anabaptists, who practised unqualified pacifism.[16] By the end of the 1620s, the government had proceeded by stages to a complete abrogation of the 'Letter of Majesty'. All protestant lords and burghers in Bohemia and Moravia, however loyal their record, had to tread the path of exile, while all peasants faced forced conversion. Meanwhile the catholic prelates regained their rank as the first estate of the realm, 200 years after the Hussites had humbled them. Ecclesiastical lands were reclaimed, or in lieu of that a financial settlement was stipulated. New churches and monasteries began to spring up and the Jesuits laid claim to a dominant rôle in the purified educational system.

In all this, of course, the régime identified heresy as the badge of rebellion, and it took equally firm steps to enforce political obedience in the future. The purely retributive measures were severe enough: not so much the execution of 27 ringleaders (which, however often invoked in Habsburg demonologies, appears mild by the standards of, say, Tudor England) as the widespread confiscation, or at least sequestration, of lands owned by persons implicated, however slightly, in oppositional activity. There followed a package of fundamental changes in which the intimidated estates perforce acquiesced. The hereditary succession of the house of Habsburg was confirmed. The Bohemian diet lost its right to initiate legislation. New appeals procedures strengthened the hand of the sovereign in the judiciary. Officers of the crown became servants of the king, answerable to him by oath and subject to regular confirmation in post. The monarch also gained control over the procedure of naturalization (*inkolát*) which helped him to manipulate the administration further. Finally, and again in the interests of administrative convenience, the German language was declared of equal official status with Czech, a final repudiation of Hussite linguistic priorities which had been reaffirmed as recently as at the diet of 1615.[17]

These enactments, although cast in the traditional mould of a revised land ordinance (the *Verneuerte Landesordnung* of 1627), signified a constitutional revolution, to accompany the confessional revolution as counter-reformation took hold and the social revolution in which over 50 per cent of landed wealth changed hands. Moreover the whole operation of the country's senior executive under the Chancellor now followed the court to Vienna, leaving a Lieutenancy

Council, which perpetuated the hated institution of 1618, to hold the fort on the Hradschin for a largely absent ruler. Yet the result – despite another of those hoary legends about the Habsburgs – was no kind of absolutism. In part the very distraction of the dynasty elsewhere limited the effect of its policies in Bohemia. Even in the 1620s much had to be left to a clique of adventurers headed by the Moravian aristocrat, Karl Liechtenstein. These individuals took time off to feather their own nests (Vienna spent decades in a largely abortive attempt to divest Liechtenstein's heirs of some of his ill-gotten gains). Then the programme was interrupted by the misfortunes of war. Swedes, Saxons and plenty of exiled natives swarmed into the country in the early 1630s. The Swedes returned to reoccupy many areas throughout the 1640s. After the Westphalian settlement, another disability slowly made itself felt. The supply of male members of the dynasty, and therefore of potential royal administrators, declined almost as disastrously as in the case of the Spanish branch of the Habsburgs. By the mid 1660s, the young Emperor Leopold I had to shoulder alone a whole range of burdens, from resisting France in the Rhineland to imposing his will upon malcontents in Hungary.

In all empires, of course, provincial mice will sometimes play. A larger reason for the survival in practice of much of Bohemia's autonomy after 1620 lay in the character of the political élite. This was a very limited group of powerful landed families, which held the reins of domestic authority in church as in state. Some of these families were indeed creatures of the ruler, newly introduced from abroad. Others, like the Dietrichsteins and Liechtensteins, Althans and Harrachs, played a bridging rôle, with some existing pedigree inside the Bohemian lands to set against their Austrian ancestry. Yet the names of the rest still sounded a roll-call of noted native clans: Martinic and Slavata (particularly prominent), Lobkowitz and Czernin, Kinsky and Sternberg, Kolowrat, Nostitz, Schlick. . . . But for the hubris of Wallenstein and his Czech friends, whose vastly swollen possessions suffered confiscation in the 1630s, the preponderance of traditional families would have been still greater. As it was, they continued to call the tune. Their willingness to espouse the essential aims of the Habsburgs and thereby to purge the protestant, even perhaps insurrectionary, skeletons from many an ancestral cupboard, reaped a rich reward from conservative and preoccupied emperors, grateful to them and their clients for the dutiful and, at times, heroic defence of the country against invasions in the 1630s and 1640s.[18]

In the hands of this 'old-new' oligarchy, Bohemia's noble estates preserved much of their influence. Diets continued to meet, annually as a rule, and soon recovered the right to make modest representations as well as to argue the toss with their ruler. The chief officials of the king, sitting on the Lieutenancy Council, remained land officers too and were drawn almost exclusively from ancient Bohemian clans. Their functions as transmitters and often modifiers of the royal will gained institutional underpinning from 1714, when a 'National Committee' (*Landesausschuss, Zemský výbor*) was established under the Grand Burgrave to co-ordinate the estates' activities. Below them, the local administrative structure survived the *Verneuerte Landesordnung* untouched, much of it serviced by lesser nobles and urban patricians. So also did all other privileges of the Bohemian nation not specifically revoked in 1627.

The powers of the estates over taxation, one area of vital concern to the

Habsburgs, actually grew. The Thirty Years War brought devastation, depopulation and stagnation unique in Bohemia's history. Yet, when the conflict gave way to one of her longest eras of peace and security at home, the country remained the dynasty's richest resource, supplying well over 50 per cent of the revenue from direct taxation throughout the seventeenth century. The estates jealously guarded their right not only to give formal approval for, but also to assess and collect, ever greater sums. These were usually subdivided in the ratio of five parts from Bohemia proper, three from Silesia, and two from Moravia.[19] War ruined the towns for generations, thus both depriving the crown of the opportunity to play them off against the aristocracy, and leaving the latter's demesne farming as the only prosperous sector of the economy, especially since the tax burden associated with demesne farming could be largely shifted onto the shoulders of the peasantry. When, after 1700, new manufactures began to confirm Bohemia's economic leadership within the Habsburg lands, the wealthiest nobles and monasteries were first to develop them.[20]

In two further respects Bohemia, while being ruled in far from absolute fashion after 1620, could be held in tolerably well-balanced loyalty to the Habsburgs. Provincial particularities diminished hardly at all. With a total disregard for the unity of the crown, the Lusatias were entirely abandoned – ceded to the Lutheran prince of Saxony in the militant 1620s without even a battle! In Silesia the government gained ground in some duchies, but had to allow certain rights to Protestants after 1648 and again after 1707. The installation of a few great Bohemian families as local rulers in parts of Silesia did something to strengthen the Habsburgs' grip. So did the wider powers now wielded through all the provinces by the Chancery and the Court of Appeal. By the same token, Moravians (rather less rebellious in 1618–20, rather less harshly treated by their own *Verneuerte Landesordnung* of 1628) tended more than ever to look now to Vienna for their lead, less than ever to make common cause with any Bohemian discontent.

What politics kept divided, culture did a little to unite. Czech language and Czech literature notoriously suffered, even though this was because of neglect rather than active persecution. They did not, however, disappear from public life overnight. The Czech language was retained, for instance, at formal sessions of the diet, and the loss of predominantly German Lusatia actually furnished some slight compensation. Yet *Bohemian* culture, mainly Latinate or visual, flourished, a more harmonious and original achievement than its pre-1620 counterpart. As at that time, it fed on growing international contacts, now redirected towards the sources of catholic Baroque. And while it came to incorporate some distinctly patriotic features significant for the future, its basically cosmopolitan character allowed educated and adaptable Bohemians easy *entrée* into a broader Austrian world.[21]

Here there appeared the crucial corollary of the first stage of Bohemia's 'provincialization': an export of individuals and influence. As the lands of St Wenceslas became more closely attached to the rest of the monarchy, especially to its thriving metropolis of Vienna, so selected Bohemians fitted themselves for a wider rôle. The first example, grand but idiosyncratic, is Albrecht von Waldstein, whose meteoric rise from an impoverished branch of senior Czech nobility to become generalissimo of the imperialist armies and duke of Friedland, Sagan and Mecklenburg needs no introduction. Wallensteins's fall yielded a cautionary moral, and the fact that over-mighty Bohemian commanders could be as suspect as Bohemian Protestants was not lost on seventeenth-century Habsburg rulers. Yet it did not hinder the advance of a series of confidants from the same quarter, mostly from old-established families. They were joined by the amphibious Austro-Moravian Liechtensteins and Dietrichsteins, whose ascendancy – notwithstanding the foibles of Karl Liechtenstein – also dates back to the same period.[22]

The next clan to be drawn into the inner circle were the Lobkowitzes. Zdeněk Vojtěch Lobkowitz, an essential prop to Ferdinand II's ambitions for Bohemia both before 1618 and after 1620, remained merely a national figure, and a slightly disgruntled one by the end. However, his son, Wenzel Eusebius, became President of the War Council, and then chief minister to Leopold I in the years around 1670. Lobkowitz, who as duke of Sagan even earned himself one of Wallenstein's titles, likewise fell into disgrace before his death. Yet his successors retained a foothold in the Viennese corridors of power, as did several Waldsteins who served in the entourage of Leopold as foreign diplomats. One of that Emperor's most intimate friends was Humprecht Jan Czernin. Leopold's correspondence with him reveals how quickly Habsburg memories of Bohemian rebelliousness (which had cost one Czernin his head) could be replaced by a bond of profound trust, while still allowing occasional scope for persiflage.[23]

The integration of Bohemians in Vienna was much helped by the presence there of the Chancellery, which both directed administration and worked to harmonize legal procedures (contrast the continued separateness of Hungarian courts, or of Scottish ones within Great Britain). In the decades after 1683 four members of the Kinsky family occupied the post of Bohemian Chancellor. The first of them, Franz Ulrich, also served as an outstanding diplomat at the Nijmegen peace negotiations, and then in Germany, before acting effectively as foreign minister during the 1690s. A Moravian aristocrat, Dominik Andreas Kaunitz, succeeded him in this role and became the first Czech to head the Imperial Court Chancellery (*Reichshofkanzlei*). A clutch of other Bohemian ambassadors, like Karl Ferdinand Waldstein and his son Karl Ernst, Georg Adam Martinitz, and Johann Wenzel Gallas, later Viceroy of Naples, vied for prominence with Bohemian soldiers, of whom perhaps the most famous was Kaspar Kaplíř, commander of Vienna during the siege of 1683.

Such men, sharing a community of interest, came to form something like a 'party', and lent a decisive new impulse to the existing triangular relationship between the Habsburgs, Bohemia and the Holy Roman Empire. Bohemia still belonged formally within the Reich. From 1708 she even regained her voice at the imperial diet where her envoy actually represented the Austrian lands too.[24] Yet her spokesmen at court from Lobkowitz on (perhaps the same had been true earlier in the century with Wallenstein) tended to be at odds with the German priorities of much Habsburg policy. They tended, for example, to look to alliance with France instead – this was the initiative which unseated Lobkowitz in 1674. The other prong of their campaign pointed south-east. As the Turkish threat receded, the resentment of Bohemians hardened towards the privileged position of Hungary within the monarchy. They stood at the forefront of attempts to administer to the Magyars some of their own 1620s medicine. Lobkowitz played an important advisory part in the assault on Hungary's liberties after 1670 just as Kinsky did in the acquisition of Transylvania as a separate province during the 1690s.

After 1700 the great expansion of Austria might have seemed propitious for the further advancement of Bohemian interests within it. Yet the reverse proved to be the case. Emperor Charles VI's favours were bestowed elsewhere; career opportunities at his court were afforded rather to Spaniards, Italians and Germans. Hungary fought the Habsburgs to a stalemate by 1711 and the comparative autonomy of her estates' administration in Pressburg clearly trumped that of the *Landesausschuss* in Prague. At home, the maintenance of empire demanded ever greater financial sacrifices. Bohemia found herself still bearing 50 per cent of the tax burden. This proportion rose still higher by the 1730s although, precisely because of the military triumphs under Prince Eugen, there appeared to be no direct threat to her. Moreover, extraordinary war taxation, levied on all, undermined the traditional exemption of nobility and clergy in respect of their own demesnes. Meanwhile new excise taxes could bypass supervision by the estates altogether. At the same time direct government interference in other spheres grew, notably through its first halting steps to aid a peasantry which oppression rendered increasingly rebellious. Such frustrations and sense of neglect coincided with the exuberant patriotic culture of the Bohemian High Baroque, symbolized by ostentatious veneration of two national saints, ancient and modern: Wenceslas and John Nepomuk. In the embarrassing absence of a male heir, the Habsburgs' future was ostensibly secured for Charles's daughter, Maria Theresa, by the Pragmatic Sanction, which the Bohemian lands acknowledged in 1720. Yet contemporaries vaguely realized that other options might be available.[25]

The age of absolutism

The nine years from 1740 to 1749 form a pale, but in some ways uncanny, reflection of those from 1618 to 1627. Again there was disloyalty and retribution, mainly in the guise of a tough reform programme. Again there was a 'winter king', but this time his arrival preceded the defection from Habsburg rule. Again an important religious dimension came into play, now not so much domestically (though Maria Theresa wanted Prague's Jews, the only non-Catholics still tolerated, to be scapegoats), as in the international confrontation with Prussia, which confirmed the need for a new brand of Catholicism. Again Moravia, and perforce Silesia, acted quite independently of Bohemia. Again the crown suffered the amputation of one of its limbs. And again the ensuing wars ravaged the country intermittently for over two decades.

On the death of Charles VI, Frederick II immediately asserted Prussia's very sketchy genealogical claims to Silesia. With his encouragement, the Bavarian Elector, Charles Albert, presented shortly afterwards a claim to the rest of the Bohemian lands. Hardly more convincing than Frederick II's, it was founded on an interpretation of marriage treaties entered into two centuries earlier by Ferdinand I.[26] The Bavarian challenge, while it may remind us of 1526, involved a curious reversal of sides since 1620. Few, if any, of Maria Theresa's subjects had actively plotted with the enemy. Nevertheless many members of the estates kept their powder dry: the diet session which approved the Pragmatic Sanction had been attended by only 25 lords and 18 knights. When Charles Albert reached Prague in late 1741 a clear majority of office-holders, clergy and towns, and a narrow majority of the whole nobility, offered homage to him as King Charles III of Bohemia. Their pressure on him to reside in the country and to guarantee all privileges and traditions of the Bohemian nation indicates the (perhaps contradictory?) nature of dissatisfaction with the old régime. Meanwhile in Silesia, where Protestants still constituted a majority in many areas, willingness to see the back of the Habsburgs was yet more manifest.[27]

The fortunes of war soon changed. In a little over a year, Maria Theresa's armies recaptured all Bohemia and Moravia, but only the southern tip of Silesia. Exactions by the Bavarians' French allies alienated domestic opinion and the next invasion in 1744–5 enjoyed no local support. When hostilities ended for a time in 1748, Maria Theresa exacted her revenge. Although any principle of 'Austrian clemency' is as much a figment of historians' imagination as the blacker legends of Habsburg cruelty, the reckoning proved in this case to be remarkably mild and strictly practical. In the long run, the loss of Silesia was to have incalculable consequences both for the monarchy and for the rest of the Bohemian lands, where, among other things, it confirmed Czech speakers as a clear majority of the population. In the short run, however, the need was for a brisk reform programme to emulate and, if possible, surpass the Prussian state.

Thus was inaugurated the second and more intense stage of Bohemia's incorporation into the Habsburg monarchy. From 1749 the Empress rapidly combined the Bohemian Chancellery with the existing Austrian one, and established a single Supreme Court in Vienna. She reorganized local government and formalized the liability of nobles and church to pay direct taxes. Participation by the estates in administration was correspondingly reduced. Under Joseph II it ceased altogether for a time. Yet the personnel at the top remained much the same as before. Individual aristocrats from old-established families, anxious to make amends, manned senior positions in Bohemia as if nothing had happened. One example is provided by the career of Philipp Kolowrat, the acting head of the régime in Prague under the Bavarians. He then served as Grand Burgrave from 1748 until his death in 1771. Moravian lords, who had preserved a scrupulous loyalty during the early 1740s, co-operated still more readily.[28]

After the interruption of the Seven Years War, the modernization of the Habsburg lands accelerated. To institutional changes were added economic and cultural ones. Under the paternal stimulus of government, manufactures expanded rapidly and new agrarian techniques took root. Both developments were concentrated in Bohemia. Mass textile production dates from this period, especially in the districts north-west and north-east of Prague and at Brünn (Brno) in Moravia, where a total of nearly 200 000 workers was employed by 1780. There, too, experiments in land tenure, crops and cropping methods found most support.[29] At the same time, a transformation began in relations between church and state as the régime sought to utilize ecclesiastical resources more efficiently, inculcate rational, unprejudiced attitudes and simpler forms of observance among the clergy, and take control of the educational system. Again Bohemia was the crucible for such endeavours, as in the work of the priest-pedagogue, Ferdinand Kindermann. They culminated in the patents issued by

Joseph II after his accession in 1780 which abolished serfdom and granted religious toleration.

Bohemia and Moravia thus became the twin heartlands – distinct, but developing in parallel – of the movement known to historians, from its radical Habsburg protagonist, as 'Josephinism'. They provided the Emperor (as we shall see) with his leading policy-makers. They also gave him some of his closest personal friends such as Count Friedrich Nostitz or Prince Johann Karl Dietrichstein. They evolved a symbiosis of loyalty with enlightened patriotism which proved fruitful for generating moderately progressive ideas, identified with the country. Aristocrats old and new – Franz Anton Nostitz, brother of Friedrich, a long-serving Grand Burgrave and lavish patron, is a striking example – presided over a flowering of talented commoners, particularly around the Society (later Academy) of Sciences, founded during the 1770s, and the freemasonic lodges: Stepling, Dobner, Pelzl, Seibt, Born, Dobrovský. . . . Even society at large was stirred by such gestures as Joseph's handling the plough himself on a Moravian peasant plot, and the widespread admiration for the Emperor-Liberator acquired the status of a national cult.[30]

Not that tensions, sometimes grave ones, were absent. One of the catalysts for change in the 1770s was old-fashioned peasant revolt and confessional strife. The excesses of reform in the 1780s, together with the harshness of Joseph's manner, alienated not a few supporters as well as conservatives. Then the coming of the French Revolution was a sobering experience for the government and it stimulated certain kinds of opposition. Yet discontent proved fairly easy to contain after the Emperor's death in 1790. There were hardly any 'Jacobins' in Bohemia, even if the radical Viennese clubs numbered a few Bohemian members in their ranks. The authorities were able to forestall any serious reaction with timely limited concessions to the resurgent estates. In the period of wars against Napoleon, Bohemia repeated her conduct during the anti-French coalition exactly a century previously and gave no real hint of dissent or independence of action.[31]

The decades after 1815 represent for our purposes an epilogue, the last phase of the Austrian *ancien régime*, the last stage in the subordination of Bohemia to overall Habsburg purposes. Maria Theresa's institutional structure survived intact, with the United Chancellery in Vienna transmitting the imperial will to provincial authorities (*Gubernia*) on Prague's Hradschin and in Brünn, presided over by officials who still bore the time-honoured titles of Grand Burgrave in Bohemia, and *Landeshauptmann* in Moravia and rump Silesia. Beneath the surface, it is true, things were altering. Considerable material advance characterized these years, with the introduction of steam-power in factories and communications and the rise of new agrarian staples like sugar-beet. So too did intellectual advance as the Slav vanguard of a Germanized regional culture began to reorientate itself and its new national institutions into openly Czech channels. For the present, however, the mutation remained discreet, genteel and at least semi-official, supervised by members of the great historic families, above all by another Kolowrat, Franz Anton, Grand Burgrave between 1809 and 1825, by his successor until 1843, Karel Chotek, and in Moravia by Anton Friedrich Mittrowsky.

Yet if Bohemia had come to form a mere province of Austria, Austria was now governed to a remarkable degree by that some oligarchy from Bohemia. The process of takeover had palpably quickened since the 1740s, drawing upon and feeding the notable ideological understanding reached between the dynasty and its chief supporters there. One of them, Wenzel Anton Kaunitz, grandson of Dominik Andreas, occupied for 40 years a pre-eminent position in both the foreign and domestic affairs of the monarchy. On the international stage, Kaunitz clearly inherited the mantle of the 'Bohemian party'. His most celebrated coup was the revival, in the early 1750s, of a French alliance at the expense of reconciliation in the Holy Roman Empire. In other ways too, such as the proposed swap of the Austrian Netherlands for Bavaria, he proved himself ready to ride roughshod over imperial traditions. From 1760 he also operated increasingly as a senior bureaucrat, with a leading voice in the new State Council (*Staatsrat*). As Councillor, this exquisite salon politician pursued papal pretensions and the ecclesiastical establishment with all the tenacity of a born-again Hussite, while renewing the attack on Hungarian privileges, at first covertly, but later in harness with the aggressive Joseph.[32]

Kaunitz's chief rival during his rise to power was a Silesian aristocrat, Friedrich Wilhelm Haugwitz, the instigator of the whole programme of administrative reform which had as its cornerstone the union of the Bohemian and Austrian Chancelleries. At the head of that combined institution during its four initial and most vigorous decades stood a succession of Haugwitz's fellow-countrymen: Joseph Chotek in the 1750s, then his brother Rudolf, then Heinrich Cajetan Blümegen between 1771 and 1782 and Leopold Kolowrat (son of Philipp) between 1782 and 1796. Meanwhile Kaunitz shared control of the State Council with a further Bohemian count, Karl Hatzfeld, who served as its chairman from 1771 to 1793. Hatzfeld had previously been President of the Imperial Court Chamber, the Austrian treasury, a job in which he was followed for no less than 25 years by the indefatigable Kolowrat (who later managed to combine it with being Chancellor).

Wherever we look in the Austrian government of this period we find Bohemians.[33] Even the highest dignity of the Reich in Vienna, the post of Imperial Vice-Chancellor, had passed to them, in the person of Count, later Prince, Rudolf Colloredo, who served over half a century in the office before being succeeded by his son Franz. Admittedly the Imperial Chancellery fell into deepening shadow, upstaged by Kaunitz, and some Dietrichsteins, Liechtensteins, Wrbnas and the like occupied largely ceremonial positions at court. But most of these Habsburg servants were very far from holding sinecures. In the area of church reform, for example, leading Josephinists threw themselves into a bruising conflict with the clerical hierarchy. Franz von Heinke, son of a customs official in Prague, was a leading Erastian and scourge of the traditionalists, whilst Franz Karl Kresl von Qualtenberg moved from the Bohemian administration to be the Emperor's right-hand man in ecclesiastical and educational affairs. Even Stephan Rautenstrauch, Abbot of Břevnov, just outside Prague, the country's most important Benedictine monastery, lent his full support.[34] In the army too, some of the most enterprising officers came from the Bohemian lands, notably Franz Josef Kinsky, co-founder of the Society of Sciences in Prague and an educationalist who instituted the teaching of Czech in the Military Academy established by him at Wiener Neustadt.

After 1792, as reform from above subsided into reaction under Emperor Francis, the bureaucracy continued to expand and a broader army of Bohemians manned posts throughout Austria, often sustaining aspects of enlightened practice at the same time. Two divergent instances are both typical (but atypical in that, much later, those involved wrote down their experiences). Karl Friedrich Kübeck, son of an artisan at Iglau, who gained a good progressive education in Vienna, enjoyed rapid advancement in central government whilst the ultramontane Catholic, Ignaz Beidtel, again from an impoverished Moravian background, served mainly in the province while gaining his encyclopaedic, jaundiced and highly critical insights into the whole system.[35] Such men represent the tip of an iceberg. In other walks of life too Bohemians from simple circumstances began to make a massive contribution to the Austrian scene. One of the few fields to have received much study is music. From Gluck's generation onwards, composers and performers flooded to Vienna – Vanhal and Vranitzky, Gyrowetz, Voříšek and others (even Kübeck began work as a music teacher and protégé of Beethoven). The last official court composers to the Habsburg dynasty were the Praguer, Leopold Koželuh, and the Moravian, Franz Krommer-Kramář. Both are good evidence for the Bohemian connection as well as for the Emperor Francis's inability to recognize genius. Other talented immigrants were the growing numbers of Jews, following in the footsteps of Josef von Sonnenfels, ideologue of the Austrian Enlightenment, but son of the rabbi at Nikolsburg (Mikulov).

Even more striking, however, is the continuing hold by Bohemians over the state apparatus of Austria. The ageing Leopold Kolowrat watched over the retreat from Josephinism – when he retired in 1806, by then as chairman of the Staatsrat, he had served for 63 years! His compatriots included Ignaz Chorinsky, Prokop Lažansky, yet another Chotek (Johann Rudolf) and the Emperor's close associate, Rudolf Wrbna. Then came Metternich, who, of course, grew up far from the Habsburg lands. Yet Metternich acquired, besides a large estate in Bohemia to add to the family's ancestral possessions there, the residue of the foreign-political programme of his grandfather-in-law, Kaunitz: pursuit of good relations with France, a remarkably unfeeling attitude towards his native Germany, and a tough line against Hungarian autonomy, at least until the 1840s. Shifts in his policy then had much to do – apart from the influence of his pupil Kübeck – with attempts to outmanoeuvre Metternich's main rival, who was none other than Franz Anton Kolowrat, transferred to Vienna since 1826 as Minister of State. And plenty more historic Slav names resounded through the faction-ridden corridors of government in *Vormärz* Vienna, like those of Josef Sedlnitzky, the infamous chief of police, or of Mittrowsky, who moved at the same time as Kolowrat in order to take over the United Chancellery.

In 1848–9 the immobile edifice of late Habsburg absolutism collapsed. What followed in Bohemia was a genuine revolution in that, for the first time since 1526, the outcome did not strengthen, but began to weaken, her bonds with Austria. The forces for cohesion had always been oligarchic. Democracy would now gradually turn the tide and undermine them. It would also dramatically polarise domestic politics, since in an age of rising nationalism, those forces, despite the bridging efforts of Czechophile aristocrats, had become ever more associated with German interests, and the Habsburgs could never quite undo the damage in the future.

This logical conclusion to the present investigation also refers us back to our starting-point of 1526. The situation by 1848 reversed that earlier one. The once independent and self-contained kingdom had been provincialized in its own public life, whereas some of its citizens now exercised decisive sway over the destiny of a great empire . At the same time a powerful inverted symmetry can be discerned, since, as Vienna had drawn away local talent, the vacuum was coming to be filled once again by a majority Czech language and culture. Thus 1526 and 1848 stand at the end and the beginning of two periods of Bohemia's separate development based on cultural transformation: her declining spiritual distinctiveness in the age of reformation being matched by her rising intellectual distinctiveness in the age of romanticism. Moreover, there existed a direct link between the two, for secular Czech culture after 1848 drew heavily on the Hussite legacy from before 1526, while the political movement for Bohemia's state rights in the nineteenth century aimed specifically to overturn the whole constitutional evolution since 1526 (or at least since 1620). Some of the former difficulties remained, particularly the reservations of Moravia which, still having more to lose from separatism and resenting dominance by Prague, continued to seek her own solutions as late as 1905. Yet in the end modern nationalism would bind together societies and provinces more effectively than Utraquist religion (or even the Catholic Church of the Habsburgs) had ever succeeded in doing.

For a time, nevertheless, much of the old fabric could be stitched together again, and by protagonists in the traditional mould. The saviours of Austria in 1848–9 were two Bohemian generals and a Bohemian statesman: Field-Marshal Prince Alfred Windischgraetz, brought up there on estates acquired by his father, as free-thinking a friend of Joseph II as his son was diehard; Field-Marshal Count Josef Wenzel Radetzky, offspring – as becomes more evident if we respell his surname 'Radecký' – of an ancient, if previously undistinguished, Moravian line; and Prince Felix Schwarzenberg, whose family were the richest landowners of all. But the last word would belong to a fourth compatriot, to František Palacký, Czech political leader and foremost historian of his country. Early in 1848, adapting the time-honoured 'Bohemian' foreign policy of opposition to Germany and Hungary – and to Russia, doing duty now for the Turks of old – Palacký could still coin a celebrated *bon mot* about the need to invent the Habsburg Monarchy as a protector if it had not already existed. By the 1860s he delivered himself, in despair, of an equally celebrated prophecy: 'We were before Austria; we shall be after her too.'[36] Significantly enough, Palacký's own pioneering historical narrative stopped short at the very year 1526.

NOTES FOR CHAPTER 8

* Senior Research Fellow of Brasenose College, Oxford and University Reader.

1 Only a skeletal annotation for such a long period is possible in the context of this chapter and the references are restricted to a few recent titles. For helpful and up-to-date summaries of the whole period, with good bibliography, see K. Richter and G. Hanke, *Handbuch der Geschichte der böhmischen Länder* (ed. K. Bosl) ii: *1471–1848* (Stuttgart, 1974); Jaroslav Purš and Miroslav Kropilák (eds.), *Přehled dějin Československa* i, part 2:

1526–1848 (Prague, 1982); Jörg K. Hoensch, *Geschichte Böhmens von der slavischen Landnahme bis ins 20. Jahrhundert* (Munich, 1987). There is nothing remotely adequate in English.

2 Ferdinand I (1503–64), second son of Philip the Fair, recognized as ruler of the hereditary Austrian possessions of Upper and Lower Austria, Styria, Carinthia, Carniola Tyrol, etc. married Anna, daughter of King Vladislav II of Bohemia and Hungary in 1521. After the death of her childless brother, Louis II, at the battle of Mohács in 1526, Ferdinand claimed the succession to the crowns of Bohemia and Hungary for himself. He was crowned Holy Roman Emperor in 1558.

3 The circumstances of the election are related in detail in Josef Janáček, *České dějiny. Doba předbělohorská*, 2 vols., (Prague, 1968–84), i; summarily in Kenneth J. Dillon, *King and Estates in the Bohemian Lands, 1526–1564* (Brussels, 1976).

4 The latest survey of the Hussite phenomenon is František Šmahel, *La Révolution hussite: une anomalie historique* (Paris, 1985).

5 On the early years of Ferdinand's reign in general see Alfons Lhotsky, *Das Zeitalter des Hauses Österreich. Die ersten Jahre der Regierung Ferdinands I* (Vienna, 1971); Paula Sutter Fichtner, *Ferdinand I of Austria: The Politics of Dynasticism in the Age of the Reformation* (New York, 1982); Günther R. Burkert, *Landesfürst und Stände: Karl V, Ferdinand I. und die österreichischen Erbländer im Ringen um Gesamtstaat und Landesinteressen* (Graz, 1987).

6 These issues deserve more attention than they normally receive; but see now the excellent Moravian-eye view of Josef Válka, *Přehled dějin Moravy*, Bedřich Čerešňák *et al.* (ed.) ii: *Stavovska Morava, 1440–1620* (Prague, 1987).

7 Winfried Eberhard, *Konfessionsbildung und Stände in Böhmen, 1478–1530* (Munich, 1981).

8 Eberhard, *Konfessionsbildung*; and *idem, Monarchie und Widerstand. Zur ständischen Oppositionsbildung im Herrschaftssystem Ferdinands I. in Böhmen* (Munich, 1985), a very important, though somewhat indigestible and problematical work.

9 Details of this revolt in Janáček, *Česke dějiny*, ii, and Eberhard, *Monarchie und Widerstand*; summary in Dillon, *King and Estates*.

10 New approaches to this important diet in A. Míka, 'Z bojů o náboženskou toleraci v 16. století', *Československý Časopis Historický*, xviii (1970), pp. 371–80; J. Pánek, 'Zápas o charakter české stavovské opozice a sněm roku 1575', *ibid.* xxviii (1980), pp. 863–86. Cf. J. Pánek's broader study of the opposition, *Stavovská opozice a její zápas s Habsburky, 1547–77* (Prague, 1982).

11 R. J. W. Evans, *Rudolf II and his World. A Study in Intellectual History, 1576–1612*, 2nd edn (Oxford UP, 1984). Latest in the rapidly growing body of literature on Rudolfine culture, especially visual: Thomas DaCosta Kaufmann, *The School of Prague. Painting at the Court of Rudolf II* (Chicago UP, 1988); *Prag um 1600: Beiträge zur Kunst und Kultur am Hofe Rudolfs II.* (Freren, 1988); *Prag um 1600: Kunst und Kultur am Hofe Rudolfs II. Katalog der Ausstellung, Essen, 1988* (Freren, 1988), with an article by Evans on the political background.

12 Josef Janáček, *Pád Rudolfa II.* (Prague, 1973).

13 New studies of these events will appear in *Crown, Church and Estates in Central Europe, 1526–1711*, ed. R. J. W. Evans and T. V. Thomas (London: forthcoming).

14 See the earlier sections of J. V. Polišenský, *The Thirty Years War* (London, 1971); *idem* (with F. Snider), *War and Society in Europe, 1618–48* (Cambridge, 1978); G. Parker *et al., The Thirty Years War* (London, 1984); and – for a domestic Czech view – František Kavka, *Bílá Hora a české dějiny* (Prague, 1962). Hans Sturmberger's taut narrative in *Aufstand in Böhmen. Der Beginn des dreissigjährigen Krieges* (Munich, 1959), remains valuable.

15 Robert Bireley, *Religion and Politics in the Age of the Counter-Reformation. Emperor Ferdinand II, William Lamormaini, S.J., and the Formation of Imperial Policy* (North Carolina UP, 1981), stresses this element in Ferdinand's overall policy.

16 *The Chronicle of the Hutterian Brethren*, i (Rifton, NY, 1987), p. 633ff.

17 A survey of these developments in R. J. W. Evans, *The Making of the Habsburg Monarchy, 1550–1700. An Interpretation*, 2nd edn (Oxford UP, 1984), chs. 2 and 6; rev. edn, with new bibliography, as *Das Werden der Habsburger-monarchie, 1550–1700. Gesellschaft, Kultur, Institutionen* (Vienna, 1986).

18 *Ibid.*, ch. 6; P. Čornej, 'Vliv pobělohorských konfiskací na skladbě feudální třídy', *Acta Universitatis Carolinae, Philosophica et Historica*, 1976, 1, pp. 165–94; Eila Hassenpflug-Elzholz, *Böhmen und die böhmischen Stände in der Zeit des beginnenden Zentralismus* (Vienna, 1982). In deference to the dominant German linguistic culture of Bohemia after 1620, I have spelt most of these surnames in their German form.

19 In the absence of reliable overall statistics, the exact burden borne by Bohemia remains uncertain. But see now Jean Bérenger, *Finances et absolutisme autrichien dans la seconde moitié du XVIIᵉ siècle* (Paris, 1975), p. 320ff.; P. G. M. Dickson, *Finance and Government under Maria Theresia*, 2 vols., (Oxford UP, 1987), ii, p. 185ff. The income from regalia – crown lands, mines, customs and excise, etc. – is a separate calculation, but one which would not materially affect this conclusion.

20 Much detail in Arnošt Klíma, *Manufakturní období v Čechách* (Prague, 1955), partly summarized by the author in *Historica*, xi (Prague, 1965), pp. 95–119.

21 Protracted neglect of the Bohemian Baroque is remedied in Milada Součková, *Baroque in Bohemia* (Ann Arbor, Mich., 1980); Zdeněk Kalista, *Tvář baroka* (Munich, 1982); Jan Kučera and Jiří Rak, *Bohuslav Balbín a jeho místo v české kultuře* (Prague, 1983).

22 As a general phenomenon, the Bohemian presence in Austria stands in need of the attention of historians. For the latest 'Bohemian' view of Wallenstein see Josef Janáček, *Valdštejnova smrt* (Prague, 1970); for the Liechtensteins see Volker Press and Dietmar Willoweit (eds.), *Liechtenstein – fürstliches Haus und staatliche Ordnung* (Vaduz and Munich, 1987).

23 Z. Kalista (ed.), *Korespondence císaře Leopolda I s Humprechtem Janem Černínem z Chudenic*, i (only) (Prague, 1936). Thomas M. Barker, *Army, Aristocracy, Monarchy; Essays on War, Society, and Government in Austria, 1618–1780* (New York, 1982), discusses Lobkowitz.

24 J. Veselý, 'K otázce lenního vztahu k římské říši v českých dějinách', *Sborník Archivních Prací*, xxix (1979), pp. 56–110.

25 There has been little discussion of this disenchantment (as of Charles VI's rule as a whole). Even Hassenpflug-Elzholz, *Böhmen und die böhmischen Stände*, considers its consequences rather than its causes. For cultural frictions see Pavel Preiss, *Boje s dvouhlavou saní: F. A. Špork a barokní kultura v Čechách* (Prague, 1981).

26 L. Hüttl, 'Die bayerischen Erbansprüche auf Böhmen, Ungarn und Österreich in der frühen Neuzeit', in Ferdinand Seibt (ed.), *Die böhmischen Länder zwischen Ost und West*, (Munich, 1983), pp. 70–88.

27 Hassenpflug-Elzholz, *Böhmen und die böhmischen Stände*, (especially p. 38ff., p. 374ff., for the 1720 diet).

28 F. Roubík, 'K vývoji zemské správy v Čechách v letech 1749–90', *Sborník Archivních Prací*, xix (1969), pp. 41–188; Dickson, *Finance and Government*.

29 Klíma, *Manufakturní*; abdsloí Herman Freudenberger, *The Waldstein Woolen Mill: Noble Entrepreneurship in Eighteenth-Century Bohemia* (Harvard UP, 1963); idem, *The Industrialization of a Central European City: Brno and the Fine Woollen Industry in the Eighteenth Century* (Edington, Wilts., 1977); William E. Wright, *Serf, Seigneur and Sovereign: Agrarian Reform in Eighteenth-Century Bohemia* (Minneapolis, 1966).

30 The general thesis of Eduard Winter, *Der Josephinismus: die Geschichte des österreichischen Reformkatholizismus, 1740–1848*, 2nd edn (Berlin, 1962), remains important. See now the social-cultural surveys by Walter Schamschula, *Die Anfänge der tschechischen Erneuerung und das deutsche Geistesleben, 1740–1800* (Munich, 1973); A. S. Myl'nikov, *Epokha prosveshcheniya v Cheshskich zemlyach* (Moscow, 1977); Josef Haubelt, *České*

osvícenství (Prague, 1986). Moravia at last receives her due in Jiří Kroupa, *Alchymie štěstí. Pozdní osvícenství a moravská společnost* (Brno, 1988). For Joseph's personal ties to Bohemia, see Derek Beales, *Joseph II*, i (Cambridge UP, 1987), especially chs. 10–11.

31 There is a good new survey by Pavel Bělina, 'Politické události let 1789–1797 v názorech měšťanské inteligence a lidových písmáků v českých zemích', *Československý Časopis Historický*, xxxv (1987), pp. 844–72. Květa Meydřická, *Čechy a Francouzská revoluce* (Prague, 1959), and J. Polišenský, *Napoleon a srdce Evropy* (Prague, 1971), make what they can of evidence of discontent.

32 For Kaunitz see Grete Klingenstein, *Der Aufstieg des Hauses Kaunitz* (Göttingen, 1975); a biography by Franz A. J. Szabo is awaited. On the religious side cf. F. Maass (ed.), *Der Josephinismus. Quellen zu seiner Geschichte in Österreich, 1760–1850*, i–v (Vienna, 1951–61), *passim*.

33 Again (cf. above, note 22) there is nothing systematic. There is a mass of miscellaneous information in C. von Wurzbach, *Biographisches Lexikon des Kaiserthums Oesterreich*, i–lx (Vienna, 1856–91). Dickson, *Finance and Government*, i, chs. 12–13 and associated tables, is now very useful for the reign of Maria Theresa.

34 Maass (ed.), *Der Josephinismus*, iii (for Heinke); Beda Franz Menzel, *Abt Franz Stephan Rautenstrauch von Břevnov-Braunau* (Königstein i. T., 1969).

35 M. von Kübeck (ed.), *Tagebücher des Carl Friedrich Freiherrn Kübeck von Kübau*, i–iii (Vienna, 1909–10); Ignaz Beidtel, *Geschichte der österreichischen Staatsverwaltung, 1740–1848*, i and ii (Innsbruck, 1896–8). The best general picture remains that in C. A. Macartney, *The Habsburg Empire, 1790–1918* (London, 1968), pp. 147–305.

36 'Byli sme před Rakouskem, budeme i po něm!', printed in his *Radhost: sbírka spisův drobných*, iii (Prague, 1873), p. 229. For the circumstances of Palacký's 1848 remarks, printed *ibid.*, pp. 10–17, see Stanley Z. Pech, *The Czech Revolution of 1848* (North Carolina UP, 1969), p. 80 ff.

9

The Annexation and Integration of Silesia into the Prussian State of Frederick the Great

PETER BAUMGART*

During his 46 years as king of Prussia, Frederick II extended his state by three provinces. Silesia was annexed.[1] East Friesland fell to the crown in 1774 through a dynastic inheritance which was not undisputed.[2] Finally, West Prussia came into the hands of the House of Hohenzollern in the wake of the First Partition of Poland in 1772.[3]

Of these three acquisitions, that of Silesia was of the greatest territorial and economic importance and would also have the most significant historical consequences in the long term. The acquisition of Silesia put into stark focus the great dispute between the old-established House of Austria, the dominant force within the Holy Roman Empire, and the state of Brandenburg-Prussia which had been, until that date, a rather peripheral power of secondary significance. The dispute would only finally be resolved in 1866. An older historiographical tradition, which can be traced back to the historian Johann Gustav Droysen in the last century, interpreted Austro-Prussian 'Dualism' as beginning in the seventeenth century, at least as far back as the time of Elector Frederick William.[4] Silesia's acquisition, along with the later military and political efforts to defend this valuable former Habsburg province in the course of three wars, gradually transformed Brandenburg-Prussia into a member of Europe's leading states, respected by the other Great Powers. Its annexation provided the basis for a government which, when combined with the political objectives of the dynasty and its territorial concentration in the north-east of the Holy Roman Empire, made it a Great Power, the fifth in terms of importance in Europe. Silesia provided Prussia with the territorial and economic basis to assert and defend such a pre-eminence.

It was precisely because the incorporation of Silesia into the Prussian state had such momentous consequences, and because the circumstances of its annexation (even in an age of absolutist high politics with its exchange of territories and ruthless partitioning of states) were so unusual, that reactions amongst contemporaries were strongly divided. It was also for these reasons that historians have tended to be controversial in their assessments of the event. Most historians have understandably concentrated more on the personality and overall political objectives of Frederick II rather than on the specifically Silesian aspects of his politics.[5]

But some historians have treated his actions towards Silesia as the yardstick by which to judge his policies as a whole. A further difficulty is that historians took up either pro-Prussian or pro-Austrian positions and either unequivocally applauded the king's motives and actions or, on the other hand, equally vehemently rejected them. It goes without saying that the historical interpretations of both sides were influenced by the developments towards a nation-state which so preoccupied nineteenth-century Germany. Historical perspectives were inevitably profoundly coloured by the contemporary debates over a 'unification of Germany' and, in particular, by the founding of Bismarck's Reich.

Opinions ranged very widely. On the one hand, Droysen and others saw the annexation of Silesia as a 'necessary' step on the way to a 'Little German' (*kleindeutsch*) solution to the Germany question.[6] On the other hand, Onno Klopp was the first to claim that Frederick's Silesian policies had sealed the fate of the supporters of a greater Germany including Austria.[7] Between these two extremes lay the conclusions of many professional historians at the turn of the century, such as (for example) Reinhold Koser, who did not deny the nationalist underpinning of the German Reich within the borders of 1871, but interpreted the policies of Frederick II in a far more realistic fashion than some of his predecessors.[8] Such debates are now, more than 40 years after the dissolution of Prussia as a state and the eclipse of the nineteenth-century notion of a nation-state implied in Bismarck's Reich, past history. This is not to say, however, that their influence upon the discussion has entirely evaporated. As the public debate over the Prussia Exhibition in Berlin and the 'Prussia Year' in 1981 demonstrated, the concept of Prussia continues to be an emotive issue.[9] Different sets of diametrically opposed preconceptions, drawing on the political transformation in German history, continue to determine not only German public opinion but also the conclusions of its professional historians.[10]

Even after making allowances for these historiographical debates and their effects upon contemporary historians, there are still considerable difficulties in interpreting Frederick the Great's Silesian policy. The circumstances and preconditions which led to his crossing the 'Rubicon' on 16 December 1740 and marching into Silesia must first be analysed.[11] The House of Brandenburg had, of course, dynastic claims to some of the individual Silesian principalities. It laid claim to the territories of Liegnitz, Brieg and Wohlau by virtue of an agreed dynastic treaty concluded with the House of Piasten, then the holders of the territories in 1537, and which had died out in 1675. The treaty had meanwhile been adjudged null and void by King Ferdinand of Bohemia and Hungary in 1546. There was also a claim to the principality of Jägerndorf. However, this territory had been confiscated by the Emperor and conferred elsewhere after the support offered to the Bohemian Winter King Frederick V by John George, Margrave of Brandenburg, at the beginning of the Thirty Years War.[12]

These were dynastic claims which Frederick William, Elector of Brandenburg, had sought to reactivate in the aftermath of the Peace of Westphalia when he was offered by the French and the Swedes the Silesian dukedoms in return for Pomerania which Sweden had laid claim to.[13] In 1670, he drafted a memorandum envisaging the acquisition of all Silesia although this seems to have been a response to the particular circumstances of the possibility of the extinction

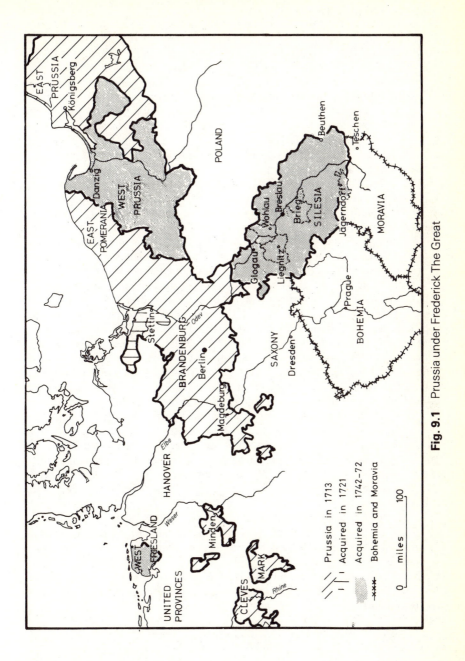

Fig. 9.1 Prussia under Frederick The Great

Prussia in 1713

Acquired in 1721

Acquired in 1742–72

Bohemia and Moravia

0   100

miles

of the male line of the Austrian Habsburgs rather than the appearance of a fully matured long-term plan for annexation.[14] What is more significant is that the Elector did not exploit the extinction of the Piasten House in Silesia to pursue energetically his claims to the dukedoms of Liegnitz, Brieg and Wohlau. He evidently regarded the dynastic treaty of 1537 as a dead letter and it was only towards the end of his rule that the Great Elector's determination was once more roused, the meagre results being the secession to him of the area around Schweibus in full settlement of his rights of inheritance. At the same time, however, in a private communication from the Elector's son and heir to the Emperor, he promised to return this small enclave to the Habsburgs after his father's death, as, in fact, transpired in 1695.[15] At a subsequent date, this convenient ploy would serve as proof of the legitimacy of Prussian claims to the smaller Silesian duchies.

The implausible dynastic claims which had been abandoned by Frederick William I were given credence by Frederick the Great for tactical reasons because they added public legitimacy to his proceedings and conduct when referred to by his jurists.[16] In private, it is well-known that he did not take them seriously himself and gave little weight to the discursive conclusions of Johann Peter von Ludwig of Halle on the matter.[17] Nevertheless, these claims were part of the nexus of considerations which Frederick formulated in the wake of the dawn of a new political age. What had set – as he put it – the stone of Nebuchadnezzar rolling was the totally unexpected demise of the Emperor Charles VI on 20 October 1740. According to Frederick's interpretation of events, this would lead to a 'total transformation of the old political order'.[18] He had contemplated the possibilities of just such an eventuality whilst he had been crown prince[19] and he summarized his reasoning in a memorandum of 6 November 1740 as follows:[20] 'Silesia is precisely that part of the imperial inheritance to which we have the most substantial claim and which is most favourable to our cause. It is just and proper to uphold her rights and to fulfil the opportunities afforded by the emperor's death in order to realize our lawful claims. The military superiority which we enjoy, the speed with which we can mobilize it, in short, the clear advantage we enjoy over our neighbours gives us, in this opportune and quite unexpected turn of events a great advantage over all the other European Powers . . . Having but once taken possession there, then the outcome will be successful for us. Negotiation on its own would provide us with nothing save highly onerous obligations in return for trifles'.

In this way Frederick attempted to justify to himself a course of action which was fraught with difficulties. Indeed, his personal emotional approach to the affair he revealed in a surprisingly frank letter to Jordan as early as 1741, and these were sentiments he re-emphasized in his *Histoire de mon Temps* (History of my Times). He maintained that he rode out to this 'rendezvous with glory' out of youthful ambition, curiosity and the wish to read his 'name in the gazettes and ultimately to go down in history'.[21]

Frederick's apologia for his expansion into Silesia points over and beyond a psychological explanation to, above all, Prussian interests of state (*l'intérêt de l'état*) as the motivating force behind his conduct.[22] At an early stage, *droit légitime* (as it was understood by his predecessors) came, in his mind and characteristically so, to be combined with *droit de bienséance*, such that (in the case of the acquisition of territories) states must enlarge if they want to make their mark in the competitive world of the European Powers.[23] What inspired his ambitions was the desire to win for his state the position of being a Great Power. He wanted Prussia no longer to inhabit 'that limbo between Electorate and Kingdom'.[24] And here, according to G. P. Gooch, it was not a question in his mind so much of 'stealing a portion of his neighbour's vineyard', but rather of ushering in 'a new chapter in European history'.[25]

Frederick's action, which subsequently was to bring his state to the brink of extinction, was a once-for-all adventure. But, in terms of the high politics of those who attempted to retain the balance of power in international affairs, hardly unique. Frederick's policies were not, in principle, different from those of his rivals or from other members of the less powerful German princes. The Electors of Bavaria or Saxony, for example, were also just waiting for a (favourable) political and military conjuncture, such as occurred in 1740, in order, with French assistance, to make territorial gains at the expense of the bankrupt estate of the Habsburg monarchy, which looked as though it was about to vanish.[26] They too hoped to obtain a share of the loot from the collapse of the Pragmatic Sanction, so stubbornly advocated by the late Emperor Charles VI. Extensive schemes for the partition of his inheritance had already been drawn up.

Frederick differed from these his fellow princes merely in his higher ambitions, his greater political intelligence and his willingness to take larger risks. Considerations of a national Germany or the political future of the Empire obviously played no part in prompting his annexation of Silesia. It was purely and simply the interests of his own state which were uppermost, a kind of Prussian *raison d'état*.[27] However one defines this *raison d'état*, it was clearly going to disrupt the existing balance of powers within the European system. In attempting to gain an entry by force into the circle of the Great Powers, the King was calling into question not just the Austrian position in the Empire, but the whole hegemonic system by which the European Great Powers ruled, a system that had been in place since the pacifications of Utrecht and Stockholm/Nystad. Thus he was threatening the right to rule claimed by the European powers and exercised in accordance with the doctrine of the Balance and the principle of mutual accord. They had no intention of sharing their 'aristocratic collective hegemony' in Europe with the 'expansionist cravings and desire for superior power' of a newcomer.[28] This is why the allies during the Seven Years War proved so persistent in their attempts to retake Silesia and why, through this, they were intent on restricting Prussia to being a *'puissance très sécondaire'*.[29]

The way in which Frederick annexed Silesia after 1740 must be assessed according to the political system to which he himself belonged. It is only then that criteria can be established against which it may be measured. These criteria, established by means of careful comparative analysis of absolute rule elsewhere in the eighteenth century, are the only way by which historians can avoid the pitfalls of arriving at over-subtle or anachronistic conclusions. These criteria need to be established not just in relation to Frederick's annexation of Silesia, but more broadly in the overall assessment of his rule.

The seizure of large portions of Silesia, including its capital, Breslau, despite its declaration of neutrality during the winter months of 1740–1, occurred swiftly and without serious difficulty.[30] A full-scale military conflict was delayed until spring by the inclement winter season and the slow preparations of an under-prepared opponent and the political confrontation was dependent upon the responses to the invasion from the European Great Powers. The first inkling of the direction events would take appeared at the battle of Mollwitz on 10 April 1741 which, although the king left the field prematurely, still gave his infantry a victory over the Austrian forces. This military victory also changed the foreign policy constellation decisively to his advantage. France abandoned the guarantee she had given to the Pragmatic Sanction and, from that point onward, she supported the Bavarian claims and ambitions to the Imperial succession, by virtue of the treaty of Nymphenburg. Thus the initial isolation of Prussia disappeared and the Austrian War of Succession began.

Frederick's main concerns from then on were not the widening or prolongation of the war but simply the consolidation of the additional territories which his surprise offensive had won him. This was clearly the case at the much discussed Secret Convention of Kleinschnellendorf concluded with the Austrians on 9 October 1741 and which was only intended to provide a breathing space for both sides.[31] It was confirmed by his subsequent conduct of the war after the battle of Chotusitz (17 May 1742) which led to the preliminary Peace of Breslau (11 June 1742), subsequently confirmed by the definitive Peace of Berlin (28 July 1742).[32] At the Breslau negotiations, conducted under English mediation, the Prussian king still raised claims to North Bohemian territories and was even willing to abandon Upper Silesia in return for them. Maria Theresa, however, was quite unwilling to accept such an offer and, instead, offered to cede Upper and Lower Silesia in their entirety (including the county of Glatz and the Moravian enclaves) to him (Article V), retaining only the principality of Teschen, the town of Tropau, as well as parts of the principalities of Troppau, Jägerndorf and Neisse. For his part, Frederick relinquished all his remaining territorial claims against Maria Theresa, agreed to assume the greater part of the Silesian state debt and explicitly undertook (in Article VI) to uphold: 'the status quo with regard to the catholic faith in Silesia and the complete freedom of conscience for those of the protestant religion, the rights of sovereignty notwithstanding'.[33]

Having secured the military annexation of Silesia and its confirmation in a treaty, Frederick was prepared to bide his time for the moment. To his minister, Podewils, he wrote; 'One has to have the ability to stop at the right time. To force one's good fortune is to lose it, and to demand more and more is to sacrifice contentment'. As far as foreign policy was concerned, he now perceived his task as: 'to acclimatize the cabinets of Europe to seeing us in the state which this war has accorded us, and a measure of moderation and equanimity will assist us in this goal. It is my hope that we would assert our position at the height of our rise to power with dignity . . .'.[34] This prognosis, however, went unfulfilled. It was only after two further wars, and only after the peace of 1763 that Frederick achieved in Hubertsburg his political objectives of seeing Prussia established as a Great Power.

The king of Prussia had not waited for the treaty arrangements over Breslau and Berlin before initiating a thoroughgoing change in the governing arrangements for occupied Silesia. Having annexed the state, he at once began to change its constitutional, administrative and financial structure. The instrument which he initially designated for this process was the 'General War Commissary' (*General-Feldkriegskommissariat*).[35] It is not possible to date with precision the installation of this interim administration. However, the Chief Financial Secretaries Reinhardt and Münchow from the General Directory had been chosen as its chiefs as early as November 1740. As its name suggests, this was initially a military directorate to oversee the needs of the army. But it rapidly turned into a unit of general administration and became the basis for the new Prussian administration throughout Silesia. The king had already presided on 3 and 5 January 1741 over the dissolution of what had been until then the Habsburg administration in Silesia, the Governing Council (*Oberamt*) and the Silesian Council (*Kammer*).[36] The General War Commissary took over from the nobility in the interim and it was at this moment that it immediately became clear that the integration of the newly won territories into the Prussian state was simply not possible on the basis of the constitutional and administrative status quo.

Unlike the Prussian provinces, which had been unified to a considerable extent under Frederick's predecessor, the Silesian principalities (formerly dependencies of the crown of Bohemia, over which Frederick was declared, on his instructions, 'sovereign and supreme Duke' on 7 November 1741)[37] presented a complicated political structure. Amongst the Bohemian territories administered by the Bohemian Court Chancellory in Vienna, Silesia, with its population recorded as around a million in 1736, was always the exception.[38] This was because of its ethnic composition and also because of its confessional circumstances.[39] The latter were a problem because, since Silesia was part of the Habsburg monarchy, the religious guarantees of the Peace of Westphalia did not apply to it.[40] In addition, the Habsburg monarchy had never succeeded in limiting the powers of the Silesian estates in the same way as had taken place in Brandenburg-Prussia since the days of the Great Elector. At all levels, the dukedom of Silesia remained a territory governed through the influence of its estates.

On the eve of the annexation, therefore, alongside the mechanisms of the monarchy such as the 'Governing Council' or *Oberamt* (which emanated originally from the estates but which was by then a monarchical institution) and the 'Chamber', there was also the surviving older constitution of the territory with its estates general and its nobility. The *Conventus Publicus* still met in the form of the 'Assemblies of the Notables' (*Fürstentagen*) of the particular estates of Silesia's individual principalities as well as on their own and had powers to levy taxes.[41] The dukedom of Silesia was fragmented into a multiplicity of particularist principalities each of which still preserved important powers, for example, the power to make law in their own locality. On the eve of Prussian annexation, there were nine so-called 'inherited principalities' (*Erbfürstentümer*) which were directly subject to the crown and in which the kings of Bohemia exercised their authority as provincial rulers.[42] In addition there were seven palatine principalities (*Mediatfürstentümer*) which owed allegiance to the king of Bohemia but whose rulers possessed their own jurisdiction as well.[43] In addition, the Silesian constitution also recognized six free noble lordships (*Standesherrschaften*), mostly in the possession of old-established Silesian noble families.[44] The city of Breslau was accorded a special status whilst a further 10 royal cities provided deputies for the third chamber in the General Assemblies of Notables at Breslau.[45] There was no separate clerical order in the estates. Together, all these various constituent elements composed the *status maiores* at the *Conventus Publicus*, the grand Silesian 'Assembly of Notables' which had existed since the year 1662 as a permanent body of deputies who represented the territories. Alongside these, however, were the 24 lordships directly subject to the king of Bohemia who had no rights of representation and who were roughly the equivalent in Silesian terms to the Imperial Knights. All the remaining members of the notables in turn had their own estates, organized upon tri-cameral principles. There, next to the prelates, the landed nobility played a dominant rôle. Those who possessed large noble estates enjoyed considerable seigneurial jurisdiction in their estates. The substantial differences in land tenure – ranging from predominantly freehold farms and secure leaseholds in Lower Silesia on the one hand to outright serfdom, especially prevalent in 'Polish Silesia', led to great economic and social differences within the province.[46]

This cluttered multiplicity of political institutions and legal status was scarcely compatible with Frederick's conception of an effective state administration. It was an obvious barrier to the more intensive financial and economic exploitation of the province for the benefit of the state as a whole which the king had very much in mind. Therefore by excluding or at least considerably restricting their existing authority whilst still retaining certain provincial posts characteristic of the old Silesia, Frederick managed, within the space of less than two years, to put it on to a 'Prussian' footing and reorganize it along the lines of the rest of Brandenburg-Prussia.[47]

The old administrative entities were swept aside and a completely new administrative as well as judicial machinery was quickly installed in the province. Silesia was divided into two parts, each with its own chamber, one sitting in Breslau and the other at Glogau.[48] In response to a royal decree, the two civil Chambers (*Kriegs-und Domänen-Kammern*) replaced the general War Commissary alone on 1 January 1742 and inherited its personnel as well as (in part) its institutional framework.[49] Its administrative chiefs, Reinhardt and Münchow were nominated interim presidents of the chambers in Breslau and Glogau. Normally, the new province would have been the responsibility of the General Directory in Berlin but the king preferred to have a completely free hand. 'I am now the Ministerial Head of Silesian Affairs until it is all properly established' Frederick wrote in the margins of one report.[50]

Frederick wanted these chambers to function in accordance with the administrative principles introduced by Frederick William I. He therefore required them to be properly established as part of the cameral administration of the state.[51] As a matter of principle, but also because there was a shortage of properly qualified Silesian administrators, Frederick relied upon officials from other provinces of the state. These were uprooted from their posts and transferred to Silesia, although they were rewarded with higher salaries because of the higher costs of living there.[52]

This kind of cameral administration was entirely characteristic of the Prussian monarchy. It involved separate administrations for town and country with two different sets of officials each collecting different sorts of tax, one mainly indirect and the other direct. These arrangements were progressively introduced into Silesia as well.[53] The installation of the tax officials as those responsible in the towns on behalf of the king was combined with the abolition of the autonomous town constitutions.[54] The Silesian towns lost their voting rights in a fashion which followed the pattern already established in Prussian municipalities, whose corrupt oligarchic government and disposal of municipal revenues at will they shared. In the provincial capital at Breslau,[55] whose privileges were of great antiquity, the Prussian administration replaced the post of First Mayor with that of a Director but it left other members of the city council in office, whilst installing a strict supervision over its whole workings and forcing the commune to pay over superfluous funds into the provincial treasury.

Although there had never been a post comparable to that of a tax official in the Silesian towns, the institution of local officials (the *Landräte*[56]) representing the central government (crown) as well as the landed aristocracy in the countryside was based on the precedent of the 'Provincial Elders' (*Landesältesten*) drawn from the ancient districts. In both the Breslau and Glogau departments, a modified version of the districts formerly utilized by these Elders was established.[57] The incumbent 'Provincial Elder' retained his title but became a paid local official.[58] It was expressly stated that these posts were to be chosen from among the 'members of the well-established nobility in the district', i.e. chosen by the district assemblies of the nobility and subsequently proposed to the king for appointment. In this way, the quasi-noble character of the position of local official, albeit a representative of monarchical power, was preserved in the province. Every subsequent reform of the provincial administration intended to limit the position of the nobility met with great difficulties as the provincial minister von Schlabrendorff would later discover.

The mental outlook of the cameral executive as it began its work in Silesia in 1742 was remarkable. Its ideals (even though they were not always realized in practice) are illustrated in the opening address of the President of the Glogau Chamber, von Münchow. According to von Münchow, the very fact that the king had 'even in the course of a war which unsettled the whole of Europe established a Domain and War Chamber' in Silesia should 'convince them of the importance of their office'.[59] Their perpetual duty, and this was how he defined their responsibilities, was 'not merely to increase royal revenue but rather, above all, to advance all that was in the interests of the province, to promote its well-being, to increase its population, to encourage the advancement of its trade and commerce and give order to both town and countryside'. Von Münchow was in no doubt, he said, that they would all have 'genuine delight' in executing their daily duties to the full 'and that not a day, nor even (were it possible) an hour should pass except that they render the king some service or, in whatever way possible, advance the best interests of this land to his satisfaction. Whomsoever has fully experienced this sense of satisfaction will affirm with me that therein alone lies rewards for all one's efforts, a sense of satisfaction to be more highly prized than some small increase in remuneration or some superficial promotion.'

Ludwig Wilhelm von Münchow (1712–53) was the first provincial minister for Silesia.[60] The son of the president of the Chamber of Küstrin who in his day had instructed the Crown Prince in the Prussian administration after his attempted flight from his father's court, von Münchow had just turned 30 years of age when he took up the appointment. Well-educated and amenable, he belonged to a close circle of confidants around the monarch. He was one of the few to hold high office whom the king really trusted. He was eminently suited to represent the new ruler of Silesia in the face of a nobility which was still restless and a clergy whose loyalties varied from the mistrustful to the openly hostile. Von Münchow sought wherever possible to avoid conflict and to present the annexation in the best possible light to the Silesians.

Von Münchow, whom Frederick had ostentatiously created Count on the occasion of the province's new oath of allegiance, was appointed the president of both chambers on 19 March 1742.[61] Reinhardt, his administrative colleague, was posted back to Berlin just prior to his appointment for reasons which are far from clear.[62] In addition to the doubling of his official salary of 4,400 *Reichstaler*, von Münchow received the title of 'senior Privy Councillor' (*Wirklicher Geheimrat*). As provincial minister in Silesia, he was answerable to the king alone. He enjoyed an exceptional position in this respect, but it is impossible to say at this point whether the king intended that this should be the case permanently for Silesia. With an eye upon the House of Austria's determination to recover the province and the constant threat which that entailed, Frederick paid particular attention to the situation in Silesia. In many respects, Silesia enjoyed more favourable treatment than the older provinces but, at the same time, he extracted financial concessions from the province. The mild but well-directed régime of the first provincial minister von Münchow,[63] whose contribution was much appreciated by the king and who died, possibly through overwork, in 1753, had a considerable rôle in this achievement. When issuing his instructions to von Münchow's successor, Joachim von Massow (an inflexible man of military background who only held office briefly from 1753 to 1755), the normally hypercritical Frederick found nothing to criticize in the dispositions for the province of von Münchow.[64] The special position of the Silesian Provincial Minister, by then firmly established, even though it ran counter to the Prussian administrative hierarchy, was preserved until 1807. The king himself recommended it to von Münchow's successors, von Massow and Ernst Wilhelm von Schlabrendorff (Minister from 1755 to 1769) as 'la plus belle place que j'ai à donner dans le civil'.[65] 'You depend on me alone' he wrote, 'It is to me alone that you have to render account'. No other minister in the eighteenth-century Prussian monarchy enjoyed such a degree of independence.

Among the tasks of the new Provincial Ministry and its officials was from the outset the establishment of 'an orderly and specified balance sheet',[66] the regulation of expenditure and the raising of income, and the placing of the entire financial structure of the province on a sound basis to the advantage of its ruler. To put it another way, the chambers were first and foremost the organs of finance, taxation and the economy throughout Prussia. Only secondarily were they in charge of the provinces and the well-being of the local inhabitants.

But a financial policy aiming to raise revenue could not succeed on the basis of the tax system inherited from the Habsburgs. Nor, indeed, did such a policy correspond to the wishes of the Silesian estates who, at the beginning of Prussian rule, bombarded the crown with petitions about their privileges to grant tax contributions and their exceptional and voluntary nature – appeals which fell on deaf ears.[67] The old Silesian tax system[68] was based on the one hand on a repartitioned tax based on the assessed value of land, introduced as early as 1527, and only slightly modified thereafter. It was highly inequitable and unjust. On the other hand, there was also an excise tax which had been introduced in the 1660s. These taxes were levied both in the towns and the countryside, such as was not the case in Brandenburg-Prussia. The income from taxation was administered and controlled by the General Tax Office, whose posts were filled by the estates, and which functioned in co-operation with the Governing Council.

The Habsburgs had tried on several occasions to change this unproductive system which had, over the years, grown severely distorted. Each new attempt at reforming the tax structure led to prolonged negotiations and the further strengthening of the nobles' rôle. The only way in which the new Prussian administration could introduce a new order effectively was, in keeping with absolute rule, to dismiss the claims of the Silesian estates to have a say in the running of the province. In the late Autumn of 1741, the General Assembly of Nobles was dissolved.[69] In the following summer of 1742 Frederick established a Land Survey Commission (*Klassifikationskommission*),[70] staffed by Prussian officials who, assisted by subcommittees, travelled through the localities and compiled a systematic cadastral survey with which, at the king's request, a Prussian system of tax contributions on a landed basis could replace the old structure. The new tax laws were also to apply in Upper Silesia and the County of Glatz and were to take effect from 1 June 1743. To consolidate Prussian rule, the king issued an edict at the instigation of von Münchow with the intention of alleviating provincial alarm. In the edict it was explained that there was no intention in the government's mind ever to alter the cadastral registers again or even to propose that the tax rates would 'never be raised or increased'.[71]

The new taxation structure encompassed all the population in a similar way as in East Prussia so that the nobility did not enjoy total exemption. The crown lands were also taxed. The rates were set at between 28 and 34 per cent of net returns. It was thus a tax related to landed productivity. Significantly church properties were more highly taxed, although there were rebates for the spiritual Orders of Knights, and, above all, for vicarages and school lands.[72] The basic income from this tax came to around 1 700 000 *talers*, to which one should add the additional income of 600 000 *talers* from indirect taxes.[73] The latter had also been transformed since late 1741 and were now in line with other Prussian provinces. They were therefore confined to the towns, were collected purely on behalf of the state and according to a uniform set of tariffs. So Silesia found itself with a tax structure which was much more effective than it had been under the Habsburgs. There is no evidence to suggest that it was regarded as particularly inequitable. Taxation 'on a Prussian footing' was more thoroughgoing than under the preceding régime but it was also more logical and equitable. It also delivered exactly what Frederick wanted in terms of an increasing revenue.

The first Silesian provincial budget[74] was prepared (although not for the Berlin General Directory) for the year 1743. Of a total of around 3 500 000 *talers*, about 800 000 *talers* came from crown lands, land rents, forest dues and regalian rights. The remainder came from taxes. Expenditures included 225 000 *talers* for salaries and a further 200 000 *talers* which were set aside for land improvements. The lion's share of what remained, 2 150 000 *talers*, went to pay for the military forces stationed in the province. Lastly, the king set aside a sum of around 800 000 *talers* from the income of the province and placed it at his own disposal. Save for writing off the payments to the Silesian provincial debts and the building of new fortifications, this sum went directly to the state treasury.[75] The Silesian provincial treasurers were instructed to deliver these sums directly to the king rather than to the general treasury in Berlin.

This new administrative and financial structure was established in the conquered province of Silesia in a short period of time. It was put in place without great difficulty or even resistance from the native population. There is no doubt that it was effective to the degree that it furthered Frederick's objectives for the state as a whole. But it would not be legitimate to identify these interests with the wishes and conceptions of the Silesians themselves. But in assessing these measures we must still attempt to do so according to the criteria of the period itself. And, in those circumstances, the evaluation of Otto Hintze in 1909 still retains its value:[76] 'These administrative patterns . . . served, in the first instance, the power of the state rather than the well-being of its citizens. Historically, they put Silesia (and particularly its towns) under a heavier burden than was felt anywhere else in the Prussian state'.

It is, however, significant that after two fruitless wars waged to win back Silesia it was precisely this administrative and financial system which was adapted by the Habsburg monarchy under Maria Theresa to institute a total reform of the state.[77] By adopting the Prussian system she hoped to achieve for the Habsburg monarchy the military prowess necessary to recover this prized province. Her most influential councillor was the Saxon-born Frederick William, Count Haugwitz (1702–65). As President of the 'Royal Bureau' set up in Troppau as from 23 January 1743 in the little of what remained of Austrian Silesia, he was able to follow at close hand the way in which Prussia set about reform in Silesia.[78] Whilst the Silesian nobility, supported by the Bohemian Court Chancellery in Vienna, refused to maintain two further cavalry regiments even as Frederick invaded, the Prussian king supported an entire army from its resources and yet without bringing about its ruin. Haugwitz's plans for a full-scale reform of Maria Theresa's state and administration, formulated in 1749,[79] were intended to be a turning-point in the financial and military fortunes of the Habsburg monarchy. However, the 'General Government Directory' (*Directorium in Publicis et Cameralibus*), the new overall authority for the Interior and for Finance (established along Prussian lines) under the presidency of Haugwitz was not able to reverse what had taken place in 1740. Prussia's entry into the circle of the Great Powers was not to be stopped in that way.

To consolidate Frederick's rule in Silesia the judicial constitution had also to be brought into alignment with the changed circumstances. It is evident that he proceeded much more cautiously with the administration of justice than was the case with the administration in general or with that of taxation. Prussian state interests were only indirectly involved. While the intention was that the multiplicity of courts should be reduced and the fragmented legal system unified wherever possible and a common and consistent framework of law evolved for the province of Silesia, until such aims were achieved, things would have to be left as before and determined in accordance with 'traditional law and practice'.[80] The lesser seigneurial courts of princes and nobles remained intact, as did the courts of town magistrates.[81] But at the same time, two 'Senior Official Government Tribunals' (*Oberamtsregierungen*)[82] were established in Breslau and Glogau as the supreme courts of the province. Beyond them, appeal lay only to the Supreme Tribunal in Berlin or through a petition to the king. An appeal to the courts in Prague or Vienna became, inevitably, a thing of the past. At the same time, there was a reform of the practices of advocacy and matters concerning legal costs and fees as well as the remuneration of judges. These measures were intended to speed up the legal procedures which sometimes dragged on. They were also designed to strengthen the guarantee of proper redress.

Of particular importance was the fact that while posts in the judicial sector (unlike those elsewhere in the government) were to be filled with qualified persons and 'without regard to religion',[83] what mattered most was that unlike those elsewhere in the administration they should be occupied by native Silesians. The first president of Breslau's Senior Official Government Tribunal was the prince of Carolath-Beuthen, one of the few Calvinists amongst the ancient noble lineages of Silesia and also a president of the 'High Court of Nobles' (*Oberfürstenrecht*), a body whose existence Frederick had retained. As president in Glogau, Frederick nominated Count Karl Albrecht von Reder auf Malnitz.[84] The reorganization of the Silesian judicial system was entrusted to two ministers of justice in Berlin, Samuel von Cocceji and Georg Dietloff von Arnim. The former was present to introduce the new bench of judges to their offices on 1 February 1742.[85] Cocceji was formally nominated 'Minister of Justice' for Silesia in March 1743[86] but before the end of the year he had relinquished the post to von Arnim.[87] However, spiritual affairs now came within the scope of the Minister of Justice and the Silesian Upper Consistory courts were subordinated to the two Senior Official Government Tribunals in Breslau and Glogau.[88] Cocceji's Catholic background and his policies towards the churches in fact proved a considerable stumbling block to him, particularly in his relations with the Catholic clergy and the Prince Bishop of Breslau.[89]

The new judicial constitution which was at first confined to Lower Silesia was extended, in the aftermath of the Peace of Berlin, to the newly annexed areas of Upper Silesia, and this was achieved by the establishment of an additional Senior Official Government Tribunal in Oppeln. It began work there in March 1744,[90] but was then subsequently transferred to Brieg in 1756.

Rather more serious difficulties were encountered in implanting Prussian military traditions in Silesia than was the case in the civil domain where, initially at any rate, scepticism or disavowal might be expressed but where there was no lasting resistance from the province. Permanent garrisoning of the rich province to ensure its preservation was vital. 'The future security of our new acquisitions', wrote Frederick in 1742, 'rests, I believe, on a good and numerically large army, a well-filled Treasury, and fortifications that instil fear and respectable alliances.'[91]

But the stationing and maintenance of large bodies of troops, the erection of garrisons, the development of forts and the enormous importance assumed by the military presence in the province, were unusual experiences in the extreme for its inhabitants.[92] Coming to terms with this was not easy since the military contingent was at least 10 times the size it had been under the Habsburgs, and stood at over 35 000 men. Even aside from the inevitable direct and indirect effects of the two Silesian wars, the billeting of troops upon the towns, and the subsidies levied on their behalf since 1742, became an oppressive burden. Sharing this burden equitably amongst the towns presented considerable difficulties in itself.

Of greater significance to the concerned local inhabitants was the introduction of the Prussian military call-up system (*Kantonsystem*) in Silesia through the decree of 16 August 1743.[93] This was to ensure that at least half the troops were recruited from within the province. The yearly quota of those actually recruited in the province came to about 1 400 men.[94] The intention was not to introduce universal conscription[95] but rather the establishment of clearly-defined recruiting districts (*Enrollierungs-Kantons*) for the troops newly stationed in the province. There were numerous exemptions for specific trades and professions, even for whole regions, such as the six mountain districts with their commitment to the production of linen or for the provincial capital Breslau. Such exemptions represented a degree of alleviation of the burden. But the unease felt about the matter was widespread. It led to a higher than average increase in desertion from the ranks of the Silesian regiments, and to the flight of a large number of young people across the borders into Saxony and Bohemia.[96] A recruitment drive for volunteers had preceded the introduction to this call-up system. But because of the frequent abuses which had resulted, and the strenuous complaints which he received about them, Frederick sought to soothe the local population.[97] He therefore issued a series of decrees intended to restore calm and these either severely curtailed recruitment by force or entirely prohibited it.[98] Only when these measures failed did he extend the recruitment regulations already applied in Prussia to Silesia. But success in this area eluded him for it took a long time for the local population to accept it.[99]

The military decrees undoubtedly constituted the major source of discontent with, and criticism of, the new Prussian rule. It is therefore hardly a matter of surprise that Frederick's opponents in Vienna attempted to exploit his vulnerability here to their own ends. They sought to woo Silesians away from Prussia by focusing on this issue. During the second Silesian War, Maria Theresa starkly contrasted Silesia under the old régime with Silesia under its new ruler.[100] Silesians were asked to recall 'the great mildness with which you were governed in the past by Our Glorious Predecessors' whilst she pointed out that King Frederick had not only violated the provincial constitution, robbed the estates of their property, encroached upon the rights of the church, but also had 'reduced the entire province to eternal bondage through the introduction of the "Recruiting Districts"'. These appeals and promises of a return to 'good government' under the Habsburgs contrasted sharply with the realities of the war situation, for it was precisely in Upper Silesia, which would have been especially receptive to such appeals, that the incursions and indiscipline of the Habsburg Hungarian troops did most damage.[101] Neither in 1744–45 nor during the widespread misery of the Seven Years War was there any large-scale disaffection besides the inevitable desertions from the army. In a personal memorandum to the king, dated August 1744, the provincial minister von Münchow reported that the mood in the province was perfectly calm. He noted the distinction between the loyalty of Upper and Lower Silesia.[102] Whilst one could scarcely find any inhabitant in Breslau or its surrounding communities 'qui n'aime beaucoup plus perdre son bien et sa vie que de passer sous un autre règne', he had 'taken all precautions (toutes les mesures imaginables)' to make sure of the loyalty of the inhabitants of Upper Silesia.

The process of integration of the two parts of the province into Brandenburg-

Prussia varied in pace and intensity. This was in no small measure due to its disparate denominational structure and the rôle of the Catholic clergy in the province of Silesia. For understandable reasons there are no reliable statistics for the confessional mix of the Silesian population on the eve of the Prussian king's seizure of power.[103] It seems, however, clear that, in 1740, the Protestant share of the population was very much higher than one would have expected, given the thorough counter-reformed policies of the Habsburgs in Silesia towards church matters.[104] Emperor Charles VI had remorselessly pursued the objective (laid down since at least the Peace of Westphalia in 1648) of reconverting Silesia completely to Catholicism through a restrictive interpretation (and, in part, circumvention) of the Convention of Altränstadt. The latter had been concluded with Charles XII of Sweden in 1707 and it was supposed to provide for a measure of freedom of religious expression.[105] It appears to have been a relatively simple matter for both the strongly Protestant population of Lower Silesia, as well as for all those who were either secretly or openly Lutheran, to look to Brandenburg-Prussia for protection. So, in seizing the province, Frederick II could reckon from the outset on a good deal of friendly understanding amongst the greater part of the Protestants whilst, from the Catholics, he could only expect to receive a guarded mistrust.[106]

Annexation not only altered the Silesian areas strongly influenced by the Bishop of Breslau, but also the religious composition of the Prussian state. Up until then, the regions with large Catholic populations were only to be found in a few of its western provinces. After the annexation, the state had a more substantial religious pluralism, and this could potentially cause difficulties both in its dealings within the Empire and with other foreign powers. It was an issue which was given an airing within Prussia itself. During the first Silesian War, the argument that it was a 'War of Religion', aiming to suppress the Catholics of Silesia, cropped up repeatedly.[107] It was seized on and exploited, of course, by the Viennese Court, and it was an argument which found favour in Poland too. To counter this propaganda, and in order to avoid a polarization of relations between the government and the clergy of the province who, for the most part, looked to the Habsburgs, Frederick's policy towards Silesia's religious communities[108] was, from the outset, conciliatory. The provisions of the various peace treaties were to be adhered to, and the status quo as regards the churches was to be maintained.[109] What the king wished to see extended to Silesia was his own basic tolerance in matters of faith, a tolerance which was fed by the Enlightenment, and which he had often publicly expressed since his accession to the throne. This was also the attitude he adopted towards the Prince Bishop of Breslau, Cardinal Philipp Ludwig Count Sinzendorf. One handwritten communiqué from the king stated:[110] 'Since the peaceful practice of one's religion is an integral part of what man perceives as his happiness, I shall never deviate from my firm resolve to protect the rights and liberties of every religion. The disputes of clerics are in no way the concern of princes, and baseless quarrels over meaningless definitions . . . shall never tempt me to decide either in favour of, or against, the various . . . protagonists.'

Frederick's detached attitude towards the various faiths could hardly be called typical of his generation.[111] He genuinely wished to guarantee freedom of religion to the Protestants of Silesia and wanted to assist them to regain their lost rights but, at the same time, he wanted to protect his catholic subjects. He therefore resisted the demands of his protestant subjects for the return of all churches appropriated since 1621 or the abolition of all tithes for the catholic clergy, since such an abolition would conflict with his stated principles.[112] Also in keeping with the principles just outlined, all forms of polemics from the pulpit were forbidden.[113]

In the course of his reorganization of the ecclesiastical affairs of Silesia, his guiding principles were to respect the rights of catholic bishops whilst, at the same time, also preserving protestant rights and, above all, sacrificing none of his own sovereign rights in the province. In the 'Decree' (*Notifikationspatent*) which established the Senior Official Government Tribunals in Breslau and Glogau in January 1742, the principles for the management and administration of ecclesiastical jurisdiction were codified.[114] Catholic subjects were to be specifically guaranteed a 'complete freedom of conscience as laid down and established in the *Instrumentum Pacis*'. The Senior Official Government Courts were required to swear under oath that they would protect 'our catholic subjects in their religious principles'. The existence of the episcopal ecclesiastical court was confirmed, but 'in such a fashion as it shall only take cognisance of ecclesiastical matters (*Causas vere ecclesiasticas*) and thus refrain from all civil matters (*Causis civilibus*), even in such cases as involve clerics'. In practice this inevitably limited clerical jurisdiction severely. The newly established consistory court was also referred to in the decree. It was to consist of a protestant and a catholic clergyman and two lay assessors. Its competence was to extend to the supervision of churches, sermons and schools as well as to matrimonial matters. This consistory was to be involved particularly in the case of mixed marriages. In matters of dispensation, Catholics were referred to the Senior Official Governing Tribunal. The Berlin Supreme Tribunal was declared the Court of Appeal for the decisions of the episcopal consistory.

Cardinal Sinzendorf saw these stipulations as an infringement upon consciences.[115] The Minister for Justice, Cocceji, however, gently reminded him that they had merely copied from Austrian practice.[116] Cocceji was a strong proponent of the view of church–state relations which allowed of no appeal by an ecclesiastical court to any body outside the state, either to a foreign diocese or to the Roman Curia.[117] Here he foreshadowed the trends of 'early Josephinism' which were to appear at a slightly later date in Austria itself.[118] Cocceji was thereby also able to advance the plans, which had long enjoyed the king's support, to create a General Vicariate for the entire country of Prussia and to place the Prince Bishop of Breslau in charge of it.[119]

The Cardinal Count Sinzendorf (1699–1747) was an educated, experienced and adaptable son of the Austrian High Chancellor.[120] He was installed in his well-endowed bishopric in 1732 against the strong opposition of the Breslau cathedral chapter thanks to imperial 'commendation'. Because of his collaboration with the Austrians, he was first arrested when the Prussians invaded. Then he was allowed to travel to Vienna after von Podewills intervened. But eventually he returned to his bishopric in Breslau and took the oath of allegiance made by the Lower Silesian estates along with his cathedral clergy. In so doing he specifically acknowledged the Prussian king as the ruler of the province and thus was treated with the most elaborate civility by Frederick.[121] Where possible, the king attempted to obtain the cardinal's acquiescence in all matters regarding church policies. Sinzendorf initially went along with the plans for a General Vicariate. Although such a plan had been rendered redundant (since it touched upon the status quo of the Silesian church constitution) by Article VI of the Berlin Peace Treaty of July 1742 it was still pursued until the problem of the choice of coadjutor[122] for the bishop came to dominate and impair the relationship between the Prussian king and the Prince Bishop.

The question of the coadjutor became one of prestige for the noble cleric who, though in some ways politically weakened by ill-health, had certainly not tired of office. It touched on the sensitive issue of who was to succeed him in the bishopric, and it was also a matter of prestige for the king who, in this matter, wanted to establish his monarchical powers within the state, including the church. In this, he succeeded, it is true, but the installation of Count Philipp von Schaffgotsch (1716–95) soon turned out to be an illusory triumph. Canon Schaffgotsch had been an engaging conversationalist at the royal table, a known Freemason, and was apparently a sufficiently staunch supporter of the king's viewpoint to attract his favour. He had convinced Frederick that he should be installed as coadjutor in Breslau. Despite the bitter opposition of the cathedral chapter, of the Roman Curia and, at first, even of Bishop Sinzendorf himself, Frederick succeeded in installing him in the post in early 1744. 'The late Emperor used the same means when it came to choosing Cardinal von Sinzendorf, as I myself have used when it came to choosing Prince Schaffgotsch as coadjutor' is how he sought to justify his proceedings.[123]

Sinzendorf died young in September 1747 and Schaffgotsch was installed in the lay administration of the bishopric of Breslau. Then, at the beginning of the following year, he was elected bishop with the agreement of the pope. Even before this, a change of attitude had indeed taken place, one which transformed the noble bishop and favourite of the king into a decided opponent of Prussian policy toward the church. In the course of the Seven Years War after the Prussian defeat at Kollin (18 June 1757) Schaffgotsch went over openly to the Austrian side and quit the province.[124] The general amnesty of the Peace of Hubertsburg included the bishop as well, but he nevertheless chose to go into exile again in 1766, and died in 1795 at the Johannesberg Castle in the small Austrian part of his diocese. Throughout this period, the suffragen Bishop of Breslau carried out his spiritual duties while the episcopal income from the Prussian part was appropriated by the state.

Even the spectacular defection of the supreme head of the Breslau diocese, coupled with the rapidly deteriorating political and military situation in the final years of the Seven Years War still did not persuade the catholic population of Silesia, and with it the majority of its clergy, to change allegiance. The proposition that this was a 'War of Religion' which the propagandists had resurrected, lost all conviction. Nevertheless, the confessional climate in the province during the war years remained strained and tense, not least because of the influence of the then Minister for Silesia, von Schlabrendorff, whose negative reports to the suspicious monarch did not fail to influence Frederick and resulted in various restrictive edicts.[125] A lasting relaxation of tension was only possible after peace was concluded in 1763 when the status quo of the Breslau and Berlin peace treaties was once again specifically re-stated (Article XIV). Thereafter the tolerant spirit of the Enlightenment[126] began to take full effect in the province, and the secular religious beliefs of the epoch further weakened these religious conflicts. Neighbouring Austria quickly lost its attractions for the Silesian clergy as the radical measures in the policies of Joseph and Maria Theresa towards church and cloister appeared in their turn. What also contributed to the rupture of what had once been the many close connections of the catholic clergy to the Habsburg territories were the attempts emanating from Vienna to redraw the diocesan borders,[127] along with a royal decree of 1779 which limited the candidature for the ministry in Silesia to those who had studied at the Breslau Academy.[128]

The annexation of Silesia was certainly welcomed by the protestant sections of its population for the freedom of religion which it gave them. Both Protestants and Catholics enjoyed an uninterrupted practice of their religious worship. In this respect, little had changed in practice from the days of Habsburg rule. Yet the church only gradually arrived at a *modus vivendi* with the Prussian state which was fully intent on exercising its rights in accordance with the principles contained in the theories of the rights of the church under a territorial prince and enlightened despotism. In this respect, Prussia was not out of step with contemporary trends. Nevertheless, the conditions were established in Silesia under Frederick the Great for the peaceful coexistence of the two faiths and for that specifically 'Silesian tolerance' which was to endure into the following period.[129]

The fundamental change in the structure, the organization of the administration, and the finance department, the introduction of the Prussian military system, the reform of the judiciary and the new order in the relationship between church and state characterize the political aims consciously pursued during the annexation of Silesia by Frederick the Great's Prussia. The annexation was tested firstly during the Silesian wars. In the longer term, the inner consolidation of the new province took place along with, overall, its smooth integration into the Prussian monarchy. Whether this also holds true for its economic integration must remain, for the moment, an open question.[130] Despite some important monographs, research in this area has so far not been able to provide a clear and convincing global picture of the economic development of Silesia during the second half of the eighteenth century. What has aroused controversy has been the effects of Frederick's economic policies on the province. This can be explained in part by the differing perspectives of those who write the history of Silesia and Prussia.[131] It may also be explained by the fact that the king did not appear to have any uniform objectives in terms of economic policies so far as Silesia was concerned. Instead, he let foreign policy rather than economic matters determine things. It must also be remembered that economic change occurs only gradually and that external factors must also be taken into account.

With all this in mind, it is possible to characterize Frederick's economic policies towards Silesia as 'mercantilist', that is to say, broadly protectionist. They were intended in the first place to give encouragement to indigenous manufactures to the detriment of commerce. He actively encouraged the founding and protection of manufactures through privileges, monopolies and state subventions. At the same time, he greatly impeded foreign and transit trade through prohibitions and duties to the detriment of all concerned. This in turn had, of necessity, largely negative consequences on the traditional Silesian 'principal manufacture' of linen, based on the growing of flax and the spinning of yarn, an industry which was geared to export throughout Europe.[132] It has now been proved to have been the case that the Silesian linen industry suffered a decline in the period from 1741 to 1806, when the sharp rise in prices and the rising population is taken into account. However the second important branch of Silesian textile industry, its production of cloth from home-produced or imported wool and cotton, presents a different pattern.[133] This industry expanded independently of the political changes consequent upon war. But, as government statistics show, the 30 or so newly established 'industries', with their centres of production geared to export and reliant upon international trade, made little significant impact upon the economy as a whole.[134] The numerous new manufacturies often did not last very long, in Silesia as elsewhere. Even with mining and the related foundry industries which, during the nineteenth century laid (on the basis of coal and iron) the foundations for a transformed Silesian economy, their productivity and overall contribution was relatively slight in the first decades of Frederick's rule.[135] It was only in the later period, under the aegis of the energetic Minister von Heinitz who, in 1777, took over the Mining and Foundry department in the Berlin General Directory (founded in 1768), that it became more significant.[136] He was among a few government officials who were critical of Frederick's customs and trade policies.

The annexation of Silesia into the Prussian state demanded that the Silesian economy, and particularly its merchant classes, grew accustomed to and adapted themselves to the Prussian internal market. Old trade connections were abruptly shattered in 1740 or were interrupted by the broader political changes. This was especially the case for the traditional economic ties with the neighbouring Habsburg territories,[137] ties which had been interrupted by Maria Theresa and which, because of the restrictive trade policies of Frederick in response, were doomed. The same was true of those trading links with the Electorate of Saxony, with whom a formal trade war was waged, with Hungary, and also with Poland.[138] Suddenly, markets and sources of supply unexpectedly vanished, either because through partition they had become, like West Prussia in 1772, a Prussian province, or else, because (like Galitia) they were in hostile hands. It seems as if the Silesian economy and, in particular, the commerce centring around Breslau did not adapt either quickly or effectively enough. The new province, although prosperous, found itself at a disadvantage (because of royal restrictions and taxation) when compared to the economically less developed central provinces.[139] Prussia was not a uniform economic entity at this period. But it was Potsdam and the capital Berlin which tended to enjoy advantages at the expense of Silesia.

From its provincial perspective, Silesia was almost bound to regard itself as disadvantaged and this has been the judgement reached (with some justice)[140] by its historians. Prussian historians of the older school tend to present the Prussian annexation of Silesia, again with a measure of justification, as the beginning of a new epoch, a turn for the better in Silesian economic affairs, as in other matters.[141] It is now possible to interpret the various aspects of this now-closed chapter of Silesian history in more generous terms. Any judgement about the economic consequences of annexation must therefore, in the absence of conclusive research, be an ambivalent one.

The widely held reservations initially felt by the Silesian population towards the annexation and towards the individual measures adopted by Frederick II were short-lived. By the close of the Seven Years' War in 1763, a war which again inflicted heavy damage on the province, all the uncertainties were finally at an end. A period of re-establishment began in which the king provided large sums of money to Silesia to make good the ravages of war and to assist in the reconstruction which brought about the final consolidation of the province under the Prussian monarchy.[142]

That its inhabitants now were a part of the Prussian state was no longer a matter for debate. Silesians even came to view it in a more positive light. They began to identify with the state, or at least with its monarch, and to be reconciled to Frederick II. Not only did a fundamental change of attitude occur in every part of public life in the province, but also amongst the population at large. There is no better moment of proof of this than at the close of the long reign of Frederick the Great. According to the unreliable but often shrewd commentator Count Mirabeau, the capital, Berlin, appeared almost relieved at the death of the 74-year-old monarch, but according to other sources in Silesia, the public displays of mourning seemed spontaneous, genuine and uninhibited.[143] Christian Garve, a representative intellectual in Silesia of the period, gave the king a fitting monument in his published essay: *An Essay depicting the Spirit, Character and Rule of Frederick the Second*. He may be taken as representative of the *litterati* of Silesia who had at first seen the king of Prussia as a conqueror and who now came to appreciate his achievements.

NOTES FOR CHAPTER 9

* Professor of Modern History, University of Würzburg.

1 This chapter originated in a paper presented and discussed at the Universities of Gießen and Regensburg in 1978. The footnotes take some account of literature published up to the year 1983. The text was originally published in P. Baumgart (ed.), *Expansion und Integration. Zur Eingliederung neugewonnener Gebiete in den preußischen Staat* (Cologne and Vienna, 1984). It has been translated by Rick Cavanagh of the Department of Germanic Studies, University of Sheffield and the editor. The critical apparatus has been shortened in the English translation; (. . .) indicates significant omissions. The chapter is published with the kind permission of the author and publisher, Böhlau Verlag.

2 For a brief account of this annexation, see P. Wagner, 'Zur Geschichte der Besitznahme Ostfrieslands durch Preußen' in *Jahrbuch der Gesellschaft für bildende Kunst und vaterländische Altertümer zu Emden* xi (1895), p. 137ff. For a more detailed perspective concerning the estates, see C. Hinrichs, 'Die ostfriesischen Landstände und der preußische Staat, 1744–56 . . .' in *Ibid.*, xxii (1927) pp. 1–268. There is more detail on the immediate circumstances in East Friesland in 1744 in J. König, *Verwaltungsgeschichte Ostfrieslands bis zum Aussterben seines Fürstenhauses* (Göttingen, 1955).

3 The fundamental work here remains Max Bär, *Westpreußen unter Friedrich dem Großen* (2 vols., 1909; new edn, Osnabrück, 1965). Cf. the overview of Walther Hubatsch, *Frederick the Great of Prussia; Absolutism and Administration* (trans. 1975), p. 181ff.

4 Alfred Kohler, 'Das Reich im Spannungsfeld des preußisch-österreichischen Gegensatzes. Die Fürstenbundsbestrebungen 1782–85' in *Fürst, Bürger, Mensch* (Munich, 1975) surveys the older literature on this subject.

5 See Walther Bußmann, 'Friedrich der Grosse im Wandel des europäischen

Urteils' (1951) reprinted in *Wandel und Kontinuität in Politik und Geschichte*, ed. Werner Pöls, (Boppard, 1973). For a recent analysis of Frederick in the light of the conquest of Silesia and his motives, see Theodor Schieder, 'Macht und Recht. Der Ursprung der Eroberung Schlesiens durch König Friedrich II. von Preußen', in *Hamburger Jahrbuch für Wirtschafts- und Gesellschaftspolitik*, xxiv (1979), p. 235ff. and also his 'Friedrich der Große und Machiavelli. Das Dilemma von Machtpolitik und Aufklärung' in *Historische Zeitschrift*, ccxxxiv (1982), p. 265ff.

6 Johann Gustav Droysen, *Geschichte der Preußischen Politik* Part 5 (4 vols. Leipzig, 1874–86).

7 Onno Klopp, *Der König Friedrich von Preußen und seine Politik* (1st edn, 1860); cf. Bußmann, 'Friedrich der Grosse', p. 270ff.

8 Reinhold Koser, *Geschichte Friedrichs des Großen* (4 vols. Repr. Darmstadt, 1963).

9 See Manfred Schlenke, 'Von der Schwierigkeit, Preußen auszuestellen. Rückschau auf die Preußen-Ausstellung 1981' in *Geschichte in Wissenschaft und Unterricht (GWU)*, xxxiii (1982). Also Klaus Zernack, 'Preußen-Welle unter dem Primat der Innenpolitik. Einige konträre Überlegungen' in *Politik, Gesellschaft, Geschichtsschreibung. Gießener Festgabe für Frantiček Graus zum 60. Geburtstag*, eds. H. Ludat and R. Ch. Schwinges (Cologne and Vienna, 1982), p. 427ff.

10 See the initial remarks in P. Baumgart, 'Epochen der preußischen Monarchie im 18. Jahrhundert' in *Zeitschrift für Historische Forschung*, vi (1979) p. 287ff.

11 '... dans deux heures je passerai le Rubicon' (Frederick II – von Podewils, Crossen, 16 December 1740) in *Politische Correspondenz Friedrichs des Großen* (henceforth cited as *PC*), i (Berlin, 1879) No. 20. (. . .)

12 Conveniently summarized in Ludwig Petry, 'Politische Geschichte unter den Habsburgeren' in the History of Silesia prepared by the Historical Commission for Silesia, ii *Die Habsburgerzeit, 1526–1740* (Darmstadt, 1973) pp. 15ff., 57ff. and 74ff. Also Peter Baumgart, 'Schlesien und Pommern in der Politik des brandenburgisch-preußischen Staates' in *Schlesien und Pommern in den deutsch-polnischen Beziehungen vom 16. bis 18. Jahrhundert* (Brunswick, 1983) p. 17ff.

13 *Ibid.*, p. 27.

14 See also the interpretation of Schieder, 'Macht und Recht', p. 244. The document is now conveniently reproduced in Richard Dietrich (ed.), *Politische Testamente der Hohenzollern* (Munich, 1981) p. 80ff.

15 The various agreements are printed in Theodor von Moerner (ed.), *Kurbrandenburgs Staatsverträge von 1601 bis 1700* (Berlin, 1867; repr. 1965) no. 286 (22 March 1686); nos. 289, 290, 382 (10/20 December 1694). Cf. the older interpretation of Koser, *Geschichte Friedrichs*, p. 282. (. . .)

16 See Gustav Berthold Volz, 'Friedrich Wilhelm I und die preußischen Erbansprüche auf Schlesien' in *Forschungen zur Brandenburgischen und Preußischen Geschichte* (henceforth cited as *FBPG*), xxx (1918) p. 55ff.

17 Reprinted in Reinhold Koser (ed.), 'Preußische Staatsschriften aus der Regierungszeit König Friedrichs II', *Stratsschriften aus der Regierungszeit Friedrichs II*, i (Berlin, 1877) p. 41ff.

18 '... c'est le moment du changement total de l'ancien système de politique; c'est ce rocher détaché qui roule sur la figure des quatre métaux ...' (Frederick II – Voltaire, 26 Oct. 1740) in *Oeuvres de Frédéric le Grand* (henceforth cited as *Oeuvres*) xxii (Berlin, 1853), p. 49. Cf. Frederick II – Algarotti, 28 Oct. 1740 (xviii, p. 199) and Koser, *Geschichte Friedrichs*, i, p. 233. These quotations are assessed in Peter Rassow, 'Die Angliederung Schlesiens an Preußen 1740 in ihrer Bedeutung für das System der großen Mächte' in *Beiträge zur ostdeutschen Kultur- und Geistesgeschichte* (University of Cologne, 1953) p. 12ff.

19 Schieder, 'Macht und Recht', p. 240.

20 Memorandum entitled: 'Idées sur les projets politiques à former au sujet de la mort de l'empereur' in *PC*, i, no. 140.

21 Frederick II – Jordan, 3 March 1741 (*Oeuvres*, xvii, p. 91).

22 In his Political Testament of 1752 the formulation is: 'L'intérêt de l'état [est] l'unique motif qui doit décider dans le conseil des princes' – see *Die Politischen Testamente Friedrichs des Großen*, ed. G. B. Volz (Berlin, 1920) p. 48.

23 See Friedrich Meinecke, *Machiavellism: the Doctrine of Raison d'Etat and Its Place in Modern History* (trans. 1957) p. 272, 298ff.; also Erika Bosbach, *Die 'Rêveries Politiques' in Friedrichs des Großen Politischem Testament von 1752* (Cologne and Graz, 1960) p. 73.

24 Frederick's *Histoire de mon temps*, *Oeuvres* ii, p. 53.

25 G. P. Gooch, *Frederick the Great* (1947) p. 8ff. On Gooch's interpretation see Bußmann, 'Friedrich der Grosse', p. 284ff.

26 See Fritz Wagner, *Kaiser Karl VII und die großen Mächte 1740–45* (Stuttgart, 1938).

27 As defined in F. Meinecke, *Machiavellism*, p. 272ff. Cf. Walter Hubatsch, *Das Problem der Staatsräson bei Friedrich dem Großen* (Göttingen, 1956). Hubatsch's views are summarized in English in 'Frederick the Great and the problem of *Raison d'état*', *Studies in Medieval and Modern German History* (1985) p. 70ff.

28 In addition to Heinrich Triepel, *Die Hegemonie. Ein Buch von führenden Staaten* (1938, repr. Aalen, 1961) p. 221 consult Johannes Kunisch, *Das Mirakel des Hauses Brandenburg. Studien zum Verhältnis von Kabinettspolitik und Kriegführung im Zeitalter des Siebenjährigen Krieges* (Munich and Vienna, 1978) p. 35ff. (. . .)

29 See Kunisch, *ibid.* p. 17ff.; but for the East-European aspect see now Michael G. Müller, 'Rußland und der Siebenjährige Krieg. Beitrag zu einer Kontroverse' in *Jahrbücher für Geschichte Osteuropas*, xxviii (1980) p. 198ff.

30 See Koser, *Geschichte Friedrichs*, i, p. 253ff. and, for the ensuing circumstances, p. 304ff.

31 Ibid., p. 356ff.

32 Ibid., p. 368ff. Concerning the frontier lines, see Colmar Grünhagen, *Schlesien unter Friedrich dem Großen*, i (Breslau, 1890) p. 194ff., 207ff.

33 In the Berlin peace treaty, the Austrian plenipotentiary agreed to a clause restricting the sovereign rights of the king of Prussia: 'de sort pourtant, que S[a] M[ajesté] le roi de Prusse ne se servira des droits du souverain au prejudice du status quo de la religion catholique en Silesie' – see Max Lehmann (dir.), *Preußen und die Katholische Kirche seit 1640* . . . (Publikationen aus den K. Preußischen Staatsarchiven, x, 1881. Repr. Osnabrück, 1965) no. 168, p. 146. On these important religious questions see Georg Jaeckel, 'Die Bedeutung der konfessionellen Frage für die Besitzergreifung Schlesiens durch Friedrich den Großen' in *Jahrbuch für Schlesische Kirchengeschichte*, xxxiv (1955) p. 78ff., esp. p. 97.

34 '. . . beaucoup de modération et de douceur envers tous nos voisins . . .' (23 June 1742) – *PC*. ii, no. 905. Cf., however, no. 902 where Frederick wanted the occupation supported 'sur une bonne et nombreuse armée, un bon trésor, des forteresses redoutables'.

35 See Fred Schädrich, *Das Generalfeldkriegskommissariat in Schlesien 1741* (Breslau, 1913).

36 Ibid., p. 34. On the development of these institutions under the Habsburgs see, among others, Petry, 'Politische Geschichte', pp. 26, 88, 127ff.

37 Documents printed in *Acta Borussica. Denkmäler der preußischen Staatsverwaltung im 18. Jahrhundert* . . . (Henceforth cited as *AB, BO* (Berlin, 1894 etc.) vi, Part 2, no. 123.

38 Besides Petry, 'Politische Geschichte', Hans Hübner, *Die Gesamtstaatsverfassung Schlesiens in der Zeit des 30 jährigen Krieges* (PhD Thesis. Frankfurt, 1922). See the informative overview from Otto Hintze in *AB, BO*, vi, Part 1, p. 495ff., and also Norbert Conrads, 'Die schlesische Ständeverfassung im Umbruch. Vom altständischen Herzogtum zur preußischen Provinz' in *Ständetum und Staatsbildung in Brandenburg-Preußen* (dir. P. Baumgart with the collaboration of J. Schmädeke (Berlin and New York, 1983) p. 335ff.

39 Statistics are given from the censuses of 1736, 1770 and 1796 in the table

published by Colmar Grünhagen, 'Schlesien im Jahre 1797. Bericht des Ministers Grafen Hoym' in *Zeitschrift des Vereins für Geschichte und Alterthum Schlesiens,* xxxiii (1899) p. 355ff. (. . .)

40 On the confessional position in Silesia after 1648 see Petry, 'Politische Geschichte', p. 95ff. For other literature, see Max Lehmann, 'Staat und Kirche in Schlesien vor der preußischen Besitzergreifung' in *Historische Zeitschrift,* vii (1883) p. 193ff. Cf. Jaeckel, 'Bedentungder confessionallen Frage', p. 85ff. An important minor problem is illuminated in the monograph of Norbert Conrads, *Die Durchführung der Altranstädter Konvention in Schlesien 1707–9* (Cologne and Vienna, 1971).

41 See Norbert Conrads, *Durchführung* and also Jürgen Rainer Wolf, *Steuerpolitik im schlesischen Ständestaat. Untersuchungen zur Sozial- und Wirtschaftsstruktur Schlesiens im 17. und 18. Jahrhundert* (Marburg/Lahn, 1978). (. . .)

42 These were Schweidnitz and Jauer, Glogau, Oppeln and Ratibor, Breslau, Liegnitz, Brieg and Wohlau. See the specialized studies of Gustav Croon, *Die landständische Verfassung von Schweidnitz-Jauer . . .* (Breslau, 1912) and the more recent account of Wohlau by Richard Juhnke, *Wohlau. Geschichte des Fürstentums und des Kreises* (Würzburg, 1965).

43 Amongst these were the principality of Teschen, ruled over by Franz Stephan, of the House of Lothringen, Maria Theresa's husband, as well as the old episcopal province of the bishop of Breslau at Neiße Grottkau, the principalities of Oels, Troppau, Jägerndorf, Sagan and Münsterberg.

44 Wartenberg, Pleß, Militsch, Trachenberg, Beuthen and Carolath-Beuthen.

45 The 10 royal cities were Schweidnitz, Jauer, Reichenbach, Glogau, Sprottau, Oppeln, Neumarkt, Liegnitz, Brieg and Wohlau.

46 For the rural conditions of Silesia see Günter Dessmann, *Geschichte der schlesischen Agrarverfassung* (Strasbourg, 1904) and, for the later period of Frederick's rule, Johannes Ziekursch, *Hundert Jahre schlesischer Agrargeschichte. Vom Hubertusburger Frieden bis zum Abschluß der Bauernbefreiung* (Breslau, 1913). Ernst Emil Klotz, *Die schlesische Gutsherrschaft des ausgehenden 18. Jahrhunderts* (1932; repr. 1978). Victor Loewe concentrates on conditions in upper Silesia in *Oberschlesien und der preußische Staat,* i, (1740–1815) (Breslau, 1930) p. 64ff.

47 Conrads, 'Die schlesische Ständeverfassung', writing from the perspective of the estates, even wrote of the 'destruction of the constitution of the estates'.

48 The original plan had been to transfer the offices to Breslau and Liegnitz. Cf. *AB, BO,* vi, no. 128 (Plan of Reinhardt and Münchow for the organization of the Silesian chambers of 11 Dec. 1741) and no. 126 (Royal Ordinance for the same day); cf. Schädrich, *Feldkriegskommissariat,* p. 100.

49 Royal Ordinance to the *Feldkriegskommissariat,* Berlin, 27 Nov. 1741, *ibid.,* no. 141; cf. also nos. 124 and 126.

50 Marginal note to the document of 8 Nov. 1741, *ibid.,* no. 132.

51 On the establishment of the two chambers, see *ibid.,* nos. 128, 129, 130, 131 and 141.

52 Cabinet instruction of 27 Nov. 1741; *ibid.,* nos. 128 and 141; cf. Schädrich, *Feldkriegskommissariat,* p. 101ff. with a list of the chamber officials.

53 See the detailed instruction of 1 Sep. 1741 in *AB, BO* vi, Part 2, no. 120; for a criticism of the 'often unsuitable personnel' in the established Silesian tax administration, Johannes Ziekrusch, 'Zur Charakteristik der schlesischen Steuerräte (1742–1809) in *Zeitschrift des Vereins für Geschichte und Alterthum Schlesiens* xliii (1909) p. 131ff.

54 See Schädrich, *Feldkriegkommissariat,* p. 53ff.

55 See Colmar Grünhagen, *Breslau und die Landesfürsten* esp. part ii (in *Zeitschrift des Vereins für Geschichte und Alterthum Schlesiens,* xxxvi (1902) p. 236ff.; and also iii (in *ibid.,* xxxviii (1904) p. 1ff).

56 See Schädrich p. 85ff.; 'Royal desiderata for the establishment of "properly

constituted *Landräte*", 11 Oct. 1741', *AB, BO*, vi, Part 2, no. 126; cf. Ursula Schulz, 'Die schlesischen Landräte unter Friedrich dem Großen' in *Jahrbuch der schlesischen Friedrich-Wilhelm-Universität*, xviii (1973) p. 56ff.

57 *AB, BO* vi, Part 2, no. 140 (Establishment of the lower Silesian *Landräte*, 25 Oct. 1741); no. 147 (Instruction, 19 Dec. 1741); no. 214 (Establishment of the upper Silesian *Landräte*).

58 Initially there were 19 of these Elders in the Breslau districts and 16 in the Glogau districts, each receiving an annual stipend of 300 Reichstaler.

59 *AB, BO*, vi, Part 2, no. 152 (2 Jan. 1742).

60 Thus described by Colmar Grünhagen, 'Die beiden ersten schlesischen Sonder-minister' in *FBPG*, xx (1907) pp. 429–64 esp. p. 430ff. Cf. Koser, *Geschichte Friedrichs* ii, p. 12.

61 Royal Ordinance to the *Generaldirektorium*, *AB, BO* vi, Part 2, no. 199. Cf. no. 259 (Münchow's Commission, 24 Sep. 1742); Cf. Colmar Grünhagen, 'Die Entstehung eines schlesischen Sonderministeriums' in *FBPG*, xx (1907) p. 105ff.

62 Royal instruction of 3 Feb. 1742 with comments on Reinhardt's appointment, *AB, BO*, vi, Part 2, no. 185; cf. no. 199. Also Grünhagen, 'Entstehung', p. 116ff.

63 But see reservations of Grünhagen, 'Die beiden ersten Sonderminister', p. 441ff.

64 *AB, BO*, ix, no. 377 (Instruction, 5 Oct. 1753); cf. viii, no. 411. On Massow, see Grünhagen, 'Die beiden ersten Sonderminister', p. 455ff.

65 On von Schlabrendorff, see Herman von Petersdorff, 'Ernst Wilhelm von Schlab-rendorff' in *Schlesier des 18. und 19. Jahrhunderts* . . . (Breslau, 1926) p. 1ff.

66 Already in the royal ordinance to the *Feldkriegskommissariat* of 22 Nov. 1741, *AB, BO*, vi, Part 2, no. 141.

67 Now studied in detail by Conrads, 'Die schlesische Ständeverfassung . . .', p. 346.

68 Summarized in Hintze, 'Behördenorganization . . .', p. 521ff., besides which see Felix Rachfal, *Die Organisation der Gesamtstaatsverwaltung* p. 261ff. and for a study of a particular aspect, Wolf, *Steuerpolitik* . . . , p. 11ff, and esp. p. 93ff.

69 The king addressed the Estates in session on 25 Oct. 1741 and said 'the hitherto customary *Conventus Publici* in Silesia, and its associated former *Generalsteuer-Amtes* of the honourable Lords, Princes and Estates were no longer necessary'; the intention, however, was to create 'a very different constitution'; see the 'Landes-Diarium de Anno 1741 et usque ad ult. Junii 1742' published by Gustav Adolf Stenzel (ed.), *Actenstücke, Berichte und andere Beiträge zur Geschichte Schlesiens seit dem Jahre 1740* (Breslau, 1851), p. 175; also *AB, BO*, vi Part 2, no. 98. Extracts from the diary are also quoted in Conrads, 'Die schlesische Ständeverfassung . . .', p. 347ff.; cf. Grünhagen, *Schlesien unter Friedrich dem Grossen*, i, p. 313ff.

70 The decisions are contained in *AB, BO*, vi, Part 2, no. 232; cf. Grünhagen, *Schlesien unter Friedrich*, i, p. 370ff. (. . .)

71 *AB, BO*, vi, Part 2, no. 232.

72 Cf. Koser, *Geschichte Friedrichs*, ii, p. 124.

73 *Ibid.*, p. 15; for the revenue from the excise see Schädrich, *Feldkriegskommissariat*, p. 63ff.

74 See Koser, *Geschichte Friedrichs*, ii, p. 110 and 123. The budget for 1763 was not markedly different in its essentials.

75 Cf. Reinhold Koser, 'Der preußische Staatsschatz von 1740 bis 1756' in *FBPG*, iv. (1891) p. 529ff.; also 'Die preußischen Finanzen 1763–1786' in *FBPG*, xvi (1903) p. 445ff., esp. pp. 455 and 472. Also, see Colmar Grünhagen, 'Der schlesische Schatze 1770–1809' in *Zeitschrift des Vereins für Geschichte und Alterthum Schlesiens*, xxvii (1893) p. 204ff.

76 Otto Hintze, in his review of the study of Johannes Ziekursch, 'Das Ergebnis der friderizianischen Städteverwaltung und die Städteordnung Steins, am Beispiel der schlesischen Städte dargestellt' in *FBPG*, xxii (1909) p. 284. (. . .)

77 See Friedrich Walter, *Theresianische Staatsreform von 1749* (Vienna, 1958); also 'Preußen und die österreichische Erneuerung von 1749' in *MIÖG*, li (1937) p. 415ff. and 'Die ideellen Grundlagen der österreichischen Staatsreform von 1741' in *Zeitschrift für Öffentliches Recht*, xvii (1937) p. 195ff.

78 Walter, *Preußen*, p. 429. (. . .)

79 Besides Walter, 'Staatsreform', see also Hans Haussherr, *Verwaltungseinheit und Ressorttrennung vom Ende des 17. bis zum Beginn des 19. Jahrhunderts* (Berlin, 1955) p. 77ff.

80 *AB, BO*, vi, Part 2, no. 143 (Protocol of the first conference on Silesian Justice, Berlin, 8 Dec. 1741); see also Grünhagen, *Schlesien unter Friedrich*, i, p. 354ff.

81 Details on the organization of justice etc. in *AB, BO*, vi, Part 2, no. 170.

82 *Ibid.*, nos. 143, 149, 150 with a description of the office, no. 151, no. 170.

83 *Ibid.*, no. 143.

84 The king had selected these members of the Silesian court already in November 1741 – *ibid.*, no. 133. Cf. Grünhagen, *Schlesien unter Friedrich*, i, p. 326ff.

85 Reports, protocols etc., *AB, BO*, vi, Part 2, no. 182.

86 *Ibid.*, nos. 169 and 200.

87 *AB, BO*, vi, Part 2, no. 420 (royal ordinance to von Podewils of 25 Dec. 1743).

88 Regulations in *ibid.*, no. 170.

89 In further detail in Koser, *Geschichte Friedrichs*, ii, p. 129ff., esp. 134.

90 Documents in *AB, BO*, vi, Part 2, nos. 362 and 367.

91 *PC*, ii, no. 905 (Frederick II – Podewils, encamped at Kuttenberg, 23 June 1742); also no. 902.

92 See also for the following, Grünhagen, *Schlesien unter Friedrich*, i, p. 390ff. On the recruitment and garrisoning of regiments in Silesia, as well as the overall military operations, see Curt Jany, *Geschichte der preußischen Armee vom 15. Jahrhundert bis 1914*, ii ('Die Armee Friedrichs des Großen 1740–1763') (New edn, Osnabrück, 1967) p. 14ff.; 49ff.; 78ff.; also Colmar Grünhagen, 'Die Errichtung des Militärwesens in Schlesien bei dem Beginn der preußischen Herrschaft' in *Zeitschrift des Vereins für Geschichte und Alterthum Schlesiens*, xxiii (1889) p. 1ff.

93 Jany, *Preußischen Armee*, ii, p. 79.

94 Grünhagen, *Schlesien unter Friedrich*, i, p. 408.

95 *Ibid.*, p. 405; also Koser, *Geschichte Friedrichs* p. 125. On the origins, introduction and development of the canton system, see Curt Jany, 'Die Kantonsverfassung Friedrich Wilhelms I' in *FBPG*, xxxviii (1926) p. 225ff.; also Otto Büsch, *Militärsystem und Sozialleben im alten Preußen 1713–1807* (Berlin, 1962) p. 17ff.

96 Until 1746 the decree of the canton-system caused 10–12 000 representatives 'of the young menfolk' to cross the border to Saxony (Koser, *Geschichte Friedrichs* ii, p. 126).

97 Letters patent from the Silesian *Feldkriegskommissariat* of 20 Nov. 1741, 25 Dec. 1741, 15 Aug. 1742 in *AB, BO*, vi, Part 2, no. 138. Royal instructions to Reinhardt, 2 Jan. 1742 (*ibid.*, no. 156). (. . .)

98 Jany, *Preußische Armee*, ii, p. 78.

99 Sharp reproach and criticism of the king was evident in 1744 and 1747; Koser, *Geschichte Friedrichs* p. 126.

100 Her appeal of 1 Dec. 1744 extracted in Koser, ed., 'Preußische Staatsschriften', i, p. 528; also the Prussian response.

101 See Jany, *Preußische Armee*, ii, pp. 113 and 117.

102 Contemporary report of 25 Aug. 1744 published in Lehmann (ed.) *Preußen und die katholische Kirche*, ii, no. 600. For the development in upper Silesia, see Viktor Loewe, *Oberschlesien*, pp. 5ff.; 27ff.

103 See above, note 39.

104 In addition to the literature cited in note 38 above, see also C. Weigelt, 'Die

evangelische Kirche in Schlesien zur Zeit der preußischen Besitzergreifung und ihre Entwicklung von 1740–1756' in *Zeitschrift des Vereins für Geschichte und Alterthum Schlesiens*, xxiii (1889) p. 60ff.

105 Conrads, *Durchführung der altranstädter Konvention*, p. 250 provides a positive assessment of the convention when he emphasizes that it gave 'Silesian Protestantism a new irrefutable basis in law'. (. . .)

106 This was also the firm conclusion of Jaeckel, 'Die Bedeutung der konfessionellen Frage', p. 119.

107 Contemporary report of 28 Feb. 1741 in *Preußen und die katholische Kirche* ii, no. 24; cf. Jaeckel, *ibid.*, p. 92; also now Friedrich Schwencker, 'Die Toleranz Friedrichs des Großen und die schlesischen Kirchen' i (1741–47) in *Zeitschrift des Vereins für Geschichte und Alterthum Schlesiens* lxxv (1941) p. 138.

108 Now also Georg Jaeckel, 'Zur fridericianischen Kirchenpolitik in Schlesien' in *Jahrbuch für Schlesische Kirchengeschichte* liv (1975) p. 105ff.

109 See note 33 above.

110 Letter in French to Sinzendorf of 20 Oct. 1741 in *Preußen und die katholische Kirche* ii, no. 51. (. . .)

111 Schwencker, *Toleranz*, p. 81; Weigelt, 'Evangelische Kirche', p. 69.

112 Detailed in Jaeckel, *Bedeutung*, p. 99. Weigelt, 'Evangelische Kirche', p. 96ff.

113 Decree on the episcopal 'vicars-general' of Breslau, Berlin, 16 Aug. 1742, in *Preußen und die katholische Kirche* ii no. 181; cf. no. 182.

114 Decree in *A.B.B.O.* vi Part 2, No 170 (. . .).

115 *Preußen und die katholische Kirche*, no. 86 (Sinzendorf – Frederick II, Breslau, 25 Jan. 1742 and no. 87 (the reply, Olmütz, 2 Feb. 1742); cf. no. 103.

116 *Ibid.*, no. 89.

117 The principle Cocceji followed was embodied in the phrase: 'Nam quod quisque in se statuit, in alio improbare nequit'.

118 There are striking parallels in the church–state politics of the Enlightenment period. For the development in Austria there are the standard works of E. Winter, F. Valjavec and F. Maaß, especially Ferdinand Maaß, *Der Frühjosephinismus* (Vienna and Munich, 1969). The European context is clarified by Elisabeth Kovacs, 'Burgundisches und theresianisch-josephinisches Staatskirchensystem' in *Österreich in Geschichte und Literatur*, xxii (1978) p. 74ff. also Jan Roegiers, 'Die Bestrebungen zur Ausbildung einer Belgischen Kirche und ihre Analogie zum österreichischen (theresianischen) Kirchensystem' in *Katholische Aufklärung und Josephinsmus*, ed. Elisabeth Kovacs (Vienna, 1979) p. 75ff.

119 On the plan for a general vicariate see the short summary in Koser, *Geschichte Friedrichs* ii, p. 13.

120 Biographical sketch in Jaeckel, *Bedeutung* p. 93; also Koser, *Geschichte Friedrichs* ii, p. 131.

121 Examples in *Preußen und die katholische Kirche* ii, no. 109.

122 The details of this issue cannot be entered into in this context; see Koser, *Geschichte Friedrichs* ii p. 132ff.; also Jaeckel, *Bedeutung*, p. 101 and his 'Zur fridericianischen Kirchenpolitik', pp. 108ff., 116ff.

123 *Preussen und die katholische Kirche*, ii, no. 583 (Frederick – Cardinal Tencin, Potsdam, 29 June 1744).

124 On the rôle of Schaffgotsch in the ecclesiastical politics in the Seven Years War see, above all, Jaeckel, *Bedeutung*, p. 107ff.

125 Examples in *Preußen und die katholische Kirche* iii, nos. 815, 823; also iv, no. 45, etc.

126 Although less satisfactory, see the thesis of Rudolf Martin Ritscher, *Versuch einer Geschichte der Aufklärung in Schlesien während des 18. Jahrhunderts* (Göttingen University, PhD Thesis, 1912) p. 133ff.; some new material in Joseph Gottschalk, 'Die katholische

Kirche in Schlesien während der Aufkärung, Forschungsaufgaben' in *Archiv für schlesische Kirchengeschichte*, xxx (1972) p. 93ff.

127 Cardinal Sinzendorf had already proposed to amalgamate the dioceses and their boundaries – see Jaeckel, 'Zur friderizianischen Kirchenpolitik' p. 108. (. . .)

128 *Preußen und die katholische Kirche* v, no. 384 (Frederick – bishop Strachwitz, Breslau, 14 May 1779).

129 Universally praised in the writings of Jaeckel, Schwencker, Weigelt, etc.; the toleration of Frederick was a principal motif of the preachers and funerary orations at the time of his death, as seen in Hans Jessen, 'Schlesiens Trauer beim Tode Friedrichs des Großen' in *Zeitschrift des Vereins für Geschichte und Alterthum Schlesiens*, lx (1936) p. 18.

130 See, for the debate over the extent of the material effects, the various works of Hermann Fechner, *Wirtschaftsgeschichte der preußischen Provinz Schlesien in der Zeit ihrer provinziellen Selbständigkeit 1641–1806* (Breslau, 1907); see the criticism of Gustav Croon, 'Die Wirkungen des preußischen Merkantilismus in Schlesien' in *Zeitschrift des Vereins für Geschichte und Alterthum Schlesiens*, xlii (1908) p. 315ff. See also the response in *idem* xliii (1909) p. 304ff.; see again Croon, 'Eine Erwiderung', *ibid.*, p. 308ff.; then Fechner, 'Die Wirkungen des preußischen Merkantilismus in Schlesien' *Vierteljahrschrift für Sozial- und Wirtschaftsgeschichte*, vii (1909) p. 315ff., a succinct statement of his position.

131 Positive assessment in William O. Henderson, *Studies in the Economic Policy of Frederick the Great* (Liverpool and London, 1963); Karl Erich Born, *Wirtschaft und Gesellschaft im Denken Friedrichs des Großen* (Mainz and Wiesbaden, 1979); also for economic policies after 1763, Ingrid Mittenzwei, *Preußen nach dem Siebenjährigen Krieg . . .* (Berlin, 1979) – see the review by Peter Baumgart in *Zeitschrift für historische Forschung*, ix (1982) p. 106ff.; cf. Hugo Rachel, 'Der Merkantilismus in Brandenburg-Preußen' in *FBPG*, xl (1927) pp. 221–66.

132 Fechner, *Wirtschaftsgeschichte . . .* , p. 730; 'Die Wirkungen', p. 317. (. . .)

133 Fechner, 'Die Wirkungen . . .', p. 318.

134 Ibid., p. 319; also *Wirtschaftsgeschichte*, p. 728ff.

135 Ibid., ch. 2. On the significance of Silesia for the 'Industrial Revolution' in Prussia see Wilhelm Treue, 'Wirtschaft und Technik in Preußen bis zu den Reformen' in *JGMOD*, xxix (1980) p. 30ff., esp. p. 35. (. . .)

136 On Heinitz and his initiatives see the monograph of W. Weber, *Innovationen im frühindustriellen deutschen Bergbau und Hüttenwesen. F. A. von Heynitz* (Göttingen, 1976). On Heinitz's criticism of Frederick's policy see Peter Baumgart, 'Tendenzen der spätfriderizianischen Verwaltung im Spiegel der Acta Borussica' in *BO, BO*, xvi, Part 2 (1982) p. xxviii and nos. 580–1.

137 Besides the other monographs of Hermann Fechner, see *Die handelspolitischen Beziehungen Preußens und Österreichs während der provinziellen Selbständigkeit Schlesiens 1741–1806* (Berlin, 1886).

138 Details in Fechner, *Wirtschaftsgeschichte*.

139 The contemporary remarks of the various Prussian ministers von Massow, von Heinitz, von Werder, Struensee are in Fechner, 'Die Wirkungen', p. 322. (. . .)

140 As Fechner, *Wirtschaftsgeschichte*, pp. 725, 731, etc.

141 See the judgement of Otto Hintze in *AB, Seidenindustrie* iii p. 295ff.; similarly R. Koser, *Geschichte Friedrichs*.

142 See Colmar Grünhagen, 'Schlesien unmittelbar nach dem Hubertusburger Frieden' in *Zeitschrift des Vereins für Geschichte und Alterthum Schlesiens* xxv (1891), p. 104ff.; 110ff. On the situation around 1763 Ernst Pfeiffer, *Die Revuereisen Friedrichs des Großen, besonders die Schlesischen nach 1763 und der Zustand Schlesiens von 1763–86* (Berlin, 1904; new edn, 1965).

143 The evidence is presented, with judicious assessment, in Jessen, 'Schlesiens Trauer'. On the atmosphere in Berlin, see Gustav Berthold Volz (ed.), *Friedrich der Große im Spiegel seiner Zeit* (Berlin, 1927) iii, p. 254ff.

10

Ukraine: From Autonomy to Integration (1654–1830s)

ZENON E. KOHUT*

The establishment of Csarist rule over Ukraine

In 1654 at Pereiaslav, in exchange for Muscovite guarantees of autonomy, the *hetman* or leader of the Cossacks, Bohdan Khmel'nyts'kyi was ready to place Ukraine under the sovereignty of the Muscovite czar. Khmel'nyts'kyi asked the Muscovite envoy to swear an oath on behalf of the czar promising that the czar would abide by the terms of the agreement. The envoy refused stating that it was unthinkable that a subject should demand an oath from an autocrat. Enraged by the envoy's refusal, Khmel'nyts'kyi and his staff walked out of the submission ceremony. In desperate need of military aid, they returned after reassurances by the Muscovite envoy and completed the submission ceremony.[1]

At Pereiaslav, two very different political systems and outlooks collided and, to some extent, accommodated themselves to one another. Muscovy was a highly centralized autocracy where, at least in theory, the power of the ruler was unlimited. In essence, the czar considered his domain as his private property. Such claims to patrimonial and unrestricted absolutist rule were hardly unique to Muscovy. But whatever their claims, western rulers were limited by the existence of autonomous corporate and regional bodies. In Muscovy, the restrictions on autocracy were practical – e.g., available resources, overcoming great distances – rather than legal or institutional.[2]

As Muscovy expanded it extended both its autocratic principle and centralized administration to the new territories. Special regional characteristics were wiped out. In its eastern and southern expansion, Muscovy had met sparsely settled and poorly organized Turkic tribes and native peoples who lacked the western traditions of political autonomy, regionalism, estate rights and legal prerogatives that would have allowed the retention of self-rule. Almost imperceptibly, Muscovy became a large, multi-ethnic yet centrally administered empire.[3]

At the time of Pereiaslav, Ukraine had been in ferment for over half a century. In the most simplistic terms, one can say that the Polish Roman Catholic magnates and the Polish state persecuted the Orthodox Church and exploited the Ukrainian orthodox peasants. The situation was further complicated by the Cossacks who had emerged in the borderlands between the Tatars and the

Polish-Lithuanian Commonwealth. The Cossacks hunted, fished and conducted raids against the Tatars and the Ottoman empire. As the Cossacks' military power increased, the Polish government enlisted the Cossacks for specific campaigns. But when dissatisfied the Cossacks revolted against the Polish administration.

In 1648 the Ukrainian Cossacks provided the military support for a massive uprising against the magnates and Polish-Lithuanian state. As Polish authority was pushed out of Ukraine a *de facto* Ukrainian Cossack polity came into existence. Needing the support of an outside power, Khmel'nyts'kyi made his agreement with the Muscovites. After a series of prolonged wars, the right-bank Ukraine (west of the Dnieper River) was reincorporated into the Polish-Lithuanian Commonwealth, but the left-bank Ukraine (east of the Dnieper) remained as a separate political entity under the protection of the czar. It is this truncated left-bank successor to the polity established by Khmel'nyts'kyi, referred to as the Hetmanate, or 'Little Russia' by contemporaries, which was ruled by the czar on the basis of the Pereiaslav agreement.

The Hetmanate was quite different from other territories under czarist rule. The Ukrainian Cossacks were used to negotiating with the Polish king and held concepts of a negotiated contractual relationship between a monarch and the Cossack estate. Such an outlook was contrary and offensive to the Muscovite view of czarist authority. Moreover, in the 1648 Revolution, Khmel'nyts'kyi had freed most of Ukraine from Polish rule. The victorious Cossacks took over a large hinterland inhabited by non-Cossacks – gentry, burghers, clergy and peasants. This resulted in a fusion of the new Cossack administration with the remnants of the old order. At Pereiaslav, the hetman and his administration represented not only the Cossack host, but also all of 'Little Russia' or the Hetmanate. Soon the Hetmanate developed a social hierarchy that more closely resembled a corporate society than a military republic. As a result, Muscovy came into contact with a complex society, with various groups – Cossacks, gentry, townsmen and clerics – claiming special 'rights and liberties'. It was Moscow's first encounter with a type of society that included at least elements of a corporate society and a strong sense of regionalism.[4]

The existence of an autonomous Cossack Ukraine was an anomaly in the Muscovite political system. In a patrimonial state in which the czar's authority was theoretically unlimited and everyone was his servant, if not his slave, there was no place for territorial privilege, corporate rights of social groups, Magdeburg Law, or the Lithuanian Statute – all elements essential to Ukrainian rights and liberties. Therefore, from the Muscovite viewpoint, Cossack Ukraine had to be treated either as a completely foreign land or as a special domain of the czar. To some extent both approaches were applied. Since all matters concerning Ukraine were handled by the *Malorossiiskii prikaz*, a branch of the *Posol'skii prikaz*, which dealt exclusively with foreign affairs, Muscovite authorities clearly recognized Ukraine as a foreign land. Moreover, in changing his title, the czar called himself autocrat of Great and Little Russia. The new title may have been no more than an announcement of the czar's possessions, but it did imply that Little Russia or Ukraine was a distinct domain or czardom, which the czar ruled.[5]

The struggle for control of Ukraine

In their dealings with Cossack Ukraine, the Muscovite authorities were guided not so much by theoretical or constitutional considerations as by pragmatic politics. The Muscovites' first step after signing the Pereiaslav agreement was to secure a firm foothold in Ukraine. They set about doing this by seeking to control the two major sources of authority: the office of hetman and the office of metropolitan of Kiev. Initially, the Muscovite authorities attempted to curb the hetman's conduct of foreign relations. The Pereiaslav agreement permitted the hetman to receive and to dispatch foreign ambassadors and to conclude agreements with foreign powers. The implication of this was that in 1654 Muscovy did not see Ukraine as falling totally under its authority or sovereignty. The hetman was required, however, to notify the czar about the content of all discussions and agreements, and he was prohibited from negotiating independently with the Polish-Lithuanian Commonwealth, the Crimea, or the Ottoman Porte. When their efforts to control the foreign policy of hetmans Khmel'nyts'kyi and Vyhovs'kyi failed, the Muscovites used Vyhovs'kyi's abrogation of the Pereiaslav agreement and his union of Cossack Ukraine with the Polish-Lithuanian Commonwealth (the Union of Hadiach of 1658) as a pretext to falsify the original articles of agreement. In 1659, at the election of Iurii Khmel'nyts'kyi, the Muscovite authorities presented a text which they alleged to be an exact duplicate of the articles signed in 1654. In fact, it was a substitute that contained many changes and additions, including the prohibition against any conduct of foreign relations by the hetman without the expressed consent of the czar.[6] Subsequently, any independent Ukrainian diplomacy was equated with treason, although controlled foreign relations were permitted until 1708.

The Muscovite authorities followed a similar policy in dealing with the Kiev metropolitan, who was head of the Orthodox Church in the Ukraine and in Belorussia. The metropolitan was under the jurisdiction of the patriarch of Constantinople. After applying extreme pressure on the Ukrainian clergy and conducting lengthy negotiations with the patriarch of Constantinople and the Ottoman Porte, the Muscovites succeeded in subordinating the Kievan metropolitan to the Moscow patriarch in 1686. This victory gave Muscovy control over both of the two major centres of authority in Ukraine.

While battling to control the hetmancy and the metropolitanate, the Muscovite authorities also strove to influence Ukrainian affairs directly by stationing military governors (*voevody*) in the major Ukrainian towns. The agreement of 1654 stipulated that military governors were to be appointed for Kiev and Chernihiv, although Khmel'nyts'kyi actually allowed one only in Kiev.[7] In spite of repeated protestations from Moscow, neither Khmel'nyts'kyi nor his successor, Vyhovs-'kyi, admitted other military governors. The articles of 1659, however, allowed for their placement in five cities. During the hetmancy of Briukhovets'kyi, the Muscovites managed to obtain the unrestricted stationing of military governors (1665). A general uprising in 1668 forced the new governors to flee from all Ukrainian towns. Afterwards they were again limited to five cities – Kiev, Pereiaslav, Nizhyn, Chernihiv and Oster. Subsequently, however, Moscow's right to maintain military governors in major Ukrainian towns was unchallenged.

The Muscovites' initial rationale for stationing military governors in Ukraine was to provide protection against foreign invasion. Each governor commanded a garrison of Russian troops and was forbidden to interfere in local municipal affairs. Gradually, however, the governors began to shield the burghers from the abuses of the Cossack administration, encouraging them to submit grievances directly to Russian officials. The Muscovite authorities not only maintained a military presence in Ukraine then, but also became frequent arbiters of Ukrainian internal disputes.

Despite these inroads, the time of 'the Ruin' (1659–79) prevented the consolidation of Muscovite gains in Ukraine. During this period, the Cossack army had split into pro-Polish, pro-Muscovite, and even pro-Ottoman factions – each with its own hetman, army and administration.[8] On the one hand, the pro-Muscovite hetman of the left-bank was more dependent on Muscovy than any hetman of a united Cossack Host would have been. On the other hand, the mere existence of pro-Polish or even pro-Turkish hetmans and Cossack armies threatened Muscovy with the loss of the entire Ukraine. The pro-Muscovite hetman had to be given sufficient authority to appear as an attractive alternative to his pro-Polish counterpart. Moreover, the ever-changing fortunes of war did at times sweep Muscovite authority out of Ukraine.

If the anarchy of 'the Ruin' prevented the Muscovites from achieving control over Ukraine, it also inhibited the consolidation of power by any Ukrainian authority. Only with the final sanctioning of Ukraine's partition (the 'Eternal Peace' Agreement of 1686), the elimination of the pro-Polish right-bank hetmans, and the creation of the left-bank Hetmanate did stability return. Subsequently, the Hetmanate experienced a renaissance. The rule of Hetman Ivan Samoilovych (1672–82) and, especially, of Hetman Ivan Mazepa (1686–1709) effected the consolidation of the Ukrainian élite into a gentry and created a more dynamic administration and a vigorous cultural life, which, in turn, gave rise to distinctive political thought, independent economic ties, and renewed interest in reuniting the right-bank Ukraine. These developments attested to the viability and vitality of the Hetmanate.[9]

The levelling of Ukrainian autonomy

A renewed autonomous Hetmanate ran counter to Peter I's attempt to transform Muscovy into a modernized Russian empire. Among Hetman Mazepa's complex motives for his break with Muscovy, one theme seems to predominate: his fear, which he shared with the Ukrainian gentry, that Peter's drive for administrative reform would violate Ukrainian 'rights and liberties'.[10] Peter's policy towards the Hetmanate's army had already shocked the Ukrainian gentry. In 1701–3, Ukrainian Cossack units were, for the first time, fighting an imperial war far from home and under the command of Russian imperial officers. Rumours of even more dramatic changes pushed Mazepa steadily away from Peter and toward the czar's enemies. A federation with the Poland of Stanislaw Leszczynski (the Swedish-backed candidate for the Polish throne) or a protectorate directly under Sweden seemed an attractive alternative to the eventual abolition of Ukrainian autonomy under Russian rule. Peter's defeat of Charles XII together with Mazepa at Poltava (1709), however, dashed any hope that the Hetmanate's autonomy could be increased – indeed, it soon had the opposite result.

After his victory at Poltava, Peter acted promptly to end 'Ukrainian separatism'. He appointed a Russian minister to the hetman's court, empowering him to read all of the hetman's correspondence and to review his appointments.[11] The czar appointed colonels directly for the first time. Candidates for the highest offices – that is, within the general staff – were selected by the *Malorossiiskii prikaz* and later by the College of Foreign Affairs and were appointed by the czar himself. The hetman's chancelleries, the general staff, and the highest court were all placed under the review of Russian officials. Peter so desired Ukrainian loyalty that he ordered Hetman Skoropads'kyi to marry his daughter to a Russian as a symbol of trust and friendship between Russians and Ukrainians.[12]

Preoccupied as he was with the Northern War, Peter, during most of his reign, supervised the Hetmanate's main administrative and judicial positions closely, but he did not attempt to take them over directly. Only after the Nystad peace (1721) did he really 'take Little Russia in hand'.[13] At the time he created a Little Russian College, composed of six Russian officers, and made it responsible for adjudicating all complaints against the Ukrainian administration. Simultaneously, he transferred the imperial administration of the Hetmanate's affairs from the College of Foreign Affairs to the Senate, symbolizing his desire to treat the Hetmanate as an integral part of the empire. Upon the death of Hetman Skoropads'kyi, the Russian authorities forbade the election of a successor. Moreover, they encouraged the Ukrainian populace to deal directly with the Little Russian College, particularly in exposing alleged abuses by the Ukrainian administration. But the General Military Chancellory, headed by acting hetman Pavlo Polubotok, resisted this attempt to take over the Ukrainian judicial and financial apparatus. In the ensuing power struggle with Russian officials, most of the top Ukrainian political figures were imprisoned, and acting hetman Pavlo Polubotok actually died in prison. In the end, the Little Russian College did wrest control of the Hetmanate's finances and judicial system from the resisting General Military Chancellory.

The Little Russian College soon found, however, that it lacked the support needed among the lower echelons of the Ukrainian administration to govern the area directly. Chaos reigned throughout the court system, and the collection of revenues was disrupted. Like other Petrine reforms, the incorporation of the Hetmanate into the 'regulated' state was first attempted without sufficient planning or preparation. Although the College was represented to the Ukrainian populace as its protector from an abusive Ukrainian administration, chaos and high cost – in both human and economic terms – of direct Russian rule generated popular discontent. Shortly after Peter's death, when war with the Turks was imminent, the Supreme Privy Council decided to abandon his policy toward the Hetmanate. In 1727 Peter II issued a decree providing that 'there be a hetman and officers in Little Russia and that they be maintained in accordance with the treaty of Hetman Bohdan Khmel'nyts'kyi'.[14]

From 1727 to the 1760s the local administration and judicial organs of the Hetmanate functioned without interference from St Petersburg. During that period the imperial authorities vacillated in their dealings with the Hetmanate's central administration. Sometimes they merely supervised the Hetmanate's central organs; at other times they created imperial offices to assume some of the Ukrainian administration's functions. During the rule of Hetman Danylo

Apostol (1728–34), one Russian was assigned to the General Military Court. The hetman was again denied the authority to select the General Military Staff and his colonels; the latter were to be chosen by the Ukrainian officers, subject to approval by St Petersburg.[15] The most significant instance of imperial centralization, however, was the assumption of control over the Hetmanate's finances. Although the Hetmanate retained a separate system of taxation and treasury, its finances were closely supervised by the College of Foreign Affairs. After Hetman Apostol's death (1734), the imperial government once more forbade the election of a hetman and created another collective body – 'Rule of the Hetman's Office' – to administer the Hetmanate. The new office nominally comprised six persons, three Ukrainians and three Russians, but was, in fact, presided over and dominated by a Russian general. For over 10 years, this collective ruled the Hetmanate while acquiring a reputation for caprice and brutality.[16]

Abolition of the Hetmancy

The levelling of Ukrainian rights and liberties was partially and briefly halted during Elizabeth's reign. It was then that the Hetmanate enjoyed the 'Indian summer' of its autonomy. Elizabeth's morganatic marriage to the Ukrainian Cossack Oleksii Rozumovs'kyi, made her favourably disposed toward the re-establishment of the hetmancy. While carefully grooming Oleksii's brother Kyrylo for the post of hetman, Elizabeth waited to announce her decision. In 1750, Kyrylo Rozumovs'kyi, then 22 years old, was duly elected hetman in the Hetmanate's capital, Hlukhiv.[17]

In contrast to his predecessors, Hetman Kyrylo Rozumovs'kyi originated from the Cossack rank-and-file, rather than from an aristocratic officer family. His formative years were spent at the St Petersburg court and in Western Europe. He was the first hetman to hold an imperial office simultaneously with the hetmancy – he served as president of the Academy of Sciences and commander of the Izmailovskii Guards. Rozumovs'kyi's close ties to the imperial family and the Russian aristocracy came not only through his brother, but also by his marriage to Ekaterina Ivanovna Naryshkina, Elizabeth's third cousin. These ties embroiled the hetman in court intrigues and he spent much time pursuing imperial politics in St Petersburg. He did not, however, neglect the Hetmanate and was able to restore Ukrainian autonomy to the extent exercised by Hetman Skoropads'kyi in 1709.

The coming to the throne of Catherine II in 1762 kindled new hope for the Ukrainian autonomists. As commander of the Izmailovskii regiment, Hetman Rozumovs'kyi played an important rôle in the coup that placed Catherine on the imperial throne.[18] Having participated on the victorious side of the revolt, the hetman reaped rewards in status, wealth and power. Courtiers, nevertheless, always risk competition from powerful rivals. Soon after the coup, Catherine reinstated into the inner circles of government the hetman's most inveterate enemy, A. P. Bestuzhev-Riumin. The hetman also clashed repeatedly with Catherine's lover, G. G. Orlov.[19] At the height of the factional struggle, the hetman asked Catherine for permission to leave Moscow and return to the Hetmanate. His reasons were twofold: Rozumovs'kyi was greatly annoyed by the presence at court of his two enemies and he was eager to resume a number of reforms in the Hetmanate which had been interrupted by the death of Elizabeth. Catherine readily granted Rozumovs'kyi a two-year leave of absence from the court beginning with the summer of 1763.

In Hlukhiv, the Hetman's capital, Rozumovs'kyi called a General Council attended by representatives from all areas of the Hetmanate, the Cossack administration and the gentry. The Council formulated a number of judicial reforms which were quickly promulgated by the Hetman's decree.[20] In addition to judicial matters, the Council discussed the problem of Ukrainian autonomy and drafted a petition to be given to the Empress. Originating from the 'Hetman, gentry, Little Russian army and people', the petition contained the most autonomist views publicly expressed since the time of Mazepa.[21] The petition depicted the Hetmanate as a separate land, with its own borders, its own head-of-state, its own government, and its own economic policy. It was connected to the Russian Empire in a special way, through a common monarch, the Russian czar. But even this 'submission' was based on treaties periodically renewed between the Ukrainian hetman and the Russian czar.

In the midst of the reforms, the Hetman received news of a change in court. His enemy, A. P. Bestuzhev-Riumin, was in disfavour and his friend, N. Panin, had emerged victorious. Believing that this was a propitious moment for a political move, Rozumovs'kyi launched his boldest project, an attempt to make the office of hetman hereditary.[22] But the Hetman badly miscalculated his position. Because of the strong tradition of an elected hetmancy, opposition developed in his homeland. Moreover, even prior to the Hlukhiv petition and the project for a hereditary hetmancy, the imperial authorities launched a very unfavourable review of the Hetman's rule in Ukraine. Instead of receiving support at court, the Hetman was recalled to St Petersburg, forced to resign, and the office of hetman was abolished.

The abolition of the office of hetman was only one aspect of Catherine's overall policy towards regional autonomy. In February 1764, at the very time she forced Rozumovs'kyi's resignation as hetman, she made it clear in a letter to the newly appointed procurator-general, Prince A. A. Viazemskii that administrative centralization and Russification should serve as guiding principles throughout the Western borderlands.

> Little Russia [the Hetmanate], Livonia and Finland [Karelia] are provinces which are governed by confirmed privileges and it would be improper to violate them by abolishing them all at once. However, to call them foreign and to deal with them on that basis is more than a mistake; it would be sheer stupidity. These provinces as well as Smolensk should be 'Russified' in the easiest way possible, so that they should cease looking [as the Russian proverb says] 'like wolves to the forest'.[23] The approach is easy if wise men are chosen as governors of the provinces. When the hetmans are gone from Little Russia every effort should be made to eradicate from memory the period and the hetmans, let alone promote anyone to that of office.[24]

While this policy decision was undoubtedly precipitated by Ukrainian autonomist demands, it also reflected Catherine's views on the rôle of government and the need for imperial reforms. Under the influence of cameralist thought, the Enlightenment and concepts of a well-ordered police state, Catherine sought to obtain greater control over the provinces, rationalize and increase revenues, and bring development and enlightenment into the empire.[25] Underlying Catherine's programme was the goal of a unitary state. Since government was to be based on reason or on universal precepts, its law and institutions should serve equally well for all the empire's subjects, regardless of whether they lived in Moscow, Siberia, or the Hetmanate. National differences, although recognized, were not considered significant and were thought to reflect differences in levels of development. Catherine believed that with administrative integration and more uniform development regional differences would recede. The ultimate goal was what Marc Raeff terms 'institutional russification' – an integration that 'was to lead to uniformity, first administrative and economic, then institutional and social, and finally cultural'.[26] In pursuing such uniformity, Catherine – like her younger contemporary, Joseph II of Austria – pitted the new rational order against the ancient 'feudal' privileges of separate historical regions. To Catherine, the latter were antediluvian relics that could only block the implementation of her major goal – the creation of a unitary well-regulated state.

Integration into imperial Russia

As a result of Catherine's policy decision, the autonomous institutions of the Hetmanate were abolished. Not wanting to spark hostility on the part of the Ukrainians, Catherine espoused gradualism – that it would be 'improper to violate the privileges by abolishing them all at once.' Moreover, in 1764, Catherine did not have an adequate model for provincial administration and had just begun plans for provincial reorganization. Progress was slow due to the first Turkish war (1769–74). However, one of the largest peasant-Cossack uprisings in Russian history led by Emil Pugachov (1774–5) demonstrated dramatically the weakness of Russian provincial administration and put provincial reform on the top of Catherine's agenda. By 1775 Catherine did have a plan for reorganizing Russia and decided to introduce the new administration into all parts of the empire, including the privileged, autonomous areas.[27]

The abolition of Ukrainian autonomy, therefore, occurred in two stages: an initial one, followed by the actual introduction of imperial administration and institutions. The first stage began in 1764 with the forced resignation of Hetman Rozumovs'kyi and Catherine's formulation of a clear policy aimed at integrating autonomous areas. From 1764 until 1782, the major Ukrainian institutions remained intact but the new Russian Governor-General, Petr Rumiantsev, attempted to inter-mesh them with the imperial bureaucracy and make them dependent upon imperial institutions. Although the Hetmanate still had a separate treasury, the Governor-general subordinated it totally to imperial agencies and requirements. He introduced a general tax, akin to the imperial capitation tax, greatly increasing the Hetmanate's fiscal contribution to the empire. Since the new regulations applied to all taxed individuals, the majority of Ukrainians were made aware of how deeply imperial practices had penetrated their homeland. At the same time, Rumiantsev acted to stamp out any overt opposition to the imperial programme and to direct the energies of the Ukrainian gentry towards socioeconomic concerns and imperial careers.[28]

By 1782 Catherine II was ready to introduce the new imperial provincial administration into Ukraine. The Hetmanate was divided into three provinces Kiev, Chernihiv, Novhorod-Sivers'k; the old Ukrainian institutions were dismantled; and the new provincial and district administration was installed. The first to be abolished was the Ukrainian treasury and all financial matters were transferred to the Treasury Boards of the three provinces. All Ukrainian institutions dealing with non-military affairs were abolished; their records were turned over to the new provincial and district administration, and any further dispensing of Ukrainian civilian offices or ranks was strictly forbidden. The Ukrainian judicial system was dissolved and the pending cases were reassigned to the new provincial and local courts. Only the Little Russian College – the highest administrative organ in the Hetmanate – continued to operate until 1786, primarily to finish its caseload as the highest court of appeal.[29]

At the same time the Cossack military organization was replaced by a system of regular imperial regiments. At first the new carbineer units resembled closely the previous Cossack units, even in name. But the carbineer units proved to be a transitional organization and, by the end of the eighteenth century, they were abolished and military recruitment and organization in Ukraine was the same as in the rest of the empire.[30]

Similarly, the Orthodox Church in Ukraine was brought fully into the imperial structure. Its wealth was confiscated by the state and its bishops, hegumens and monastics became virtual state employees. Parish priests were still responsible to the parish community, but the state determined the number of priests, deacons and other church personnel. The boundaries of the eparchies were adjusted to correspond to the newly established provinces. By the turn of the century, the church in the Hetmanate had become an integral part of an official imperial church structure.[31]

The Ukrainian social structure, however, did not correspond to the imperial order so readily. While the burghers soon became part of an ethnically heterogeneous Russified estate and the clergy were transformed into a partially Russified closed social group, and the peasants on private estates became fully enserfed, the Ukrainian gentry and the Cossacks proved more difficult to integrate. The imperial authorities, moreover, wavered in their policies toward the latter two groups. Initially, in 1783–5, virtually the entire Ukrainian gentry was admitted into the Russian nobility, the *dvorianstvo*. Then, at the turn of the century, the Office of Heraldry rescinded thousands of patents and advanced strict regulations for those who claimed rights to imperial *dvorianstvo* on the basis of Ukrainian ranks. This resulted in 25 years of struggle by the Ukrainian gentry against the Office of Heraldry and the Senate. Although most Ukrainian ranks were eventually recognized (except for the two lowest ranks) this long, drawn-out battle slowed the assimilation of the Ukrainian gentry.

Similarly, the imperial authorities vacillated in dealing with the Cossacks – a group that did not readily fit any standard category of imperial society. On the one hand, there was a strong tendency to reduce the Cossacks' status to that of state peasants; on the other, in times of military emergency, the imperial authorities sought to mobilize them as irregular troops, thus reviving their Cossack status. Finally, in the 1830s the Cossacks were definitively accorded the status of special state peasants. It was only at the end of the 1830s, therefore, that Ukrainian society at last approximated the imperial social structure.[32]

In the span of a few decades, Ukrainian self-government – rooted in historical tradition stemming from the Polish-Lithuanian period and bolstered by more than a century of practice in the Hetmanate – was replaced by an imperial provincial administration. The former functionaries of the Hetmanate exchanged their swords and colourful Cossack garb for the rapier, the powdered wig, and the provincial imperial uniform (each province had its own uniform). The successes of such a metamorphosis, however, depended on Ukrainian attitudes towards the demise of autonomy.

Ukrainian reaction to imperial integration

The initial reaction of Ukrainian society to imperial integration was quite negative. Soon after the resignation of Hetman Rozumovs'kyi, Ukrainian society had an unusual opportunity to express its views at Catherine II's Legislative Commission of 1767–9. All segments of Ukrainian society – with the exception of the peasants – were asked to draw up petitions expressing their needs and desires. Governor-General Rumiantsev attempted first to cajole and then intimidate the Ukrainian gentry into not raising such issues as the election of a new hetman and the continuation of Ukrainian autonomy. As a result, the elections to the Commission became stormy. When 36 nobles refused to retract a demand for the election of a new hetman, Governor-General Rumiantsev had them arrested, tried, and sentenced to death.[33] Although these harsh sentences were eventually commuted, they do indicate the opposition Governor-General Rumiantsev faced in the initial period of his administration.

Despite repressions and arrests, most of Ukrainian society favoured the continuation of Ukrainian autonomy. However, the concept of Ukrainian 'rights and liberties' had a multiplicity of meanings for various segments of Ukrainian society. At times the rights of various groups complemented and reinforced each other; at other times, they conflicted with and even negated each other. Each social group, however, had some tangible stake in autonomy.[34]

As the most politically conscious estate, the gentry regarded the Hetmanate as a separate political entity with an ancient history and 'confirmed privileges'. Interlaced with this political tradition were specific problems of the gentry's power, status and wealth. The Ukrainian gentry had to be reassured that at least their wealth and status in the Hetmanate would be recognized and that they would have access to positions in the central imperial bureaucracy. This approach would erode the tradition of Ukrainian political distinctness, especially if all the gentry's honours and offices were dependent solely upon the centre. Until Catherine took some measures along this line, however, the Ukrainian gentry remained the most vocal and articulate defender of the Hetmanate's political separateness.

Some of the higher clergy, especially the Kiev metropolitan, viewed the Orthodox Church in the Hetmanate as a separate autonomous entity. Corresponding to the hetman in the secular realm, the metropolitan of 'Kiev, Halych and all Little Russia' was the religious primate for the Hetmanate. Yet, while the secular hetman ruling an autonomous principality had until recently been a reality, a metropolitan governing a separate church in the Hetmanate was only a seventeenth-century memory.

Autonomy had a more limited meaning for the rest of the Ukrainian clergy. For the monks, it signified the retention of large monastic landholdings, which in Russia had been secularized, and the return of properties seized by the Cossack administration. For the two independent monasteries, Ukrainian autonomy denoted continued exemption from the local church hierarchy. For the parish clergy, it meant equal status with the gentry, which in practical terms included such prerogatives as brewing alcohol and farming estates with the help of peasant labour. The clergy attempted to prove that all these privileges were rooted in Ukrainian traditions, various guarantees and the Lithuanian Statute.

Despite the abuse the regular Cossacks received from officers and the gentry, they, too, had specific interests in maintaining Ukrainian autonomy. The only alternatives were service in the regular Russian army or peasant status, neither of which was palatable. In the existing system, at least in theory, the regular Cossacks were equal to the gentry and could elect their officers. But this nominal equality conflicted with the desires of the gentry, who wanted exclusive rights to all offices and separate courts for the nobility.

The burghers also wanted to maintain ancient rights and privileges, including Magdeburg law, but to them this meant regaining political and administrative control of the towns from the Cossack administration and subordinating all town dwellers to town authority. The burghers also wanted exclusive control of trade and manufacture, which conflicted with prerogatives claimed by the gentry, Cossacks, and clergy. All these sometimes conflicting yet cherished 'rights and liberties' were abolished only two decades later, yet the reaction of the Ukrainians was fairly mild. Had there been an opportunity to register an opinion, such as in the 1767 Legislative Commission, much of Ukrainian society would still, perhaps, have preferred to maintain their 'rights and liberties'. Even with the lack of a public forum, the gentry, the chief proponents of Ukrainian autonomy in the past, might have expressed greater dissatisfaction. Their seeming placidity stemmed from a number of causes.[35]

Ironically, it was the abolition of Ukrainian institutions which forced the imperial authorities to admit the Ukrainian gentry into the imperial nobility (*dvorianstvo*). Since nobles were to play an essential rôle in the new provincial administration, virtually all the Ukrainian gentry were recognized as nobles. It was only near the end of the century that the imperial authorities began to re-examine Ukrainian ranks. At the same time, the peasants on private estates were fully enserfed. Although Catherine issued this *ukaz* to ensure the proper collection of taxes and maintain uniformity in the empire rather than to please the Ukrainian gentry, in effect, the *ukaz* did please them.

Another powerful stimulus for the merger of the Ukrainian and Russian élites was Catherine's 1785 Charter of the Nobility. The Ukrainian gentry had claimed rights which far exceeded the privileges of the Russian nobility. The 1785 Charter of the Nobility considerably narrowed the gap between the two. Thus, only by becoming part of the Russian nobility, could the Ukrainian gentry obtain recognition of many of the prerogatives that they had claimed for over a century.

Governor-General Rumiantsev furthered this integration by a well-planned policy of drawing the Ukrainian gentry into imperial service. Imperial co-optation of the Ukrainian élite proved so successful that it was a Ukrainian, Andrii

Myloradovych (Andrei Miloradovich), and his largely Ukrainian staff who actually prepared the introduction of imperial institutions into the Hetmanate.

In fact, the Ukrainian nobility had already become dependent on local and imperial governmental positions. Although some nobles possessed immense wealth, the majority owned small estates that were barely able to provide the necessities of life. Economic conditions forced the sons of noblemen to seek careers in government service. The existence of the Kievan Academy and the Chernihiv and Pereiaslav Collegia offered the Ukrainian petty gentry better educational opportunities than those possessed by their Russian counterparts and, therefore, more ready access to bureaucratic positions. Thus, the abolition of Ukrainian institutions did not mean a loss of offices for the Ukrainian gentry. On the contrary, Catherine's provincial reforms offered the Ukrainian petty gentry an unprecedented opportunity for imperial careers, first of all in the new administration in the territory of the former Hetmanate, in the bordering provinces, in the military ranks, and in St Petersburg itself.[36]

Another factor that greatly facilitated the integration of the Ukrainian gentry into imperial society was the cultural and linguistic similarity between the Ukrainians and Russians. The identitites of the German Baltic barons or the Polish szlachta, similarly to the Ukrainian gentry, were based on historical 'rights and privileges'. However, they were also reinforced by radical differences between the Balts or Poles and the Russians in language, religion and culture. While contemporaries perceived the differences between Ukrainians and Russians, they also saw similarities in Orthodox religion and Church Slavonic cultural traditions, and the vernacular languages. As a result, the Ukrainian élite could and did readily adapt to the newly emerging Russian imperial culture. Finally, an important element of the Ukrainian gentry's collective myth was the tradition of loyal service to the czar. With the exception of a few hints of conspiracies, the Ukrainian gentry could not envision any alternative to loyal service to the czar.

Yet the co-operation obtained by the imperial government from the Ukrainian gentry cannot be interpreted as universal acceptance of imperial integration.[37] A portion of the Ukrainian gentry openly espoused assimilation, and a much larger number probably became Russified and were assimilated without ever being conscious of the process. Some of the assimilators who went into imperial service and left the Hetmanate subsequently raised the question of what rôles the Little and Great Russian traditions played in forming a 'Russian' national identity. Through their attempts to reconcile Little-Russian and All-Russian loyalties, they may have prepared the ground for Slavophilism. Another part of the gentry strove to retain or even renew various aspects of the Hetmanate's heritage. The latter group, the traditionalists, were not united in any cohesive movement but were heterogeneous in make-up and goals. Some merely espoused the continuation of the Lithuanian Statute and the Ukrainian judicial system; others utilized propitious political moments to propose the re-establishment of Cossack military formations; still others clandestinely wrote and distributed anti-assimilationist and anti-Russian political literature (*Istoriia Rusov*); and a daring few even plotted against the imperial government. Oppositionist tendencies were further reinforced by the government's subsequent reversal on Ukrainian ranks and the long struggle to gain recognition of Ukrainian ranks as bestowing automatic membership in the imperial *dvorianstvo*. In sum, while most of the Ukrainian gentry had become assimilated and at least partially Russified, the process was not as automatic as some have assumed it and encountered pockets of resistance throughout the first half of the nineteenth century.

The only protest against imperial assimilation not made by the gentry was 'The Lament of the Kievans on the Loss of the Magdeburg Law' a passionately anti-Russian poem. Kiev, with its strong traditions of self-rule and an articulate burgher class, was the exception to the rule. For the most part, the burghers, the Cossacks, the lower clergy and the peasants were the politically passive elements of society. Their dissatisfaction was expressed through flight or occasional Cossack/peasant revolts.[38]

Conclusions

Catherine seemed successful in integrating the Hetmanate into the Russian Empire. Not only were the institutions of the Hetmanate replaced by imperial ones, but a part of Ukrainian society was assimilated and Russified. A basic polarization resulted; the town, with its ethnically mixed population and numerous officials, became Russified, while the countryside, inhabited by Cossacks, peasants and nobles, remained, on the whole, Ukrainian. Later, even many of the provincial nobles became Russified and the Cossacks were merged into the peasantry. Being Ukrainian was virtually syonymous with being a peasant.

Imperial absorption of the Hetmanate had important consequences for Ukrainian developments. Since Ukraine was no longer considered a borderland but a core area of Russia, virtually any form of Ukrainian particularism – irrespective of how apolitical or innocuous – seemed to many Russians as treachery if not treason. Moreover, in a traditional society, where political leadership was the exclusive province of the upper classes, the assimilation of the native élite to another culture also meant the loss of national political representation. For Ukrainians, the whole course of 'nation-building' would have to be different from those nations that, although stateless, had fully retained their traditional élites. Unlike the Poles, whose national movement in its initial stages could be based on the historical legitimacy of the nobility and expanded to include ethnic Poles of various strata, the Ukrainians first had to develop a new stratum capable of leadership – the intelligentsia – and the subsequent national movement was based not on historical legitimacy but primarily on ethnic and linguistic considerations.

NOTES FOR CHAPTER 10

* Senior Research Specialist, Library of Congress, Washington, USA. This article is based on the author's book, *Russian Centralism and Ukrainian Autonomy: Imperial Absorption of the Hetmanate 1760s–1830s* (Cambridge, Mass. Ukrainian Research Institute, Harvard University; distributed by Harvard UP, 1988). The author is grateful to the Ukrainian Research Institute for permission to use materials and passages from the book.

1 The Muscovite envoy's report has been translated into English and published in John Basarab's *Pereiaslav 1654: A Historical Study* (Edmonton, 1982), pp. 245–58.

2 Richard Pipes, *Russia under The Old Regime* (New York, 1974), pp. 52–4; 76–9.

3 Marc Raeff, 'Patterns of Russian policy towards the nationalities', in E. Allworth (ed.), *Soviet Nationality Problems* (New York, 1971), pp. 22–42.

4 The Ukrainian 'rights and liberties' are well summarized in Leo Okinshevych, *Ukrainian Society and Government (1648–1781)* (Munich, 1978).

5 Boris Nolde discusses the Muscovite view of Ukrainian autonomy in his 'Essays in Russian State Law', *Annals of The Ukrainian Academy of Arts and Sciences in the United States*, 4, (3) (1955), pp. 873–903.

6 The substitution is discussed by John Basarab in *Pereiaslav 1654: A Historiographical Study*, pp. 230–58.

7 The question of Russian military governors in Ukraine is discussed by I. Rozenfeld, *Prisoedinenie Malorossii k Rossii* (St Petersburg, 1915), pp. 100–5, and by A. Iakovliv in *Ukrain'sko-moskovs 'ki dohovory v XVII—XVIII vikakh.* [=*Pratsi Ukrain'skoho naukovoho instytuta vol. 19*] (Warsaw, 1934), pp. 75–7, 81–92.

8 Doroshenko in *Narys istorii Ukrainy*, ii (Munich, 1966), pp. 51–135 provides a good overview of the second half of the seventeenth century.

9 Ukrainian society and politics during the Mazepa period have been well described in the following works: F. Umanets, *Getman Mazepa* (St Petersburg, 1897); B. Krupnitzky ((Krupnyts'kyi)), *Hetman Mazepa und seine Zeit* (Leipzig, 1942); O. Ohloblyn, *Het'man Ivan Mazepa i ioho doba* (New York, 1960); V. Diadychenko, *Narysy suspil' no-politychnoho ustroiu Livoberezhnoi Ukrainy kintsia XVII-pochatku XVIII st.* (Kiev, 1959).

10 The motivation of Mazepa and the Ukrainian élite in breaking with Muscovy has been analysed by O. Subtelny, 'Mazepa, Peter I, and the Question of Treason', *Harvard Ukrainian Studies* 2(2) (1978), pp. 158–83 and more recently in *The Mazepists: Ukrainian Separatism in the early eighteenth Century* (Boulder, 1981). An interesting contemporary justification for the break was written by Pylyp Orlyk, Mazepa's chancellor and, later, the emigré hetman to his former mentor, Stefan Iavors'kyi: see Orlyk to Stefan Iavors'kyi, June 1, 1721, *Osnova* (St Petersburg), 11, 1862, pp. 1–29.

11 The best summary of the rule of Hetman Ivan Skoropads'kyi and the immediate post-Mazepa period is to be found in Doroshenko, *Narys*, 2, pp. 136–82.

12 S. Solov'ev, Istoriia *Rossii* (hereafter Solov'ev), (15 vols. Moscow, 1959–66), viii, pp. 593–94.

13 The phrase of Count P. Tolstoi when reporting on Peter I's policies towards the Hetmanate, cited in Doroshenko's *Narys*, 2, p. 179.

14 *Polnoe sobranie zakanov Rossiiskoi Imperii* Ist ser. (1649–1825), 45 vols. (St Petersburg, 1830), vii, no. 5127 (July 22, 1727), pp. 828–9.

15 The rule of Hetman Apostol is treated by Borys Krupnyts'kyi, *Het'man Danylo Apostol ta ioho doba* (Augsburg, 1948).

16 Doroshenko, *Narys* 2, p. 191.

17 Hetman Rozumovs'kyi's rule is discussed in the first volume of A. A. Vasil'chikov, *Semeistvo Razumovskikh* (hereafter Vasil'chikov) (4 vols. St Petersburg, 1880–87).

18 Solov'ev, vol. 13, pp. 79–102; Vasil'chikov, i, pp. 291–300.

19 Vasil'chikov, i, pp. 304–305.

20 The decree was published by D. Miller, 'Ocherki iz istorii i iuridicheskogo byta staroi Malorossii. Sudy zemskie, grodskie i podkomorskie v XVIII stoletii', *Sbornik Khar'kovskogo istoriko-filologicheskogo obshchestva* no. 8 (1896), pp. 236–43.

21 The petition was published under the title 'Proshenie malorossiiskogo shliakhetstva i starshin, vmeste s getmanom, o vozstanovlenii raznykh starinnykh prav Malorossii, podannoe Ekaterine Il-i v 1764 godu', *Kievskaia starina* 1883, no. 6, pp. 317–45.

22 Vasil'chikov vol. I, pp. 313–17; Solov'ev, vol. 13, pp. 241–2.

23 The Russian proverb runs: 'No matter how much you feed a (captured) wolf he still looks to the forest (to escape)'.

24 Nol'de, 'Essays in Russian State Laws', pp. 889–90.

25 The views of Catherine II and the impact of cameralist and enlightenment ideas on policy has been the subject of discussion and debate. See Marc Raeff, *The Well-Ordered Police State: Social and Institutional Change Through Law in the Germanies and Russia 1600–1800* (New Haven, 1983); Robert E. Jones, *Provincial Development in Russia: Catherine II and Jacob Sievers* (New Brunswick, 1984); Isabel de Madariaga, *Russia in the Age of Catherine the Great* (New Haven, 1981), particularly ch. 10.

26 Marc Raeff, 'Uniformity, diversity, and the imperial administration', *Oesteuropa in Geschichte und Gegenwart: Festschrift für Gunther Stokl zum 60. Geburtstag* (Cologne, 1977), p. 112; de Madariaga, *Russia in the Age of Catherine the Great* pp. 582–3.

27 de Madariaga, *Russia in the Age of Catherine the Great*, pp. 277–82, discusses the provincial reforms.

28 For the 1764 to 1782 period of Governor-General Rumiantseva's rule see G. A. Maksimovitch, *Deiatel'nost' Rumiantseva-Zadunaiskogo po upravleniiu Malorossiei* (Nizhyn, 1913) and N. V. Storozhenko, 'Reformy v Malorossii pri gr. Rumiantseva', *Kievskaia starina* 1891, no. 3, pp. 478–93; 1891, no. 9, pp. 455–65.

29 Zenon E. Kohut, *Russian Centralism and Ukrainian Autonomy: Imperial Absorption of the Hetmanate 1760s–1830s* (Cambridge, 1988), pp. 209–18.

30 Storozhenko, 'Reformy v Malorossii', *Kievskaia Starina* 1891, no. 3, pp. 478–93; Kohut, *Russian Centralism*, pp. 218–22.

31 Kohut, *Russian Centralism*, pp. 222–33.

32 For imperial policies towards Ukrainian social groups, see Kohut, *Russian Centralism* pp. 237–98; and 'The Ukrainian élite in the eighteenth century and its integration into the Russian nobility', in Ivo Banac and Paul Bushkovitch (eds.), *The Nobility in Russia and Eastern Europe* (New Haven, 1983), pp. 65–97.

33 The elections to the Commission, including the arrests of the Ukrainian gentry has been covered by G. A. Maksimovich, in *Vybory i nakazy v Malorossii v Zakonodatel'nuiu Komissiiu 1767 i sostavlenie nakazov* (Nizhyn, 1917).

34 The Ukrainian wishes expressed at the Legislative Commission have been treated by Kohut, *Russian Centralism*, pp. 125–90.

35 For The integration of The Ukrainian gentry see Kohut, 'The Ukrainian élite in the eighteenth century', pp. 72–97.

36 David Saunders in *The Ukrainian Impact on Russian Culture 1750–1850* (Edmonton, 1985), traces the careers of the Ukrainian gentry in Russia, primarily St Petersburg.

37 For the reactions of the Ukrainian gentry to imperial integration see Kohut, 'The Ukrainian élite of the eighteenth century', pp. 75–85.

38 Kohut, *Russian Centralism*, pp. 285–305.

Index